Letters of Richard Reynolds: With a Memoir of His Life

Richard Reynolds

MEMOIR

OF

RICHARD REYNOLDS.

Rich.ᵈ Reynolds

⟨E. Borgstroth 347 Market St. Phil.ᵃ⟩

LETTERS

OF

RICHARD REYNOLDS,

WITH A MEMOIR OF HIS LIFE.

BY

HIS GRAND-DAUGHTER,

HANNAH MARY RATHBONE,

AUTHOR OF

"THE DIARY OF LADY WILLOUGHBY."

PHILADELPHIA:

HENRY LONGSTRETH, 347 MARKET STREET.

1855.

CONTENTS.

APPENDIX.

MEMOIR

OF THE

LIFE OF RICHARD REYNOLDS.

CHAPTER I.

UNDER feelings of deep reverence and affection, I undertake the task, which has been allotted to me, of giving some account of the life of my grandfather, Richard Reynolds. .

It is a solemn thing, to attempt to portray the character of another,—to trace the footsteps of one, who has passed away from the earth,—to collect the scattered signs and records of his mind's existence,—knowing, the while, that there is, in every human being, an inner life, which cannot be penetrated. And this is peculiarly to be felt, in the present instance, of one, whose whole conduct was governed by the utmost simplicity of truth, and a sensitive shrinking from the observation of others.

There was nothing in my grandfather's station in life, in his attainments in any branch of science or literature, or in any circumstances connected with him or his family, to render him a man of public mark or interest. It was solely through his self-denying benevolence and extended beneficence that he became so widely known in his life-time, and that he comes before us now, after the lapse of so many years since he was removed from this earthly scene. So greatly was he esteemed in his native place, that shortly

after his death a meeting was held in Bristol to consider
the most appropriate mode of recording his worth and perpetuating his name: and a charitable society was formed
and entitled "The Reynolds Commemoration Society."
And shall he who was so beloved and respected by his fel-
low-citizens, as to win from them this testimony to his
virtues and beneficence, be suffered to remain unremem-
bered, and almost unknown, in the habitations of his descendants?—shall his labours of love, and his self-denying
life, exist only in the recollection of the few, who must soon
follow him to the grave?

He departed this life, leaving behind him children, and
grandchildren, and great grandchildren,—and now his son,
—alone in his generation,—is the beloved grandfather,
whose sons and daughters, fast approaching the evening
of *their day*, look as he did on their children's children playing around their hearths,—and they would not that these
should, one day, ask, and ask in vain,—Who was the Reynolds, whose name has thus been perpetuated?

But the materials for a biography are very limited,
and it is a cause of surprise as well as of regret, that so
little remains to give a life-like picture of what he was,—
so endeared in all his domestic relations, so respected by
his acquaintance, and regarded by his intimate friends
with an affection and admiration almost enthusiastic, that
any endeavour to express this in words falls coldly upon
the ear, and does not satisfy the heart of the few who
knew and loved him. There was an attraction, a fascina-
tion about my grandfather which died with him; and it
will be difficult to give it form and permanence even to
those who knew him, and impossible to convey any adequate
impression of it to those who knew him not. Many, however, of his letters remain, which afford some insight into

his character and the peculiar make of his mind; and so retiring and uneventful was his life, that a more copious selection is given from his correspondence to supply the deficiency of information from other sources, than the intrinsic value and interest of some of the letters might seem to justify. This selection has also been the more freely made from the consideration that this sketch is intended chiefly for a family memorial, which it is hoped may not be without some interest to the members of that Society, in which whilst living he held so distinguished a place. For the public generally it will probably possess little attraction. Any attempt to heighten the interest of a biography by the reflections or remarks of the editor, is not often successful: and however deficient may be the present memoir, the reader is more favourably placed to form just conclusions, and a correct judgment of the character, than one who stands in the near and peculiar relation of a grandchild.

Richard Reynolds, born in Bristol, according to a memorandum in his own handwriting, on the 1st of November, o. s., in the year 1735, was the only son of Richard and Jane Reynolds, members of the Society of Friends. The family probably joined this sect at the commencement, as the marriage-certificate of Michael, the father of the above-mentioned Richard Reynolds, surnamed the " Honest," is dated in the year 1704, and is signed by *his* father Michael as a witness, who may therefore be supposed to have been one of the early converts to the preaching of George Fox, in the middle of the seventeenth century. This certificate is in the usual form (essentially) of these documents, as required at the present time, in the Quaker mode of conducting the ceremony of marriage in their public assemblies; and as so few of my grandfather's descendants now

remain in the Society, an extract from it is here given.
The name, parentage, occupation or station in life of the
parties being set forth, also the fact of their having given
due notice of their intention of marriage, and of their
having been declared clear of all other similar engagements, and as having consent of their parents, it thus
proceeds :—"Now these are to certify all whom it may
concerne, &c., this ffoure and twentieth day of the twelvth
month, called Ffebruary, in the yeare, according to the
English account, one thousand seven hundred and foure.
They the said Michaell Reynolds and Susanna Bromley
appeared in a publick assembly of the said people and
others mett together for that end in their publick meeting
place att Stratford aforesaid, He the said Michaell Reynolds taking the said Susanna Bromley by the hand did
solemnly and expressly declare that he did take her (the
said S. B.) to be his wife—and then and there, in the said
assembly, the said Susanna Bromley in like manner holding him (the said M. R.) by the hand, did solemnly and
expressly declare that she did take him, the said M. R.,
to be her husband—and each of them did solemnly promise
to be loving and faithful to each other in the relation of
husband and wife, until it should please the Lord to separate them by death—and the said Michaell Reynolds and
Susanna Bromley as a further confirmation thereof, did
then and there to these presents set their hands, &c., &c."
To this certificate there are about twenty signatures, three
of which are expressed by a *mark*.

Young Richard Reynolds was sent to school, at the
early age of five years, to a Friend, named Thomas Bennet, of Pickwick, in Wiltshire. The little boy, who was
leaving his home for the first time, to go to school, at a
considerable distance, was set forth on his journey in a

primitive style, under the care of a carrier, on horseback; a circumstance to which he often pleasantly referred in later years, as contrasting with the early habits of ease and indulgence which he saw encouraged in many of the families around him. Another incident, which he used to relate, was no less illustrative of the simple manners of that period, when one or two pence a week was the whole of his allowance of pocket-money, although his father was in a lucrative business as an iron merchant. On his first return to school, after the holidays, one of his companions ran up to him, as he entered the play-ground, saying, "Dick, thou owes me a penny." Dick immediately paid the penny, which was the only one that he possessed,— and he keenly felt his poverty, but he also felt the satisfaction of having discharged the debt. In after life, the principle of owing no man anything, he ever most scrupulously maintained; and when, in managing the concerns of others, he had to endure a temporary infringement of this habit of punctuality, it occasioned him a degree of distress, that would be thought by some almost a refinement upon honesty.

The defective education existing, probably. in most schools of the same class, at that period, may be inferred by a proceeding of the boys at Thomas Bennet's, which, it is to be hoped, would not occur at the present day. Understanding that a school in the neighbourhood. consisted of children whose parents were members of the established Church,—and, in the ignorance of their prejudiced minds, conceiving that a diversity of religious profession was a just ground of hostility, they resolved to go in a body, and valiantly fight the "Church boys." Sallying forth accordingly, for this especially unquakerly purpose, they encountered the other party, who, unac-

2

quainted with their design, met them with so much civility,
and in so courteous a manner, that their hearts instantly
relented, and they returned home secretly convicted, and
ashamed of their unworthy project.

Whilst at this school, Richard Reynolds was guilty of
the only deliberate falsehood, which, as he used to say,
he believed he had ever uttered in the course of his life.
He had been accused of some fault, of which he was, in
reality, innocent; but appearances were so much against
him, that the master, feeling no doubt on the subject,
urged the boy to confess, promising forgiveness to induce
him to do so, and threatening him with a flogging if he
continued obstinate.　He persisted, however, in maintaining his innocence, until he was ordered by the master to
go into the adjoining room, in which was the girls' school,
and there to ask for the instrument of this degrading
punishment.　The corporal pain, and even the disgrace,
he would have borne; but he had not strength of mind
to endure this great humiliation,—and he pleaded guilty.

For years this sin weighed heavily upon his mind, and
he was not satisfied until he had convinced the master of
his unintentional injustice, and of the injurious consequences of his severity.　There can be no doubt, however,
that Thomas Bennet took a sincere and permanent interest
in the future welfare of his pupils, and that he gained and
preserved their esteem and affection.　As characteristic
of the master, and exhibiting the mutual regard which
existed between himself and his late scholar, the following
letters, though of later date, are inserted here, where they
may not be without some interest, in connection with
Richard Reynolds's school-life.

To RICHARD REYNOLDS.

Pickwick, Fifth Month 14th, 1758.

DEAR RICHARD,

I have thy pretty and sensible letter of 10th current, intimating thy sending the books, which are received, and I accept them kindly. I find thou art desirous of receiving a line from me in answer to thine, which I now send thee, and should have written thee before had leisure and opportunity conveniently offered.

It appears to me a good sign, where any, that formerly were my Scholars, and had the best instructions I could give 'em, though at the time did not consider that my view in advising them was solely for their good, should by proper reflections on past advice, show a disposition of corresponding with their friend, and seek the company of their adviser.

This seems pretty much thy present situation; and I could not help taking notice of thy conduct and behaviour to me when last at Bristol: I plainly saw an alteration in thee for the better, and had then a secret joy and pleasure in beholding it, though I mentioned nothing of it to any one. Since, therefore, it has pleased Infinite Wisdom to extend his merciful visitation to thee, and thou hast been made measurably sensible of it, let not any thing divert thy steady perseverance in the way of thy duty to thy Maker, which, if pursued as it ought, will naturally lead thee to be dutiful to thy parents, obedient to thy master and mistress, and respectful in thy carriage to all thy relations and friends; not suffering the flashy temper incident to youth, to predominate on the one hand, nor slothfulness in effecting thy master's commands on the other; it will be a preservative against idleness and idle companions, and will be thy protector and deliverer from temptations, and the evil attending them; it will also direct and guide thee into that retirement that is essentially necessary to enlighten thy eyes, enlarge thy understanding, and correct thy depraved will, so as to give thee a knowledge of thy Maker, thyself, and the duty incumbent on thee to God and man-

kind. Thus wilt thou not only be the visited, but the saved of
the Lord. I earnestly desire that many more of our young
friends of both sexes would close in with the offers of Divine
love, extended by the merciful visitations handed forth to them
at this time, which I have been made sensible of, and I have
rejoyced to observe one here and another there embracing the
opportunities offered them, who are saying in their hearts, with
good old Jacob, "If God will be with me, and will keep me in
this way that I go, and will give me bread to eat, and raiment
to put on, so that I come again to my father's house in peace,
then shall the Lord be my God." It has been a signal providence of Infinite Goodness (who will never suffer his truth to
fall in the streets, for want of proper instruments as standard
bearers,) to raise up divers young men and young women to bear
a testimony for his truth on earth, and lead them forth in their
services to supply the places of many of our worthy ancients
called off the stage to their eternal rest; and I wish the Society
was enough sensible of this favour, that hearts full of gratitude,
for so great benevolence, might be united in thanksgiving for the
same, to the Author of all mercies, who is eternally worthy
thereof, world without end.

I have exceeded what I first intended; if too prolix for thee,
attribute it to the strength of love that prevailed in me to en-
courage thee to faithfulness, according to the gift thou hast received; and I know thou darest not make a bad use of these
hints, if thou art honest to the witness, to which I recommend
thee as the best Teacher and Instructor.

And with our united love and good wishes for thee in every
thing just and commendable, I remain and am

Thy hearty, sincere, and affectionate friend,

T. Bennet.

Pickwick, 15th Twelfth Month, 1761.

DEAR FRIEND,

Thy favour of the 10th ult. arrived in course, and should have replied sooner, but waited till I received thy second kind present of pipes : the Barclay cheese came also safe to hand, which is a very fine one, and I return my acknowledgments for both in the following manner. As thou hadst, but a little time before, been so kind to present me with a box of such fine pipes, which are not yet exhausted, so it was the more surprising that I should have the favour so soon and so generously repeated ; exclusive of the Barclay cheese, which is far more valuable than the net-cheese I sent thee as a small part of my gratitude for thy first present of pipes. As I was incapable before of justly retaliating thy former benefaction, not only respecting the thing itself, but the manner of its presentment, and the disposition of the mind then urging it, so by such reiterations I shall never be able to render any compositions for the debt thou hast involved me in ; though I am sensible that I am writing to a generous creditor, who will, rather than exact the utmost farthing, forgive the whole debt.

I now quit this subject, and proceed to another of greater weight and importance, and perhaps more intelligible and acceptable to a virtuous and religious mind, and that is to impart to thee some pleasing remarks I made on thy behaviour and conduct during thy last visit, and which I in part hinted to thy father, who was here with thee. It has been my lot to know thee from a child, when thou wast placed young under my care and tuition ; whilst thou pursued that good principle implanted in thee, thou acted right, and was a pleasure to thy ffriends, and a comfort to thyself : but the contrary, when at any time thou forsook it. Since thy juvenile state, or when further advanced towards manhood, that good hand that always supports his own, still attended thee with his gracious visits, and attracted thy affection and attention, not to the things of this life, but unto himself ; discovered to thee that true wisdom that is from above, by which thou still

2*

advanced in that only saving knowledge, and at the same time surrounded with many temporal blessings, which to some might have had quite a contrary effect, by setting them on the wing, than what I observe they have on thee. Doth not this plainly manifest, that though Divine Providence hath bestowed these temporal favours in so abundant a manner, thy chiefest treasure is elsewhere? and that thou art for seeking first the Kingdom of God and his righteousness, before these things that are necessary, and already added. I could not but take notice of the meekness of thy behaviour in all respects, when last here, and at other times also, and it always afforded me much satisfaction : and in my reflections since, I have been ready to say to thee, as if present, Dear Richard, keep fast thy hold ; let none take away thy crown. Thou wilt excuse me for mentioning these my observations after this manner, when I acquaint thee that 'tis the effect of true love, that wishes thy perseverance in the right way, and thy safety in the day of trouble. No ffriend like the best of ffriends, who will be with thee when all outward comforts fail, and who has promised not to leave or forsake such as cleave close to him. Let not this letter be exposed ; if any error is therein found pass a charitable construction thereon: if any hints therein shall prove serviceable in confirming thy resolution in pursuing thy peace, be thankfull to the Author of every good and perfect gift, and from whom we derive all our blessings.

I shall be glad to hear from thee as often as thy leisure will admit, and to see thee here when opportunity offers : and with all our joint love and respect to thy whole self and ffriends, I conclude, and am

> Thy affectionate and obliged friend,
>   T. BENNET.

To Thomas Bennet.

Ketley, Third Month 27th, 1761.

It gave me great pleasure to hear of thy welfare and of thy family's, by thy letter of the 16th ult., which, together with thy kind present, came safe to hand yesterday, and for which I return thee my grateful acknowledgments.

Convinced by experience of the justness of thy observations, and of the wholesomeness of thy advice, I recollect the many opportunities I have formerly had of improving thereby with gratitude and complacency, I grieve it has so little influenced the conduct of many who enjoyed the same advantages with me; and though I doubt not thy possessing that serene peace of mind which results from a conscientious discharge of duty, I persuade myself it would be an addition to thy *present* happiness, were all thy former scholars religious, virtuous men.

I have some thoughts of seeing Bristol this summer, and it is not the least of many inducements thereto, that I hope then to see thee in good health; for I never intend to go to Bristol without visiting Pickwick, whilst thou lives there.

I hope thy son and his family are well; please to remember me to him, and to Richard Painter, when thou sees him. We are told there is a time to speak, and a time to be silent; I do not suspect Richard of having spoke when he should have been silent.

If it will not occasion thee too much trouble, I shall be very glad if thou will let one of thy scholars write for me a list of the names of the boys that were at school with me, and the places from whence they came, to which, if thou will please to add, ever so concisely, where and what they now are, it would be very obliging.

If thou cannot conveniently grant that request, refuse not, I pray thee, to let me hear frequently of thine and thy family's health. A letter directed for me at Ketley, near Wellington, Shropshire, would be likely to come to hand.

It may, probably, be thought an uncommon return for one favour received, unasked for, to request two more; but give me leave to assure thee, thou need not dread a proportional increase of petitions from me, having only to desire in future, the continuance of thy kind regard, and that thou will believe me, with great esteem and love to thy whole self, in which my wife joins,

Thy very affectionate and obliged friend,
RICHARD REYNOLDS.

To Thomas Bennet, at Pickwick,
  near Corsham, Wiltshire.

Richard Reynolds was removed from Thomas Bennet's school at the age of fourteen, just as a growing taste for classical study had taught him to value the time and opportunity for making further progress, especially in the Latin language. History had also become a favourite pursuit; and it was, I believe, about this time, that his imagination was so much excited, by the bravery and heroism of the soldier's character, and the glory of skilful and successful warfare, that he had felt a strong desire himself to embrace a military life.

Of his conduct, or of anything which might mark the progress of his character, during the next six years, we unfortunately know little or nothing, beyond what may be inferred from one of his letters, written when he was twenty-three years of age, (and a copy of which is here given,) to John Maccappen, a young man for whom he had formed a sincere and ardent attachment,—a friendship which deserved the name,—in which mutual pleasure in each other's society, and a strong sympathy in each other's tastes and pursuits, was combined reverence for religion, and an earnest desire to be guided by its principles.

To JOHN MACCAPPEN.

Ketley, March 18th, 1758.

MY DEAREST FRIEND,

I have often thought one reason why many letters we receive from our friends are read with indifference, compared with others received from the same persons, is our not being in the same disposition or frame of mind with the writer. That this letter may not want that advantage, I will tell thee, I have been reflecting on the many occurrences we have been jointly concerned in since the time we first became acquainted. We were both young, apprentices to the same trade and in the same street. A similitude of circumstances and inclinations was the foundation of our intimacy, productive of very salutary effects to me. I remember with pleasure, one of our first evening walks together in the rope-walk, that our conversation was serious, and concluded with joint resolutions, that, let others do as they would, we determined to be religious. Happy would it have been for us, could we have as easily practised as resolved! but alas! I too soon gave back, too soon returned to my former follies, and added new. I fear I was the means of engaging thee in the practice of many things thou wast conscious were not right and wouldst not have done, had not my example strengthened the temptation and increased that disposition we all naturally have to what is wrong; but yet, we have great reason to be thankful to the gracious Preserver of men, that we were not suffered to be guilty of any gross sins. Oh! my friend, my dearest friend, may we be grateful, may our future conversation be influenced thereby, and may we for the time to come, be as helpmeets and incentives to each other in the way that is right! I protest, I can never reflect on the many hours we have spent together, but I am seized with a sort of tender melancholy, an agreeable pensiveness. How frequent were our excursions to Clifton and over the Downs! how often to the river-side, and the Hot-well rocks! but above all, the square was our most common resort. There, how often we talked down the summer's sun! Those days are gone, irrevocably gone, and we are separated by too great a distance ever to hope for the like again.　But let me conjure thee to come and see me, if it be but for a short time.　The spring is coming on, and I expect thou wilt be too busy when that is far advanced to come then.

Thy affectionate friend,

RICHARD REYNOLDS.

₊ John Maccappen was an early friend of Richard Reynolds, at Bristol, before he went to live at Coalbrook Dale.

CHAPTER II.

SCARCELY was the term of his apprenticeship expired, when a friend of his father's, Thomas Goldney, of Clifton, who was the partner of Abraham Darby, in the iron works at Coalbrook Dale, engaged Richard Reynolds to transact some business for him in Shropshire;—for which place he set out in 1756, on the journey which, as it afterwards proved, was to have so momentous an influence upon his future life. He arrived at the Dale, and there was introduced to Hannah, the only daughter of Abraham Darby, by his first marriage. She was possessed of great personal attractions, and her mind was one of no common order; —to a most amiable and generous disposition were united a truly humble spirit, and habits of piety and serious reflection. My grandfather, young, and enthusiastic in his admiration of beauty, and very susceptible to its influence, was equally so to goodness; and it was always understood, that his affections were first drawn towards Hannah Darby, by his witnessing (unknown to her) an instance of kindness and consideration to one whose claims were overlooked by others, in sending out of her own private allowance a liberal token of remembrance;—an action in its kindliness of nature, and unobtrusive manner of performance, in perfect accordance with his own benevolent and shrinking disposition. In a few months after this first visit to Coalbrook Dale, he was married to the object of his choice, on

the 20th of May, 1757; and having become a partner in
the iron and coal works at Ketley, about five miles from
Coalbrook Dale, he went to reside there. Few young men,
at the age of twenty-one, could begin life under more
auspicious circumstances: his domestic happiness was complete, and in the management of extensive works and a
large number of workmen, he entered on a wide sphere of
usefulness, which was calculated to call into full exercise
the various powers of his mind, and received dignity and
importance from his high integrity and active benevolence,
—whilst in the society and dear companionship of his
wife, he derived from her cultivated taste, her piety, and
her cheerful disposition, the purest enjoyment.

But, in a few short years, he was called upon to resign
this happiness; on the 24th of May, 1762, his wife died,
after an illness of only four days. From a friend who
came to their house as a guest, and who there was taken
ill of the measles, she, in the exercise of her hospitable
cares and attention, herself took the infection. On the
fourth day of her illness, the medical attendant considered
her to be going on so satisfactorily, that her husband, who
had some important business to attend to in Shrewsbury,
set out early in the morning, without communicating to
his wife that he was going from home. A short time after
his departure, an alarming alteration took place in her
symptoms, which was quickly perceived by herself, and by
those about her, as indicative of approaching dissolution.
Expressing her grief, on finding that her husband was not
in the house, she endeavoured to use the little strength
that remained to her, in making such arrangement of her
outward affairs as the time admitted; then taking a tender
leave of her two little children, a son about four years of
age, and a daughter one year and a-half old, she waited

with humble resignation and Christian fortitude the summons of her heavenly Father. A messenger had been immediately dispatched to recal her husband, who arrived in time to receive her last words and parting embrace, as she thanked him for all his kindness to herself, and commended their infant children to his care. The stroke of death was sudden; as if, by a flash of lightning, the joy of his life, the light of his home was destroyed,—the beloved wife of his bosom was taken away! His sorrow was too deep for utterance;—and never, even to the latest year of his life, did he omit, secretly to distinguish the sad hour of his bereavement, by spending a portion of the day in retirement and meditation. Some time after his loss, he thus speaks of her in a letter to a friend.—

"How often with a devotion and humility of soul that converts the ventings of sorrow into tears of joy, has she repeated from one of Watts's hymns:

> 'My God, my portion and my love,
>   My everlasting all,
> I've none but thee in Heaven above,
>   Nor on this earthly ball.'

I have *her* book before me with the leaf folded down at this place. Never, I believe, was there greater sincerity of intentional compliance with the requirings of apprehended duty, nor often greater resignation of will or acquiescence of choice with the dispensations of Providence. Such were her dispositions towards her God—towards her friends, all that can be conceived of the tenderest warmest affection 'glowed in her faithful sympathising breast'—all that constitutes happiness below, or ensures it above—

> 'These were all her own;'

and she was mine, and I was—*was* most blest."

3

Richard Reynolds continued to reside at Ketley; the works there furnished him with active employment, and his fully occupying his time and attention assisted him in maintaining that composure of mind which he worthily derived from the higher sources of religious consolation,—a strong practical faith in the wisdom and goodness of God, through which he was preserved in patient submission and acquiescence to the Divine will.

In the year 1763, he left Ketley to reside at Coalbrook Dale, in consequence of arrangements, rendered needful by the death of his father-in-law, Abraham Darby, who by his great exertions and spirit of enterprise, had extended the concerns of the Coalbrook Dale Company far beyond the locality where those works were situated, having established foundries in London, Bristol and Liverpool, and agencies at Newcastle and Truro, for the disposal of steam-engines, and other machinery made of cast iron, used in the deep mines of those districts. As the oldest son of Abraham Darby was too young to take the place of his father, the want of a person qualified to superintend this extensive business was a cause of great anxiety to the Company, and, in this emergency, they requested the assistance of Richard Reynolds. Influenced by affection for the family of his late beloved wife, and regard for his kind friend Thomas Goldney, he consented to leave his home, and relinquish his daily attention to the furnaces at Ketley and Horsehay, and to take upon himself the care and responsibility of superintending these works, in which he had no direct personal interest, as the shares which formed the portion of his wife, had been, at his own request, settled upon her children. The necessity of so much attention to a business, which called for incessant labour and activity, and took him much away from home, put it out of his power to attend, as he desired, to the safety and education of his children, and this source of care and anxiety pressed heavily upon him.   Under these circumstances, although he continued, as he ever was, a sincere mourner for the loss of her, whom he had loved with all the ardour and depth of a first affection, it was natural that he should wish to provide a mother for his helpless children, by a second marriage.   He was particularly sensible to the charms and advantages of female society; his constitutional reserve and diffidence readily yielded to an influence which drew out the varied powers of his mind, and the excellencies of his character, heightened his enjoyment of the beautiful in nature and art, and by sympathy in those religious sentiments which exercised so large an influence upon his whole character, was indeed, essential not only to his happiness, but, as he believed, to his improvement and religious advancement.   On the 1st of December, 1763, he was united to Rebecca Gulson, daughter of William Gulson of Coventry, (the intimate and dear friend of his late wife); who, by her kindness of heart, her tranquil disposition, and her regard for the memory of their mother, was peculiarly qualified to take the charge of her two children, William and Hannah Mary.   She was a woman of exemplary piety, most simple-hearted and truthful in her practice of the Christian virtues, and was possessed of much practical sound sense and understanding.   For many years she contributed largely to the happiness of her husband, uniting with him in his works of charity, taking an earnest part with him in his study of the Scriptures, strengthening his religious hopes, and sharing in his daily meditations and prayers.   She was an eminently consistent member of the Society of Friends, and conscientiously observant of plainness and simplicity in dress and domestic accommodations, not only as more consistent with her apprehension of the Christian character, but as affording additional means of relieving the wants of others, —thus, by self-denial, giving to benevolence the only distinctive quality which makes it a virtue.

The following two letters to his wife are interesting records of his affection, and are not without some biographical value.

London, Eleventh Month 18th, 1772.

MY DEAR WIFE,

It is true my letters have been short to thee, but it has not proceeded from a decrease in my affection, or a want of inclination to please thee. I have been pretty much hurried and disappointed. Barclay was to have met us with his accounts last night, but did not, nor do I yet know when he will. I am rather poorly with a sore throat and cold in my head, which renders nursing necessary, though my present situation does not admit of it. I wish for the time when I shall return to my dearest Becky, but fear it will be some time before it comes. If Richard Phillips has issued a bill to Humphrey Felton, it will not be amiss for him to advise Smith, Wright and Gray, of it, and any others, in about a week after it is drawn. I write to thee now because I have a few minutes leisure, but whether it is owing to my cold, or to having been attempting without success to adjust a long and perplexed account,—I do not know that I was ever less capable of writing to my own satisfaction, or, I think, to thine; and therefore I will suspend the conclusion till nearer the time of the post going out, in hopes of an alteration for the better, though I love thee dearly, notwithstanding my present inability to express it. I am cold, and dull, and low, but yet I hope for better times in every respect. Farewell my Becky. Remember me, as I do thee, frequently and affectionately. As I am so near the bottom of the paper I will endeavour to fill it, that I may not, by writing in company with the address at the top of the paper, discover to whom I am writing so awkwardly.

I dreamed last night of thee and Joe,* and awakened with sorrow, to find myself so far from those I love so well, and so likely to be for such a length of time.

The 19*th*.—I am at this time waiting at the counting-house for Barclay, who promised to be here long before this time. I am, through mercy, better than I was yesterday. I then began to think of my distance from the object of my affections, and the willing nurse of my infirmities, in case I should be as ill as I once was. I was then in a private house, and my father was with me; but I hope I shall be favoured with health, while absent from my Becky. And, indeed, if consistent with Divine appointment, health is very desirable at all times, and in all places; and yet I confess it is my duty, and I wish and hope it would be my endeavour, to be resigned to the dispensations of an all-wise and all-merciful Providence, whether in health or in sickness, in riches or poverty.

I have just received, and I rejoice to receive, thy kind letter, of the 16th and 17th instant. Every token of thy remembrance is delightful to me; and if that part of my letter which was written yesterday was not in some measure an answer to it, I should assure thee, that the shortness of my letters is never occasioned by the want of my being in good humour with my Becky. Of the dead and the absent people generally think well, even where there is no particular esteem or regard; but as I love thee with the tenderest affection, it is not possible I should here be out of humour with thee; indeed, it grieves me thou should admit such a thought. When I go to Bristol, and which I hope will be some time in the next week, I shall inform thee of Hannah's situation, as well as some other things. I advised brother Cowles of my coming to London, but I have received no letter from him. I presume he had nothing particular to communicate, and we do not correspond as friends merely. I can bear the slights of every body else, supposing they should slight me, better than the appearance of neglect in my Becky; and I rejoice that thy letters so effectually remove every apprehension of that kind. Do me

* His youngest son.

3*

equal justice, and be assured it is much my desire, in the words of our marriage covenant, to be unto thee a faithful and loving husband, until it shall please God by death to separate us.

RD. REYNOLDS.

London, Twelfth Month 1st, 1777.

I am come down stairs before other lodgers, and avail myself of the opportunity to begin a letter to my beloved Becky. I did not write yesterday, because nothing was done. The reason assigned now, is the multiplicity of business the lawyer has in hand, requiring immediate dispatch. Well acquainted as thou art with the impetuosity of my temper, and sensible, as I hope thou art, of the ardour of my affection for my best beloved on earth, thou may perhaps form some judgment of the disagreeableness of my situation; but it received some alleviation by the receipt of thy most affectionate letter of the 28th ult., last night. Does it not occur to thee, my Becky, that on this day nine years, I first called thee mine—my own wife—and O that I could this day, repeat in thy hearing, the endearing, the endeared epithet —which I now repeat to myself, with complacency and satisfaction, undiminished by time, and unimpaired by absence; nay if I know my own heart, I can adopt the language of the poet, and am happy in the belief, not lessened by thy last most acceptable letter, that my Becky can unite with me in acknowledging, with heart-felt satisfaction, that we are,

> "Enamoured more, as more remembrance swells,
> With many a proof of recollected love."—

I am called away by the tailor, who has brought me some clothes. I hope to add to this, by informing thee certainly this evening when we shall leave this place; for I design to leave it soon, whether the agreement is signed or not. Farewell, my dearest Becky, my nine years' wedded wife.—Love me nine times more than ever. I resume my pen while breakfast is bringing into the room, for I gladly snatch every spare minute to repeat my fond declarations, and true as fond, of continued affection to my Becky. Thou wished to hear particularly of cousin Kelsal. I drank tea with her yesterday, when she consulted me about a project she had formed, for I can call it no other, of taking a house by Westminster Bridge, the rent upwards of £70 per annum; £150 good-will, and a lease for only three years. She says, the rent will be made by letting lodgings, and her son was to occupy the shop, as an ironmonger,—without money to purchase a stock,—without interest to dispose of it,—unknown in that or any part of the town, and equally unknowing. I told her I thought it was a risk, that if they had ever so much money, prudence would not justify, and, as she had asked my opinion, I must say, I thought it absolutely unsafe, and improper, but referred her to persons of more knowledge and experience. Her son had a place, but it not being so advantageous as he thought he merited, he has left it before he knows of another. I should not my dearest Becky, occupy any part of this paper on any other subject but that of my regard for my wife, did I not hope thou would receive the preceding, written at thy request, as the effect of the desire I have to give my best beloved every satisfaction in my power. My brother Darby is come into the box, so I must conclude, and once more, my Becky, farewell.

I again resume my pen, but it will be only to conclude a letter which I am glad is already so nearly finished, as well as so amply filled; for, if I had not written before this time, though I do not love thee less, it would not have been in my power by this post to have sent so long a letter. Barclay said he would dine in town, and the rough draft of the agreement was then to be settled; but when we came to the appointed place, we were told he was gone out of town, poorly in health; but intended to return to-morrow. I am unwilling to leave unfinished what appears so nearly accomplished, after so long attendance; but if it is not done this week, I intend to leave it undone. Thou wilt sympathise on the vexatious occasion, with, my dearest Becky,

Thy affectionate, faithful
RICHARD REYNOLDS.

Love to Joe, Cousin Sukey, &c.

Richard Reynolds's engagement with the Coalbrook Dale
Company was terminated by the sons of the late Abraham
Darby assuming the direction of their own affairs; and
in 1768, he left Coalbrook Dale, and returned to Ketley,
with the satisfaction of having left the Dale works in a
prosperous state. It was whilst they were under his management, that an important change was accomplished in
the mode of converting cast or crude iron into malleable
or bar iron. This process was previously carried on in a
fire called a finery, somewhat like that of a smith's forge,
and wood-charcoal was the only fuel made use of. In this
fire the iron was exposed to the blast of powerful bellows,
and was in constant contact with the fuel. The quantity
of charcoal thus used was rapidly consuming the woods
of the country, and many efforts had been made to substitute pit-coal, when coked, for wood-charcoal; in the
first process, fusing the iron ore or iron stone, it had
answered, and had been used at Coalbrook Dale for many
years with continued and increasing success, but it was
then suggested by two of the workmen, that the coal
might also be used in the second or refining stage, the
process being performed in a reverbatory furnace, in which
the iron would not mix with the coal, but be heated solely
by the flame. My grandfather was struck with the ingenuity and feasibility of the scheme,—and the end to be
obtained was of such great importance, that he caused an
immediate trial to be made; the result was so successful,
that he communicated the discovery to the owners of the
works, doing justice to the workmen, by giving them the
credit which they deserved, and earnestly recommending
that the invention should be secured by a patent, in the
name of the " Cranages," with whom it originated. This
process is now technically called " puddling;" and it has
been the means of enabling Great Britain to make iron

in vast quantities at a small cost. At the present time, when iron railways are intersecting the earth in every direction, it may not be uninteresting to his descendants to know, that to their ancestor, Richard Reynolds, is due the credit of first employing iron instead of wood in the construction of railways. For the conveyance of coal and iron to different parts of the works, and to the river Severn, wooden rails had been in use, which from the great weights carried upon them, were not only soon worn out, but were liable to give way and break, occasioning loss of time, and interruption to business, and great expense in repairing them. It occurred to him that the inconveniences would be obviated by the use of cast-iron. He tried it at first with great caution, but found it to answer so well, that very soon all their railways were made of iron. He did not attempt to secure by patent the advantage of this invention, and the use of cast-iron in the construction of railways was afterwards generally adopted. Whilst speaking of him at this period, when he was acting for others, it should be mentioned that, through his representation to the principals, a large and profitable Government order for "cannon" was declined, it appearing to him inconsistent with the avowed principles of Friends, to manufacture weapons of war.

CHAPTER III.

AT the time when Richard Reynolds returned to his former residence, called the Bank, about one mile from the works at Ketley, his family consisted of William and Hannah Mary, the children of his first, and two little boys, Michael and Richard, the children of his second marriage: and shortly after, on the 31st of July, 1768, was born his youngest son, Joseph. Here he lived many years, carrying on an extensive business, in an enlightened and comprehensive spirit, with undeviating integrity and industry. His principle, in all cases of bargain and sale, was, according to the old adage, "Live and let live;" and, as an instance of the consistency with which he acted up to his motto, it may be adduced that, at the breaking out of the American war, when bar-iron rose to an extravagant price, and the makers of pig-iron could obtain their own terms, instead of taking an unreasonable advantage of the opportunity, he proposed to his customers that it should be left to one of themselves to name a fair price for pig-iron in the *then state* of the trade, and to determine the scale of proportionate reduction which should take place when the price of bar-iron should fall, as he foresaw that it would follow the *then* great and unsatisfied demand. The proposal was accepted, and by the scale which was then fixed-his conduct was governed, so long as he remained in the iron trade.

He early interested himself in the condition of the work-people whom he employed, establishing schools, building for them convenient cottages, and attending to their comfort. In all these objects he possessed the active sympathy of his wife, who, in her particular sphere of benevolence, was a most kind friend to her poorer neighbours, ever ready to help them with food and clothing in their time of need, and with advice and medicine in their times of sickness. Denial of self was a ruling principle of her conduct, and that she took an enlarged view of this duty was evident on one occasion, when she thought it right to remonstrate with one of her sons, upon his wearing so fine a broad cloth for his coat, as an expensive luxury. When he explained to her that, for weaving, it was necessary to separate the long wool from the shorter staple, and that, in consequence of rich people buying the fine cloth, the coarser fabric could be sold at a price within the reach of the poorer classes, she at once acknowledged its reasonableness, and said she no longer objected to all those persons wearing fine cloth who could properly afford so to do.

In 1769, Richard Reynolds lost his father, and in February, 1770, his son Michael. The death of his little child affected him deeply, and he makes touching mention of the event in one of his letters:

——We buried poor little Michael this day week. I never saw a person die before, and the scene affected me extremely. He breathed with such difficulty, that it was manifestly a labour to live, but yet discovered not the least frowardness or impatience. There is nothing so affecting as to see patient innocence in extreme suffering, what then must a parent feel when it is borne by one of his infant offspring: but the struggle is now over, the conflict is ended, and he now is, must be happy. . . . My judgment is reconciled to the event; but it will require more time to obliterate the many little engaging actions and expressions, the recollection of which moves and will continue to move the affections : and if thou should happen to recollect the innocency of his countenance, and the simplicity of his inquiries concerning his little brother, as he sat on thy knee by the fireside, however unavailing, however useless to.thyself or him, thy judgment may convince thee any emotion will be, yet I believe thou wilt not be able to recollect those circumstances, trivial as they are, without being also moved.

The state of the iron trade, in 1774, fully justified gloomy anticipations, and it is evident from my grandfather's letters, that his expectations respecting it were unfavourable; yet, as he knew the worst that could occur, and had made preparation for the worst, by keeping a balance at the credit of his stock account, to meet it, his peace and comfort do not appear to have been materially affected by anxiety on the subject. Rendered independent by the resources of his own mind, and his simple and rational tastes, his happiness was less affected by those changes and fluctuations in property, which are in general felt as so grievous an evil. At the outset of his life, the horror of debt, which never deserted him till its close, determined him never to exceed his means; and he commenced house-keeping, and made all his household arrangements, upon a system of strict economy, which enabled him unfailingly to adhere to this invaluable resolution. The advantage which he derived from acting on this principle, and his observation of the loss which others sustained from the neglect of it, induced him, as a rule, to liquidate every demand to which he was liable, previous to the annual settlement of his accounts.

He thus, at a later period, advised his eldest son, then lately married :—

——May I without offence on the present occasion, mention the word *frugality*, as including an avoidance of all unnecessary expense, till either of thy own or the Company's there is a deposit of a few thousands for such emergencies. I am aware, thy late engagements, the company thou had to entertain at Bristol, &c., as well as the length of time, must have occasioned a considerable expenditure, and if it would not savour too much of the prudence, or rather parsimony of old age, I would recommend an attention to small expenses, which, occurring so frequently, amount in the year to a sum incredible to those who have taken no account of them; but the independency which is purchased by early economy, was a sufficient inducement to me to begin life and continue it too, as long as it was necessary, upon a small scale, and I now thankfully taste the fruits of it in the enjoyment of the conveniences of life myself, and at times in assisting some others to procure them: the same conduct for a much shorter time will probably put it in thy power to retire in the manner thou wishes to do, and approves in thy father.

The care which he took, in the education of his children, was commensurate with the estimate which he had formed of its importance to their present and future well-being. He engaged for his eldest son when he was but eight years of age, a tutor who proved a valuable acquisition to his family and to himself personally, as he was a man of exemplary integrity, of refined manners, and possessed of considerable literary and scientific attainments. He preferred, so far as it was practicable, an education at home, —as being less liable to the influence of bad example than at a public school, and as affording them more rational amusements, and more frequent opportunities of observation and improvement. He was earnestly desirous, and unremitting in his endeavours to train them in "a religious life and conversation," and consistently in every respect

4

with the opinions and precepts of the Society of Friends. He paid great attention to their instruction in the Holy Scriptures, particularly in the New Testament; the "Sermon on the Mount," he regarded as the compendium of all Christian duty, and he required each of his children, as soon as they were capable of understanding it, to commit it to memory, and to repeat it aloud every Sunday evening, without missing a single word.

As a book of entertainment, Robinson Crusoe was his chosen gift to his own and other children. He had great pleasure in reading it himself, and we may suppose he was acquainted with some other of De Foe's writings, as among his papers was found a complete list, in his own hand-writing, of De Foe's works. He had great consideration for the young, liked to see them cheerful and happy, took an interest in their pleasures, and in various ways promoted their enjoyment; and although his occasionally stern manner and his undeviating punctuality kept them in some awe of him, yet was he beloved and respected by them in no common degree. In the fruit season, he would send them into the garden, with free leave to gather the fruit; and upon one day of the year, which was called "gooseberry-day," he collected a number of boys in his neighbourhood, and gave them the like permission. With his servants, he was very strict; but on the other hand he was remarkably attentive to their comfort and welfare in every respect, and was indeed their true friend, both spiritually and temporally. His temper was by nature hasty; and if, in moments of irritation, he spoke to them more strongly than the occasion justified, or with a severity which, upon reflection, appeared to himself inconsistent with the meekness and forbearance of a disciple of Jesus, he hesitated not frankly to acknowledge, and to apologize to them for his error. And in the same spirit of humility, he has been known even to follow a poor woman to her house, and ask her excuse for having either spoken hastily, or sent a sharp message to her, when she had applied to him for help at an unseasonable time. It would be difficult to express how deeply he lamented this infirmity: we know that in private, he prayed earnestly for the Divine forgiveness, and for grace to assist him in overcoming this and every other temptation to evil. He was most charitable in his judgments of others, and always discouraged, not only evil-speaking of the absent, but the trifling gossip about other persons and their concerns, which was then, and is now, so much too common; and the same charitable feeling made him slow to believe reports, injurious to the reputation of those who, not being present, were unable to explain or to justify their conduct.

My grandfather was an early riser (in the winter mornings lighting his own fire), regular and methodical in all his habits, punctual in the extreme, and very determinately exacting from others the same punctuality. Order and neatness pervaded the character of all his household arrangements; and over the fire-place in his kitchen, he had a board placed, upon which was painted in large letters, these words, "A place for everything, and everything in its place." He remarked that the adoption of this maxim of the famous De Witt's, proved often helpful to him,—" to do one thing at a time—to think, to speak of or attend to nothing else till the one thing was fairly done with; this with application will enable a man to do much business, and have sufficient leisure to write to his friends and to enjoy their company."

He was fond of animals, horses, dogs, cats, birds,—indeed his fine tortoise-shell cat, "Myrtle," generally sat by his side at meal-times. He was in the habit of feeding the birds from the windows of his study, and, one day, upon his return from a journey, taking out of his pocket a paper parcel containing small caraway comfits, and being asked, "what they were for," he said, "I brought them for the *robins*, I could not think of anything else to bring them." He rarely came home, after an absence, or entered a house where there were children empty-handed; and comfits he used often to bring for the young grandchildren, as well as for the robins.

When he was travelling with post-horses, he was careful that they should be driven slowly up long steep hills, and he invariably insisted upon their being driven with reins, as being less oppressive than by a postilion; this, it may be remarked, was then very seldom allowed by travellers. My grandfather's journeys, however, until the latter period of his life, were generally performed, as was the custom formerly, on horseback; and when at home, the long distances which separated the various branches of the iron-works obliged him to ride almost daily, and his horses were to him, as they are with most men, objects of great personal interest; and he estimated highly their different qualities, their strength, docility and swiftness. He rode remarkably well, and, being a tall handsome man, of the true Saxon race, his light brown hair, worn in long floating curls, his eyes blue, his complexion fair and ruddy, he was when mounted, a very striking looking figure. One of his grandsons, in his notes of a few of his recollections, thus writes:—"He had great amusement in telling us of one of his equestrian adventures, when he was riding, I believe, on Blackheath, where the king (George the Third) was at that time reviewing some troops. My grandfather's horse, which had formerly belonged to the cavalry, all at once started off at such speed, directly towards a circle of officers, that our grandfather, before he could rein in his martial steed, found himself, to his inexpressible confusion, within a few yards of the king."———Another anecdote, which he was fond of relating, used to divert us very much, but seems almost too ludicrous to put into *a book*,—that he once rode a race, with another young man, each of them having a young lady, seated upon a pillion behind him. Our grandfather fairly won the race; but when, on reaching the goal, he looked back, he found to his astonishment, that he had lost his fair companion, she having fallen off, at the commencement of the race, without his having perceived it.—I recollect his telling us, that once, when he was staying at Minehead, he went to see some poor women who were in an Almshouse there, and inquiring, from one of them, what were their circumstances, how they were treated, and the like; she replied, "that they were better off than they used to be, because now they were allowed 'liberty of conscience.'" This aroused my grandfather, who was always very indignant at the least interference with the rights of conscience, and he hastily asked the woman, what she *meant* by "liberty of conscience?" when he was much relieved by her replying that, "they were now allowed to go in and out when they pleased."

His enjoyment and admiration of the beauties of nature, was extreme, especially of extensive prospects over well-wooded and richly-cultivated lands. It was with intense delight that he looked upon such scenery, when it was bathed in the glorious hues of sunset; the elevated situation of his first residence afforded him this pleasure, and frequently on a fine evening, he would take his pipe, and retire to a spot, from whence he had a full view of the

4 *

Wrekin, the Ercall Woods, and in the distance, Cader-Idris,
and the mountains of Montgomery and Flintshire. There
he would contemplate in silence, the setting sun, slowly-
descending till it touched the distant hills, and, apparently
expanding, increase in grandeur and splendour, till it sunk
clear and unclouded below the horizon. He did not, however, while indulging in the soothing influence of his pipe,
allow himself to fall into a state of dreamy unconsciousness;
but, under feelings of admiration and devotion, such times
were to him, seasons of elevated thought and serious
reflection.

In a letter to his daughter, telling her of a new arbour
which he had then lately made, he says, "From thence I
have seen three or four as fine sunsets as I at any time have
seen—and if the gradual going down, and last, last twinkle of
the once radiant orb, the instant when it was, and was not,
to be seen—made me think of that awful moment when
the last sigh consigns the departing soul to different, if
not distant scenes; the glorious effulgence gilding the
western horizon with inimitable magnificence, naturally
suggested the idea of celestial splendour, and inspired the
wish that (through the assistance of His grace) a faithful
obedience to the requirings of our great Maker and Mas
ter, may in that solemn season justify the hope of my being
admitted into that city, which hath no need of the sun,
neither of the moon to shine in it, for the glory of God
lightens it and the Lamb is the light thereof."

Led by his keen appreciation of the beauties of natural
scenery, it was his practice, on his return from London,
Bristol, and elsewhere, to take in his way home places
remarkable for their picturesque beauty, or which were in
any respect of interest to a traveller, such as Cheddar
Cliffs in Somersetshire, Stowe, Hagley Park, the Leasowes

and Enville; he made frequent excursions in his own neighbourhood, to Hawkstone, and Apley Terrace; and, once in every year, he was accustomed to assemble a large party to spend a day upon the Wrekin. This hill is remarkable from its rising up alone so abruptly from the plain that it commands a most extensive view. Looking to the north may be seen Hawkstone, (the obelisk clearly visible,) and beyond, in the distance, the Cheshire, and to the left of these the Welsh hills, the Moel-Vama range and Dinas Bran. Still further to the west, in the distance, are Cader-Idris and Plinlimmon; and nearer, the Shropshire hills, the Long Mountain, Stiper Stones, the Long Mynt, and those of Church Stretton. Approaching the south may be seen, the most distant of any point, the Brecon Beacon; in the south, the Cleehills, which are the highest in Shropshire, and Malvern in the extreme distance. From the south, turning towards the east, come into view the hills of Gloucestershire, Warwickshire, and Oxfordshire, and the Bar-beacon in Staffordshire; due east, a hill in Leicestershire; and coming round again to the north, the Derbyshire Peak and hills in Cheshire. Such is the extreme boundary line; whilst nearer to the foot of the Wrekin, in the vast surrounding plain, lie Shrewsbury and other towns and villages, richly cultivated fields of different shades and colours, spread out like an immense map, interspersed with gentlemen's seats and farm-houses,—and here and there in the other direction, the smoke hanging like a mist, marks the situation of various iron-works and collieries, and, to complete the scene, the Severn,—Shropshire's beautiful Severn,—winding its way like a silver thread through the lovely landscape; between Coalbrook Dale and Shrewsbury could be counted nineteen turns where the river was lost and returned

to sight. The Wrekin is now much changed in its external character, and to those who knew it forty years ago,
is not improved, by having been planted almost to the
very top. The easiest ascent is from the Wellington approach, where, at the commencement of the carriage-road,
is a pretty cottage, built by Mr. Cludde, the proprietor of
that side of the hill. To spend a day on the Wrekin, at
least once a year, was the general custom of the neighbourhood, and one which my grandfather entered into with all
his heart. The party usually consisted of himself and
his family, his relations from Coalbrook Dale, and the
principal clerks in their employment, with their families;
and, in short, almost the whole of the members of their
small congregation were invited. On the top of the hill,
where are some large pieces of rock jutting out of the
smooth short grass, and affording some shelter from the
hot rays of the sun, the party seated themselves to partake of a bountiful supply of provisions: and a cheerful,
merry, busy party they were. After the meal was over,
surrounded by his relations and friends, their kind host
endeavoured to promote the happiness of all those whom
he had thus brought together. Sometimes, his countenance
beaming with enjoyment and genial feeling, he watched
with interest the games and sportive exercises of the young
people; at others, he would join in cheerful conversation
with the elders of the party, when the justness of his remarks, his playful wit, his expressions of delight, and his
admiration of the extensive prospect before him, charmed
all who listened. The season which he preferred for these
excursions was the time of harvest, when the richly-laden
corn-fields were spread below, and he never failed reverently
to praise that Being, from whose bounteous hand flowed
all these blessings. On such occasions, and in his walks

through the woods, he would read or repeat passages from "Thomson's Seasons," (which was frequently his pocket companion,) from "Addison's Hymns," which were familiar to him in the "Spectator," and from other authors. The grander scenery of Wales,—rivers, lakes, waterfalls,—all were the objects of his enthusiastic admiration. "But the ocean, (his son says, speaking of his father,)—the ocean, in its calm, or when stirred by the light breeze, or when the mighty winds drove the rolling billows, breaking into foam on the rocky shore at his feet,—I can find no words to describe the intensity of his emotions of wonder and delight."

His friendships were ardent and sincere, and were a source of enjoyment which engaged a large portion of his thoughts and affections. Reverence for goodness, which was a marked feature in his character, and his lowly estimate of his own religious attainments, led him to believe himself far behind those whom he esteemed for their piety and virtue, and he looked to such, not only for their sympathy, but for their counsel and guidance in the Christian path.

To one whom he thus regarded, he gave as a symbol of the durability of his affection, a small, beautifully white pebble, on which was engraved these words :—

"As firm my friendship, and as pure my love."

Possibly the idea was suggested by an ancient custom in the East, where, on the parting of friends, a white stone, on which the name of each was engraved, was broken, and divided between the two, each having his half, so that, wherever and whensoever these friends might hereafter meet, these would be the answering pledge of their fidelity, and if need were, a proof of their identity.

My grandfather had great respect and regard for a very
amiable and excellent minister of the Gospel, who lived in
his neighbourhood, the Rev. Joshua Gilpin; and it was
mainly through his exertions and personal interest that
Mr. Gilpin was presented to the living of Wrockwardine.
He also enjoyed the acquaintance of many scientific and
well-informed men. His manners, as a host, were courteous and dignified, and his conversation, when he was perfectly at ease, animated, and often diversified with a quaint
wit and humorous satire. His fine countenance beamed
with intelligence and kindliness; his eyes were piercing,
and were remarkable for the brightness which seemed literally to flash from them under strong emotion. It was
something almost fearful to meet their glance in anger or
indignation, whilst equally striking was their beautiful
expression under the excitement of admiration or affection.

CHAPTER IV.

WE are nearly without any familiar details of my grand-father's daily life : he does not appear to have been communicative to any one on personal or trifling incidents and occurrences. Letter-writing was considered by him as a substitute for conversation, and chiefly as conveying an interchange of thought or sentiment, expressed in his own case, in a didactic and a somewhat formal manner, and rarely descending to domestic or trifling subjects. His extensive correspondence, and his habit of copying every letter that he wrote, must have occupied no small portion of his time; and the invention of the copying machine was an important one to *him*.

Having made considerable purchases of land in Somersetshire, besides buying the Manor of Madely, in which Coalbrook Dale was situated, he had great enjoyment in planting and improving these estates, and laying out walks through the woods. Those upon Lincoln Hill, which were of some extent, were made expressly for the workmen, and seats were put up at different points, where they commanded beautiful views; they were called " The Workmen's Walks," and were a source of much innocent enjoyment, especially on a Sunday, when the men, accompanied by their wives and children, were induced to spend the afternoon or evening there, instead of at the public-house.

In this wood he built a very pretty rustic cottage for his daughter, containing sufficient accommodation for the persons who inhabited it, whilst three upper rooms were set apart for his daughter's use, and were by her furnished in excellent taste, with the plainness and simplicity of a real cottage ; and in this quiet retreat, she at times resided for days together. The cottage, which was beautifully situated, still remains.

So much alive was Richard Reynolds to every call of duty, he was not likely to be either negligent or oppressive as a landlord.

Archdeacon Plymley, in his "Survey of Shropshire," thus alludes to him :—" The population of the parish of Madely, in which Coalbrook Dale is situated, has increased very much. In January, 1782, it contained 440 houses, 560 families, 2690 persons ; in March, 1793, it contained 754 houses, 851 families, 3677 persons. In viewing this increase, it is pleasant to observe that the houses are increased in a greater proportion than either the families or persons, which bespeaks greater prosperity and comfort than heretofore, and has arisen, as well from the benevolence of the lord of the manor, as from the works. He has built many comfortable houses for old and distressed persons, and granted a great number of leases of waste land, in the proportion, if I recollect right, of about one-eighth of an acre to each person, to build on, they paying a fine of five guineas for a lease of ninety-nine years, and five shillings a year ground rent."

In 1772, my grandfather exerted himself to obtain an Act of Parliament for making a towing-path for horses to tow the vessels up the River Severn, considering the employment of men for this purpose as not only degrading and unseemly, but as the means of harbouring and collecting persons of bad character, and facilitating a system of plunder injurious to the trade and destructive of the morals of the people engaged in it. Some years later he became a member of an association for the purpose of improving the navigation of the Severn; but the efforts made were unsuccessful, the measure being opposed in Parliament by the inhabitants of some of the towns, who mistook their own interest, whilst others neglected to give it that support which the great and obvious advantages that such an improvement would have conferred upon them entitled the projectors to expect. In 1788 an act was obtained for making a canal from the principal iron works in Shropshire to the Severn—this was the last work of a public nature in which he took a part.

The great improvements in the steam engine, invented by James Watt, which were adopted at Ketley in 1778, gave a new impulse to the iron trade. The greater degree of knowledge and ingenuity required in the construction of these engines, and of the machinery which the use of them introduced, led to a rapid improvement in the minds and condition of the working classes, through the habits of reflection and the desire for the acquisition of knowledge, excited by the wonderful results of the genius of this great man. Richard Reynolds took a warm interest in the introduction and success of his steam-engine. For no one did he entertain sentiments of more affectionate esteem than for James Watt, and he admired and revered to the end of his life, the talents, the varied acquirements and the virtues, of this peculiarly-accomplished man.

From his correspondence with Mrs. Trimmer, and some of his letters to Earl Gower and others, we learn how deeply he was interested in the education of the work-people. It has been already mentioned that he built a school-house,

5

near his own residence, at Ketley; but, at that time, such
was the ignorance of the population by which he was surrounded, that not only were the children unmanageable
and most unwilling to learn, but the parents would only
send them on condition of being paid for their attendance.
His exertions at Coalbrook Dale were more successful.
The ministry of the excellent Mr. Fletcher, of Madely, had
produced a beneficial and lasting effect on the people in
that part of the country; and, so far from being indifferent
to the value of a good education for their children, they
eagerly availed themselves of the efforts made in their behalf. In addition to a large week-day school, two Sunday-schools were established and well supported. Nor was
his interest confined to his own neighbourhood; he contributed liberally to the Friends' school at Ackworth, and
to the building of schools in various parts of England and
Wales.

Although, by the attention of his son, my grandfather
was relieved in some degree from the arduous duties of his
position, as managing partner of a large and increasing
iron-work, other circumstances of a more public nature
called for his exertions. The distress consequent upon
the deficient harvest of 1782, induced him to unite with
the gentlemen of the neighbourhood in raising a subscription for the purchase of food, and in framing the rules and
regulations of an association for relieving the " industrious,
and truly indigent," by which the attention of the magistrates and landed proprietors was turned to other objects intimately connected with the happiness of the labouring
classes. The number of public-houses was diminished, the
provisions of the laws against drunkenness were enforced,
the practice of paying workmen at public-houses was severely
censured, and great pains were taken to abolish a custom

so demoralizing in its effects, not only on the men, the
employers, and their agents,—but also entailing, in this
time of scarcity, starvation on their families. From these
judicious measures, more effectual relief and more permanent advantages were derived by the poor people, than
from the distribution of food at low prices : which yet appeared absolutely necessary under the circumstances. Flour
or rice was, for this purpose, bought at Liverpool; and such
was the state of excitement in the country, that a guard
of men on horseback was required to protect the canal
boat, and prevent its being stopped, and the flour taken
possession of by other parties equally in want. The recurrence of a scarcity of food in 1796, again called forth
his feelings of deep commiseration for the starving and
distressed state of the poor ; and, as on the former occasion, he united with the neighbouring gentlemen and land-
holders to adopt some efficient mode to save them from absolute starvation. Meetings were called, and a committee
appointed to purchase rice, each subscriber to have the disposal of a certain quantity, in proportion to the amount
of his subscription. The urgency of the case may be inferred, from the liberality of the subscriptions attached to
the names of some of the gentlemen who attended the
county meeting,—namely,

Messrs. Bishton & Co. . . .	£1,500
Mr. Botfield, for the Old Park Co. .	1,500
Mr. Jos. Reynolds, for the Ketley Co.	2,000
Mr. R. Dearman, for Coalbrook Dale Co.	1,500
Mr. William Reynolds, for the Madely Co.	1,000

Several of £100 by private gentlemen ; and £500 as the
individual subscription of R. R.

Early in the year 1783, the horrors of the slave-trade
became generally known, and petitions to Parliament were

presented for its amelioration, and ultimate abolition. This appears to have been the first occasion on which Richard Reynolds felt himself called upon to come forward on any national question. His letter to G. Forrester, Esq., M. P. for Much Wenloch, and the draft of a petition from that borough, indicate the earnestness with which he co-operated with the early opponents of that trade in human blood; and other letters in this collection will show that his interest in this work of benevolence was never weakened, but continued in all its warmth to the close of his valuable life. Another effort being made in the year 1788, on behalf of the much injured Africans, he again solicited the aid of his friends, both in and out of Parliament; and among others, he addressed a letter to Mrs. Trimmer, though personally unknown to her, hoping that he might, through her means, influence the female sex in the cause, and also if possible, interest the Queen herself. Those who knew the writer may imagine how warm must have been the zeal which could so overcome his natural shyness and reserve, as to induce him thus to address a perfect stranger.

On the occasion of the bill for the abolition of the slave-trade being carried in 1807, he thus writes to a friend :—

I should have been glad to hear that some public manifestation of Christian rejoicing had been exhibited, or at least recommended. Thou wilt not suppose I mean illuminations or ringing of bells. I recollected, and was not without a thought of reminding the public, by a paragraph in the newspaper, of the practice of the Jews, who manifested their joy on an especial deliverance, not only by feasting and sending portions one to another, but by *gifts to the poor*. And I think it would not be amiss, if those who consider themselves, or are considered by others, as pastors, would, by example and precept, excite their flocks to discover their joy for the abolition of the slave-trade, by commiserating the sufferings of the poor in their neighbourhood, and administering to their wants, of clothing, food, and fuel, which the present severity of the cold, though less felt than common, in the course of the winter, must increase. Such, I trust, has been the case with some individuals, but I wish to have it more general.

His strong feeling on the subject, also induced him, in the year 1790, to write to Lord Sheffield, declining to vote for him, at the approaching election for Bristol, on the ground of his being opposed to the abolition of the slave-trade.

The next question of a public nature in which he took an active part, was in 1784, when it was proposed by the ministry to lay a tax on pit-coal. His letter to Lord Gower, afterwards Marquis of Stafford, shows the impolicy of this tax, and the earnestness with which he opposed it: and that to Sir Richard Hill, the representative of the county, as clearly points out the unequal pressure of others. He proposed, in lieu of these, taxes on some articles of luxury; and some of his suggestions were adopted at the time by Mr. Pitt—and others, by succeeding Chancellors of the Exchequer.

In the year 1785, the commercial arrangements with Ireland, then under the consideration of Parliament, excited an unusual degree of alarm amongst the manufacturers of Great Britain. The interests of the iron trade were considered to be peculiarly endangered; and my grandfather united, though reluctantly, in an active and effective opposition to the measures proposed. He joined some others, interested in manufactures, in forming an association for the protection of that portion of the national interest, under the title of " The United Chamber of Manufacturers of Great Britain ;" and his name, on this occasion, was associated with the names of James Watt,

5 *

Matthew Boulton, Josiah Wedgewood, and many others, to whose talent and exertions the progress of manufactures in this country is chiefly owing.* His letters to Earl Gower and Mr. Rose, and his examination taken by the Privy Council, show the value of the information conveyed by him, and those with whom he acted, on this important occasion.

He was soon again called upon, on the occasion of a commercial treaty being entered into with France, to give information to the Lords of the treasury, in order to protect the interests of the iron trade. His opinions on this subject are fully given in his correspondence with Lord Sheffield, as well as his hopes that a commercial intercourse, beneficial to both parties, would tend to prevent the breaking out of wars between the two countries, and ultimately promote the pacification of the whole world.

* Had these intelligent and right-meaning men lived at the present time, we may well believe their views on these questions would have been very different.

CHAPTER V.

RICHARD Reynolds's habits and mode of life were marked by great plainness and simplicity; the furniture of his house, his table, and his establishment throughout were strictly regulated by a desire to avoid all ornament or expensive luxury. In viewing this part of his character, however, it must be borne in mind that among Friends, domestic life and manners are so influenced and restricted by the rules and customs of the Society, that it is often difficult to determine to what extent the habits of individuals may be formed by those regulations to which they feel it right to show a deference, although in their private judgment they may not fully coincide with them. So it probably was with the subject of this memoir, whose natural disposition and tastes were unquestionably opposed in some respects to the requirements of the Society, by which not only are plainness and simplicity strongly enforced in dress and language, in the furniture of their houses and domestic economy; but a strict limitation is placed on amusements, the cultivation of music, and to a certain degree on the indulgence of a taste for paintings and the fine arts in general. Parents, too, are repeatedly warned of the duty of bringing up their children in accordance with these principles. In order that this discipline may be strictly maintained, meetings of each congregation are periodically held for this especial purpose, a series of printed

questions being read, to which written answers have to be
drawn up stating how far the several members of the congregation have been careful to act up to the principles of
the Society, regarding attendance at meeting, dress, language, the refusal to take oaths, or to engage in war, the
non-payment of tithes and church-rates, &c. Should it
be needful to notice a departure from the rules of the
Society in any of these points, two or more of the most
influential members are deputed to visit the individual or
family, and endeavour to influence their conduct by exhortation or friendly reproof. By many this system would
be regarded as a most unpleasant species of interference;
but by those brought up in the Society, it is not often felt
to be burthensome or inquisitorial, and it is indeed rarely
exercised otherwise than with gentleness and discretion.
These meetings for maintaining the discipline of the Society
were viewed by Richard Reynolds as highly important,
and he considered it his duty to attend them regularly,
and so far as his diffident disposition would permit, he took
an active part in the conduct of the business. During
forty years he was never once absent from the general
annual meeting held in London. He thus writes to a
friend on this subject;—

"Thy sentiments respecting our meetings for discipline,
and the necessity that a degree of the same spirit under
which they were established should influence those who
are active in them, are perfectly just, and under that impression there is little danger of thy too hastily interfer-
ing in the conducting of them; but let not a consciousness
that there still remains something to be done in thy own
vineyard, prevent thee from doing what may be in thy
power for promoting the good of others, whether of the
Society at large, or of individuals, assured that a faithful

discharge of duty in the ability given, will increase thy own strength as well as thy own peace : for if we defer endeavouring to serve others till there is no room for improvement at home, we shall attempt but little and effect less; nor, when we shall give an account of the talents committed to us, can we expect to receive a reward, but in proportion to our improvement of them.''

Although, then, his natural disposition and tastes would probably have led him, under the ordinary influences of society, to follow a variety of pursuits, which in themselves he could not condemn, yet he had grown up under the belief that it was his duty to yield his private opinions to those held by others, whom he esteemed more highly than himself; and as through life it was his earnest and sincere desire to be a consistent Friend, his conduct was always irreproachable, even in the small as in the more important points inculcated in the rules and precepts of the Society. There can be little doubt that his regard for these had a tendency to produce something like a perpetual warfare between his sectarian scruples and the more enlarged views suggested by his own sound sense and wise judgment; and in one so keenly alive to the slightest whisper of conscience, this raising up of artificial difficulties and conventional distinctions of right and wrong, operated upon him in a way much to be deprecated. There was a sensitiveness in his temperament, and an inequality of spirits, which predisposed him to melancholy, which gave something like a morbid colouring to his estimate of failure, or imperfection in his practice of the higher Christian virtues, and led to his taking depressing views of his own religious state. Thus he, who particularly needed encouragement and freedom to rise above the shackles of human authority, was thrown upon a close self-inspection concerning matters of mere

opinion and comparative minor importance, which told unfavourably upon his own happiness, and indirectly affected
that of others whom he loved most. He possessed a decided taste for pictures and engravings, and made a small
collection of valuable prints. But here, his scrupulous
spirit thought it right to deny self, and in consistence with
his high ideas of duty, as steward of the talents intrusted
to him, he spent very little money upon these or any similar gratifications. Books he bought more freely, yet still
under much limitation. He was fond—passionately fond
—of music; and here again the asceticism which so largely
mingles in the opinions entertained by " Friends," interfered with the full development of his mental powers;
those intellectual tastes which were given to him by his
Creator, and which would have harmonized the other parts
of his character, by counteracting, on the one hand, his
tendency to depression, and affording, on the other, an
outlet for the vivacity of disposition which was often a
cause of distress to him,—subjected to these rigid rules,
were made occasions for the mortification of self, instead
of being cultivated and encouraged as sources of innocent
pleasure and social enjoyment.

In 1776 he had a severe and dangerous attack of fever,
and now when his religious faith was called upon to meet
the possible approach of death, he experienced its sustain-
ing power; this faith, and the remembrance not of any
works of righteousness, but of the *integrity*, as he expresses
himself in one of his letters, with which *he had desired to
be made conformable to the will of his Maker*, enabled
him to attain a degree of hope, which could and did support him in the hour of trial.

He was very conscious of the effects of his physical
temperament upon his mental powers and inward peace,

from which he suffered so much, and he submitted to it as
a discipline wisely and mercifully appointed for the trial
of his faith, and the more complete purification of his
spirit. The nature and degree of this suffering are so well
described in the poem entitled "The Doubting Christian,"
a copy of which was found in his own hand-writing, that
it is here inserted, at the suggestion of one who knew him
intimately, and who had heard him read it as the expression of his own feelings.

THE DOUBTING CHRISTIAN.

A SOLILOQUY.

What shall I do to know my state,
    And read my sins forgiven?
What will be my eternal fate?—
    How shall I get to heaven?

I look within and look without,
    And both quite dim appear;
My firmest hopes admit of doubt,
    And faith is mixed with fear.

I drudge along the tiresome road,
    Few beams of comfort shine;
But seldom can I say "My God,"
    Or call the Saviour mine.

Others of holy pleasures talk,
    Which faith and duty bring,
While I with gloomy sadness walk,
    Nor taste the cheering spring.

They sail beneath a cheerful sky;
    Their peace is seldom lost;

While on the boisterous billows, I
    Of hope and fear am tost.

Fain would my soul their bliss obtain,
    And join the happy few;
Why may not I such pleasures gain,
    And be as happy too?

What is the requisite, my soul!
    Is it perfection here?
Can this alone my fears control,
    And make thy title clear?

I may pronounce that were it so,
    Assurance is a dream;
Since none are perfect here below,
    However good they seem.

I'll search the sacred records then,
    Nor thus conclude in hastè,
To find descriptions of the men
    Who shall salvation taste.

I'll pass by lesser marks for one
    That soon will end the strife,
" He that hath God's eternal Son
    Hath everlasting life."

From condemnation he is freed,
    And glory shall obtain;
But he who hath not this to plead,
    His hopes are all in vain.

This is the weight that turns the scale;
    Whatever else we boast
Are comforters that then will fail,
    When we shall need them most.

My soul thine evidences prove
  Nor longer boasting, stay;
Hast thou embrac'd the source of love
  In His appointed way ?

If a suspicion still remain,
  And fears still keep their place,
Renew thy solemn acts again
  And plead His promis'd grace.

That grace which leads thee to His throne
  Thy ruin will prevent—
He never did or will disown
  An humble penitent.

Come then, my soul, surmount thy fears,
  Let thy despondings cease !
My weeping eyes forbear your tears,
  My rising joys increase !

I bid farewell to every doubt,
  Now Jesus is in view,
He stands engag'd to bear me out
  And bring me safely through.

By no one could the commandment, "Remember the Sabbath-day to keep it holy," be more conscientiously and literally observed. It was his custom to consider the evening of the preceding day, as a time of preparation, and when the clock struck eight, all work and employment of himself and the household, of merely secular interest, were suspended. At the most active period of his life, when he was so closely engaged in business, that to save time, even his dinner was sent down to him at his office, he never transacted any business after eight on Saturday night. In this connection the following recollections of

6

Richard Reynolds, by one nearly related to him, will **not**
be out of place; and, though not containing any important
incident, and although some of the anecdotes are of a very
trifling description, they are, to some extent, characteristic.*

"Our uncle Reynolds's strict observance of the Sab-
bath, was very striking, and evidently arose from a genuine love for heavenly employment, and not from Jewish
ideas of the duty. Regularly every Saturday evening,
it was his custom to remove such books as were lying about,
which were not of a decidedly religious tendency. He
wished all his household to finish their work as early in
the day as possible, and at eight o'clock he liked to see
us put by our work, or whatever employment we might be
engaged in. On Sunday, every servant in the house attended both the morning and evening meeting, no one
staying at home to prepare dinner, which he used to say,
'is always better cooked the day it does itself, than on
any other.' After dinner, when he had taken a short rest,
the domestics were called into the parlour, each having a
Bible, and seldom appearing unaccompanied by one or more
of their friends, whom they had permission to invite on
these occasions; and I have often seen a large company.
When all were seated, the servants, after a short pause,
proceeded to read aloud a chapter selected by my uncle,
the oldest servant beginning, and the rest following, each
taking a verse successively. My uncle then read a chapter himself, generally making a few apposite remarks upon
it; then followed another short silence, and the little meeting was concluded. After tea, the whole family went
again to meeting. When we returned, we had supper,
which was a very pleasant meal—my uncle, by his own
lively manners and cheerful conversation, encouraging
those around him to converse freely. A short reading in

* These recollections refer to the latter period of Richard Reynolds's life.

the Bible closed the day. His consideration for the comfort and well-being of his servants was most exemplary, and he never received anything from them without thanking them courteously. On leaving home he always shook hands with each. He rose very early in the morning, and his study-fire was always left over-night prepared for his lighting it himself; his time was chiefly passed in reading and devotion. After breakfast, it was his habit to retire to his study, where he remained until noon—he then generally went out alone on some errand of mercy, or to attend one or another of the numerous committees on which he acted. Two mornings in the week he attended the Friends' Meeting, and on these occasions, as well as on the Sundays, no weather was ever known to keep him at home. After dinner, Sarah Allen, or some friend, who might be staying at the house, read aloud to him, to soothe him to sleep. He was a poor sleeper at night, and found it necessary to take a long rest in the afternoon, even if unable to sleep. Six o'clock was the hour for tea, and afterwards, when the season admitted, he walked out into the country. In the evening of every day, as in the morning, a portion of the Scriptures was read; when the clock struck ten, candles were brought in ready lighted, and every one was expected to retire for the night. A young relation (not a member of the Society of Friends) arriving, on a visit one evening at tea-time, my uncle said to him, ' I shall be glad of thy company as long as thou likest to stay; but remember, ten o'clock is the hour at which I choose all who are in my house to go to bed! What wilt thou do this evening?' ' I think I shall go to the play,' was the answer. ' Well, remember—ten o'clock.' The young man returned at ten; and the next morning, whilst at breakfast, my uncle was highly amused at the description of the performance,

in which a Quaker had been introduced.   The young man,
however, found the time pass so pleasantly under the roof
of his aged relative, that he did not again go to the play
during his visit.

"My uncle was occasionally severe in his manner of
administering rebuke, and forwardness or impertinence,
especially in the young towards the old, was not often
allowed to pass unnoticed.   A young Quaker of very forward and self-confident manners, one day entered the room ;
my uncle looked upon him with a scrutinizing glance, and
said 'I do not know thee, young man,—who art thou ?'
He replied, 'I am ——' My uncle, quietly, but with an
emphasis that could not be mistaken, said, 'Whose *son* art
thou ?' "

"It was painful to him to witness any species of waste,
and I remember few things of a small kind that hurt him
more than the fashion of ladies wearing long trains—'I
cannot bear to see sweeping on the ground what would
clothe a poor shivering child.'   A love of order was natural to him, and he made it a principle that whatever was
worth doing at all, was worth doing well.

"Of his extensive charitable acts so much is known that
it is almost needless to advert to them; yet those that
were hidden were particularly indicative of the quickness
and delicacy of his benevolent sympathies.   One of these
was the pleasure he took in enabling those who were themselves in limited circumstances to assist the poor and distressed, by placing money in their hands for that purpose.
I have myself been thus favoured by him, and well remember his very words on one occasion and the spot where he
stood, as he said, 'My dear, I wish thee to take this, (giving
me what appeared to me a large sum), thou canst not
always relieve the distressed as thou would'st wish—but I

charge thee tell no one—the injunction is not enough obeyed, "let not thy left hand know what thy right hand doeth."' His generosity was not confined to merely benevolent objects. Once when I was greatly disappointed in not being in time to meet a young friend who had returned home a distance of twelve miles, he very kindly ordered a chaise, saying, "Is there not some one whom thou would like to accompany thee ?—by all means send a note to her, and I hope you will enjoy yourselves."

As an instance of his readiness to serve others, and of the great good often resulting from a small action, the following anecdote related to one of the family by Dr. Jephson, of Leamington, may be mentioned. Richard Reynolds, who was travelling through Nottingham, met with some slight accident, and sent for a surgeon, whose assistant, a mere lad, came in his place. My grandfather entered into conversation with him, and in the course of it young Jephson alluded to the desire he had to attend a course of lectures on chemistry, which were at that time being delivered in the town, which would be of essential service to him, but said he had not the means of paying for them. The patient listened attentively, and with his usual kindness, interested himself in this young man, and for the purpose of encouraging him in the pursuit of knowledge, gave him five guineas. We might speculate on the possibility that, but for this timely aid, Dr. Jephson might not have risen to his future eminence.

6.*

CHAPTER VI.

By the marriage of his only daughter to William Rathbone of Liverpool, in 1786, my grandfather was deprived of one, the loveliness of whose character, superior mental endowments, cultivated mind, and devoted attachment to this beloved parent, constituted her most emphatically the joy of his life; he was to her the guardian and counsellor to whom she looked up with admiring reverence, as she was to him the intimate friend and dear companion, upon whose unfailing sympathy he could at all times, and in all circumstances, confidently rely; and the loss to himself and to his family, which was occasioned by her removal to a distance, was felt to be irreparable.

It was not long after this event occurred, that he determined to retire from the business, which for many years he had so ably conducted. He had ever regarded the possession of wealth as entailing very grave responsibilities upon the possessor; and he felt that the accumulation of property was therefore more to be deprecated than desired. He earnestly wished for more leisure for reading and reflection, and also believing that a life free from the engrossment of time and mind, which the management of so large a concern involved, would be more conducive to his own religious advancement, he gave up his shares in the iron-works at Ketley to his sons William and Joseph.

His son William was well known as an eminently scientific and intelligent man; his taste for mechanics, his eagerness in the pursuit of knowledge, his energy and activity, particularly qualified him to render valuable assistance to his father,—and he had for some time taken an active part in the management of the works. He carried out great improvements in the manner in which the collieries and iron mines were worked, introducing new machinery, and availing himself with much ingenuity of the discoveries in chemistry and the practical experience of other countries in the manufacture of iron.

He was the first to bring into successful and permanent operation the transit of canal boats by means of inclined planes, where great inequalities of surface and a deficiency of water were unfavourable to the ordinary system of locks. The first work of this kind which he executed was completed in 1788, and is thus described by Mr. Thomas Telford in *Plymley's Agricultural Report for Shropshire*, page 291 :—

" These difficulties, the inequality of the ground, and want of sufficient water, seemed insuperable, and most probably might have proved so for ages to come, had not Mr. William Reynolds of Ketley, whose character is too well-known to need any eulogium, discovered the means of effecting this desired object.

" Having occasion to improve the method of conveying ironstone and coals, from the neighbourhood of the Oakengates to the iron-works at Ketley, these materials lying generally at the distance of about a mile and a-half from the iron-works, and at seventy-three feet above their level; he made a navigable canal, and instead of descending in the usual way, by locks, continued to bring the canal forward to an abrupt part of the bank, the skirts of which terminated on a level with the iron-works. At the top of this bank, he built a small lock, and from the bottom of the lock, and down the face of the bank, he constructed an *inclined plane*, with a double iron railway. He then erected an upright frame of timber, in which, across the locks, was fixed a large wooden barrel; round this barrel a rope was passed, and was fixed to a moveable frame,— this last frame was formed of a size sufficient to receive a canal boat,—the bottom, upon which the boat rested, was preserved in nearly an horizontal position, by having two large wheels before, and two small ones behind, varying as much in the diameters, as the inclined plane varied from an horizontal plane. This frame was placed in the lock, the loaded boat was also brought from the upper canal into the lock, the lock-gates were shut, and on the water being drawn from the lock into a side-pond, the boat settled upon the horizontal wooden frame, and as the bottom of the lock was formed with nearly the same declivity as the inclined plane, upon the lower gates being opened the frame with the boat passed down the iron railway, on the inclined plane, into the lower canal, which had been formed on a level with the Ketley Iron-Works, being a fall of seventy-three feet. Very little water was required to perform this operation, because the lock was formed of no greater depth than the upper canal, except the addition of such a declivity as was sufficient for the loaded boat to move out of the lock; and, in dry seasons, by the assistance of a small steam-engine, the whole of the water drawn off from the lock was returned into the upper canal, by means of a short pump. A double railway having been laid upon the inclined plane, the loaded boat, in passing down, brought up another boat, containing a load nearly equal to one-third part of that which passed down. The velocities of the boats were regulated by a break acting upon a large wheel, placed upon the axis, on which the ropes connected with the carriage were coiled."

In 1789, a copper token, or half-penny, having a representation of this plane on one side, and of the cast-iron bridge, executed by Abraham Darby, at Coalbrook Dale, on the other, was struck, and issued by the Coalbrook Dale Company. Since the practicability of inclined planes has been established by the success of the Ketley plane, but few Acts have been passed for new canals, without a clause authorizing the Company to erect inclined planes instead of locks, if they should be found most advisable.

Other instances of William Reynolds's mechanical skill are mentioned by Mr. Telford, in connection with the canals and improvements in this part of Shropshire: and he also notices the mistake of Fulton in claiming the invention of the inclined plane.

Leaving the Ketley Iron-works then, in such good hands, in the year 1789, on the 19th February, Richard Reynolds went to reside in the house which he had formerly occupied at Coalbrook Dale. In the same year his son William married, and his son Joseph about four years afterwards. In the happiness and well-being of his children he ever manifested a deep and affectionate interest, and as years went by, surrounding him with many grandchildren, he showed a constant desire to promote their enjoyment and improvement, and as they grew up, evinced an unceasing solicitude for their progress in virtue and the highest wisdom. He liked, even when they were quite young, frequently to have them to stay with him at his own house; and some of them can well remember his indulgence to their childish faults, and his attention to their childish pleasures, one of the greatest of which was when he would take them with him in his walks, talking kindly to them, in a pleasant and lively manner, and leading them to observe and admire, as they took their way through his favourite woods, the various objects of beauty in their path,—the delicate spring-flowers, the mossy bank, and the various foliage of the trees,—while the little grandchild, holding by his hand, would skip along by his tall and commanding figure, proud and happy to be his companion.

In later years he showed great kindness, and an attention to his grand-children not very common, in encouraging them to correspond with him. A few of these letters have a place in this selection, with others of a merely personal or private character, to fill up in some measure the want of domestic incident, and the deficiency of such details as interest the affections, and give pleasure in the perusal of faithful biographies.

The year 1803 was marked by severe domestic affliction. In April, he had an attack of influenza, which had nearly proved fatal, and whilst confined to his bed, his wife was taken ill with the same disease, and, not having strength to resist it, she rapidly sank, and after a week's illness, peacefully breathed her last, closing her benevolent and exemplary life with unaffected piety and resignation.

On the 3rd of June, his eldest son, after a long and painful illness, was released from a life which had latterly been one of much suffering; and on the 12th of July, the wife of his youngest son, Joseph, was called from the oversight of a large family of young children, at a time when, humanly speaking, a continuance of her care was as important to their welfare, as her affection was essential to the happiness of their father; but He, whose very self is love, in wisdom inscrutable, removed her hence. Thus, in the short space of three months, he was bereaved of three beloved members of his family. In the course of this year he made preparations for leaving Shropshire; many of the ties, which bound him to his residence there, were broken, and as he no longer considered that he was required by any claims of duty to remain at Coalbrook Dale, in April, 1804, he removed to Bristol, having taken a house in St. James's Square. His cousin, Sarah Allen, who was attached to her aged relative by no common sentiments of affection and regard, took up her abode with him, and remained with him to the last, in every way ministering as a daughter to his comfort and enjoyment, by her unwearied kindness, whilst her intelligent and well-informed mind, and energetic character, peculiarly fitted her to be his friend and companion.

In this large city my grandfather soon found ample scope for the exercise of his benevolent desire to promote the happiness and lessen the sufferings of his fellow-creatures. He took a lively interest in the various public charities, being the founder of the Samaritan Society, and giving his warm and liberal support to others, particularly the Strangers' Friend, Misericordia, the Orphan Asylum, the Infirmary and the Alms-Houses. The increase of the population, and the diminished value of money, pressed so heavily on some of these institutions, that the intentions and expectations of their founders and original promoters could not be fulfilled without further support. He solicited personally and by letter, subscriptions on a large scale for augmenting the fund for the payment of a weekly sum to the inhabitants of the alms-houses, going from house to house,—by his own zeal kindling that of others,—and by the authority which his own liberality gave him, exercising a degree of influence which he would not otherwise have possessed over those whom he knew could afford to contribute largely. One gentleman to whom he applied, of acknowledged wealth and importance in the city, had given him a check for £500, and he left the room, but returning instantly, said he would give him back the check, as such a sum from *him* would do the cause more harm than good. The gentleman immediately wrote another for a thousand pounds, and gave it to him. He himself gave £2,000 (one of his friends says four) to this fund, and £4,000 to the Trinity Alms-houses.

The knowledge of his desire to avoid even the appearance of ostentation would make his family wish to be guided by the same spirit in speaking of him; yet, as he is now beyond the reach of human opinion, a few instances of that benevolence, for which he was in his life-time so widely known and so gratefully regarded, could not properly be left unrecorded; and it seems right to give some insight into the practical effects upon his own conduct, of the high estimate he had formed of what is required of those who are rich in this world's possessions, although no attempt will be made to give any complete statement. In another point of view, also, this testimony to the undeviating consistency with which he acted up to the principles he adopted and enforced, is desirable. He strongly disapproved of making charitable bequests by will, and left no legacies of this nature in his own; and it is therefore only doing him justice to state *some* of the cases in which he bestowed considerable amounts of money, during his life-time.

The numerous committees on which he acted brought under his notice and consideration the fluctuation to which institutions entirely dependent upon annual subscriptions were liable; with him, to become aware of an evil, was to excite the wish and the endeavour to remove it, and in 1808 he placed in the hands of trustees the sum of 10,500

pounds, which was by them invested in lands in Monmouth-
shire, the income arising from the rents of these estates,
after contingent expenses were paid, to be distributed
between seven of the charitable institutions in Bristol,
named in the deed of trust, in such a manner and proportion, either to one alone, or between any, as should at the
time appear expedient to the trustees—this, under certain
conditions, specified in the trust deed.* An addition to
the Infirmary being greatly wanted, he devoted much of
his time to that object, also subscribing £2600. It was
on this occasion that the committee received an anonymous
donation of a thousand pounds, entertaining no doubt who
was the giver; and on the following day one of their number happening to meet Richard Reynolds, thanked him,
in the name of the committee, for his acceptable donation.
He did not deny it, but said, " Thou hast no authority
for saying I sent the money;" and on the gentleman repeating, in strong terms, the acknowledgment of the Committee, and refusing to be thus satisfied, my grandfather
quietly said, " Well, I see thou art determined that I
should give you a thousand pounds;" and the next day
they received a donation of that sum with his name, thus
doubling his first contribution. To these gifts may be
added (beside his annual subscription) donations of £1260
to the Strangers' Friend, £900 to the Misericordia, £500
to the Refuge, the same to the Orphan Asylum, and to
the Bible Society £900. Of several other smaller amounts
one only from its purpose, need be mentioned—that of
£300 to Temple Parish, towards providing a better supply
of water for the poor.

Many of his letters refer to the interest he took in
various benevolent institutions and projects in other places

* See Appendix.

7

besides Bristol, and his desire to relieve distress wherever
it existed, and of whatever description. In several instances he paid the debts of persons confined for debt in
prison; one case, in 1798, was that of two men, who, with
their wives and twenty-two children, were imprisoned in a
small room in the King's Bench. Their distressing situation was made known to him, and he procured their release.
Unwilling to be known as the giver of large sums, he
frequently gave his name with his subscription, and forwarded a further and larger contribution anonymously, as
in the instance of the distress in Germany, when he
privately added £500 to the sum given with his name.
It was, for many years, his habit to employ others to act
for him in London and elsewhere, in dispensing such sums
as he wished to devote to charitable purposes, in every
case, with a scrupulous care that his name should not be
known. To one party in London he remitted £20,000,
during the distress in 1795.

He had four almoners constantly employed in Bristol,
who brought their accounts to him every week, which contained the names of each person or family who had been
relieved, the sum given, and the circumstances. He was
very particular in requiring them, when applied to by beggars, to go at the instant to their house or lodgings, as
this promptitude prevented the parties having time to prepare for the visit of inspection. Whenever he found that
any person was receiving assistance from more than one
of his agents, their name was struck off the list. It would
be tedious, and in no wise profitable to go further into
these details, or to attempt to enumerate the various societies and institutions, to which he was either a subscriber
or donor. He was equally generous in all his private
transactions, and he paid over large sums rather than al-

low the most remote possibility of error in the settlement
of an account. In one instance, where he held shares in
an undertaking, by which the contracting party for its
construction was a loser, he did not choose to be the possessor of a property for which he considered he had not
paid the cost,—and he paid to the contractor the proportion of the excess which attached not only to the shares
which he originally held, but to those which he subse-
quently purchased.

Not the least to be appreciated was the consideration
and delicacy with which he assisted many persons who
were not ostensibly objects of charity, (to use this word
in its common sense,) and many who, through relationship,
or other ties of personal interest, or estimable conduct,
were felt by him to have claims upon his kindness and generosity. He kept a minute and accurate account of this
portion, as of every other of his expenditure, but he con-
trived so to enter the sums which he gave away, that no
one could learn their precise destination.

Possessed of an annual income of many thousands, his
style of living remained perfectly simple; there was every
needful and substantial comfort, and an open-handed readiness to provide for the pleasure as well as the convenience
of those who shared his unlimited hospitality, yet without
display, or indulgence in luxuries—hence but a small proportion of his income was spent upon himself,—the remainder flowed in the continuous and bountiful stream
of a well-regulated and catholic benevolence. While receiving the heartfelt expressions of gratitude of those who
had the opportunity of personally thanking him, he always directed such feelings to the Source of all Good.
"My talent," he said to a friend, "is the meanest of all
talents, a little sordid dust: but as the man in the para-

ble who had but one talent was accountable, I am also accountable for the talent that I possess, humble as it is—to the great Lord of all."

In 1810, he had a painful and dangerous illness, from which he never recovered his wonted strength—though in the summer of that year, he went into Devonshire, in hopes that the carriage exercise and the pleasureable excitement he had ever been accustomed to derive from the beauties of the scenery, would be of service. In these hopes, however, he was disappointed. He thus writes to a friend,—"I feel with increased consciousness the effects of old age—the decrease of mental strength with lessened bodily powers,—of firmness of nerve and energy of mind. I find too, and I consider it wisely ordained in the constitution of mankind in their present state of existence, that with the power of enjoyment, the inclination declines also. I believe, few men with means so limited from education, so contracted a sphere of action, and that so occupied by the duties attached to my station in life as not to admit of much intellectual cultivation, have had a higher relish for the gay or the grand, the beautiful or the sublime, or the wonderful works of the Almighty in the outward creation; and I remember with gratitude, the admiration, the delightful astonishment, the rapture which scenes like those at present before me—the boundless ocean in its various states of awful agitation or placid expansion, excited the first time I beheld them, and frequently since. But I do not regret that the things which are seen, which are temporal and which I must so soon leave, now affect me so little; my principal, my frequent wish is, that those things which are not seen, but which are eternal, may be the objects of my solicitude in proportion to their incomparable importance, and my swift approaching, my almost *instant* interest in them." And to another friend he says,"My disposition indeed, to seek or expect happiness in or from outward things, seems to have decreased as fast as my powers have diminished. I am sometimes thankful, that my desires for an increase of spiritual-mindedness bear some proportion to the importance of it in the hour so swiftly approaching, when I shall have done with all the objects of sense, and when time shall be lost in eternity. * * * * The broken slumbers in which my nights are frequently passed, have the advantage of favouring the immediate application of heart to the Lord, which he mercifully inspires and regards; and if I cannot say much of "songs in the night," I may to thee thankfully acknowledge that, through Divine favour, a degree of the spirit of grace and of supplication has been experienced more frequently at those times, and with nearer access to the footstool of the mercy-seat, than at some more appropriate seasons."

Although his bodily strength gradually decreased, and his memory was now less obedient to his call, yet he still retained a clearness of intellect, an earnest desire to seek after the truth, and an uncompromising fidelity to its dictates. Calm and serene in his undeviating reliance on the wisdom and benignity of the Divine government, full of religious hope, of faith and charity, and his heart glowing with warm affection for his friends, he continued to the last, more and more the object of the love and veneration of his children and family; and when the time came that he was removed from them, the sense of their exceeding loss and deprivation filled their hearts with irrepressible sorrow. They could rejoice for him, that in him mortality was exchanged for everlasting life and happiness, in the presence of his Creator and Redeemer and the spirits of just men made perfect; but they wept that the beloved

7 *

father of the family, to whom they looked up as their head for so many years, was gone from amongst them.

On the 24th of June, 1816, he set out on the journey which he had been in the habit of taking once every year, to visit his children in Shropshire and at Liverpool. He arrived first at his son Joseph's house at Ketley, when his increased feebleness was very apparent, and a subdued feeling of mingled concern and pleasure was felt by my father and his family, as they welcomed him for what they all feared would prove the last time. He remained there but two days. I remember it was a beautiful bright summer morning on which he was to leave us, and we children were summoned into the parlour after breakfast, and the whole family gathered around him. His son read a chapter in the New Testament, and when the book was closed, there was silence and perfect stillness for some minutes. Presently my grandfather raised his head and looked round upon us, and we listened breathlessly, as he began to speak, saying this was the last time he should ever see us in this world —solemnly and sweetly he addressed us—then he spoke a few words of affection and hope to our father, and afterwards to his other relations; again there was silence, and we all felt that his spirit was engaged in supplication, shared in some degree by the hearts of all present. Then he arose, kissed us affectionately, and bade us farewell. We followed him into the hall, where some of the servants were waiting to see him pass. He kindly noticed them; and, accompanied by his friend Sarah Allen, was assisted to his carriage, and drove away. We had indeed seen our beloved grandfather for the last time.*

* On our return to the room where he had taken leave of us, some lilies of the valley were found lying on the table. He had worn them, as he often did flowers, in the button-hole of his coat, and as they were faded had taken them out and left them there. They were carefully preserved, and are now before me, folded in a paper, yellow with time, thus inscribed, "Lilies of the valley, worn by my grandfather, at Ketley, 1st July, 1816."

He reached Liverpool by short stages ; whilst at Green-bank, the residence of his daughter, he gained no strength, but rather the contrary, and did not remain there long, returning to Bristol on the 19th July. Shortly after his return, his medical attendants advised his removal to Chelt-enham, in the hope of relief from the biliary obstruction, which was the most obvious symptom of the decay of the bodily frame; and, although convinced in his own mind that no human means could restore the powers which a long life of more than eighty years had nearly exhausted, he was unwilling to leave any thing undone which he con-sidered was his duty, and consented to leave his own house, to which he expected never to return.

He arrived at Cheltenham on the 7th of August. From his daughter's letters to her family, we learn that he tried every measure prescribed by his medical attendants, with exemplary patience, and throughout his illness exhibited a marked gentleness of manner to all around him. He was tranquil, often cheerful, and always most affectionate and kind.

But little remains to be said of the last days of his earthly pilgrimage, and this account is chiefly derived from a memorandum, drawn up by his valued friend, Thomas Sanders.* It appears that no decided change was observ-able till the 6th of September, up to which time he had taken his usual exercise, even driving the carriage himself, accompanied by his cousin or daughter only. On the sixth he walked out before breakfast, but soon afterwards became much weaker, and towards evening declined rap-idly. On Sunday he partially revived, but sank again in

* Published in a small work entitled, Verses to the memory of the late Richard Reynolds of Bristol. By James Montgomery. Longman, Hurst, Rees and Co. 1816.

the course of that night, never to revive. His son arrived on that day from Shropshire, and two of his grandchildren from Liverpool the day following. For many
years he had not been confined to his bed a whole day,
and during the whole of this illness he had joined the family
at their usual meals; but on Monday the 9th, he was persuaded to remain in bed till the afternoon, when he rose
and drank tea with them, and did not retire for the night
till his usual time. At five o'clock the next morning an
alteration for the worse took place in his breathing. Some
of his relatives who had left the room were called, but
none of them thought his end so near. He inquired if his
servant whom he had sent to Bristol for his will had returned with it, and on being told that he had, seemed satisfied.
He had made it his earnest request to his daughter that she
would be with him at his close, and now, about six o'clock,
raising himself a little, his eye sought hers, and he signified
that she should go to the other side of the bed; when turning on his side, and taking her hand in his and pressing it,
he quietly and almost imperceptibly expired, on the 10th
of September, 1816.

At his funeral, which took place on Monday, the 18th
of September, the most marked, profound, and general
testimonies of respect were spontaneously offered to his
memory. Soon after eight in the morning, about 500 boys
from the schools of St. James's and St. Paul's formed in
two columns, extending from each side to the good man's
dwelling across St. James's Square. On the appearance
of the coffin, the boys stood uncovered. The streets were
thronged with the poor. The resident clergy, and dissenting ministers of different persuasions, the gentlemen
of the committees of various charitable societies, and other

of the leading citizens of Bristol and a numerous body of the Society of Friends, followed the procession of the family and relatives from the house.

"So great was the public curiosity excited on this occasion, and such the eagerness manifested by the poor, who had lost their best friend, to pay the last respect to his remains, that not only the spacious burial-ground was filled with spectators and mourners, but the very walls and tops of houses surrounding the area were covered in a remarkable manner. And it is but justice to add, that the behaviour of this vast concourse of people was in the highest degree decent, orderly, and respectful; the poor at the same time considered it a favour to be permitted in their turn, to approach the grave of their departed friend, and to drop the silent tear, as a mark of their regard for a man whose life had been spent in doing good."—*Bristol paper.*

In the report for this year of one of the Charitable Societies, occurs the following just and warm tribute to the memory of my grandfather, by one who knew him well; and with it I conclude this very imperfect memorial of Richard Reynolds, grieved and disappointed that his character should be so feebly depicted by the hand of a granddaughter, who had looked up to him from earliest childhood with reverential and grateful affection, and in his death first knew the sorrow of bereavement.

"But at a time, when the exertions of benevolence are barely sufficient to keep famine from the houses of the poor, it is impossible to prevent the mind from continually recurring to the loss which this society, in common with every distressed individual and every association for the good of others within what he considered as his sphere of action, have sustained, in our venerable and respected vice-president, Richard Reynolds. The views of this truly great man, in the science of political economy, were as enlightened as his benevolence was extensive. To teach the idle, the thoughtless and the improvident, the value of industry, prudence and economy, were in his opinion of the first importance in the attainment of the object of the labours of his long life—the happiness of his fellow-creatures; and though he never turned from suffering, whether the consequence of imprudence or the result of misfortune, he knew that important as is the duty of *relieving* distress, there is one still higher—that of *preventing* it. As the friend of the prudent man, therefore, this society might be called his adopted child, for without his approbation of the plan, the original promoters of it would hardly have ventured to make it public. From the first meeting which was held with a view to its establishment, to the day on which it received the sanction of the citizens of Bristol and inhabitants of Clifton, in the Guildhall, his attention to its interests was unremitted; he was amongst the most bountiful of the annual subscribers to its support; he endowed the Loan Fund with the noble donation of one hundred guineas, and his venerated name—seldom pronounced by the poor man without a blessing—gave to the Bank of Savings a stability in the eyes of those for whose benefit it was intended, which the wealth of the city would not have imparted. Where the name of Reynolds appeared, *there,* had experience taught the labouring man there was good in store for him. Your committee with pride and pleasure remind you, that he, who gave medicine to the sick, was eyes to the blind, fed the hungry, clothed the naked, bade the prisoners and the slave be free, supported the rising fabric of your society on his own shoulders till its completion. Our central stay is gone, another single pillar of equal strength and equal beauty we cannot hope to raise; but let our united efforts, like a clustered column, continue to support the building, which may prove a shelter from the storms of adversity to generations yet unborn."

LETTERS OF RICHARD REYNOLDS.

To John Maccappen.

12th of Seventh Month, 1762.

——If I had not an opportunity of sending this by——, who dines at my house to-day, I think I should not write now, being quite without inclination to write; but as thou might perhaps think it inconsistent with my professions of friendship to omit acknowledging the receipt of thy favour of the 14th, I send this, languid as it is, to prevent it,—indeed I am now in a disposition of mind, of late pretty common to me—an indifference to everything; my late loss* has rendered all the enjoyments of life tasteless, and I am very much surprised at the difference I find in myself at different times. In general I am employed all the day long in the unavoidable avocations of business, which, though they divert my mind from reflecting on scenes that never will return, exhaust the spirits, and when I return from the works to my once cheerful habitation, my unhappiness appears the more formidable, through that application to business which prevented my reflecting on scenes which every surrounding object now brings to my remembrance, with heightened anguish. No words can express what I feel in these bitter hours, and couldst thou conceive it, thou wouldst likewise be much surprised at the difference there is in me at different times; whether it is because I seldom see any company, or something else be the reason, I know not; but when I have been favoured with that of my friends, who are very few, and which is very seldom, I have at times such a flow of spirits, such an unaccountable vivacity, that though

* The decease of his first wife.

(84)

I cannot forget the unhappiness of my situation, and have, if I may use the expression, the arrow of affliction deep fixed in my soul, I believe as though it were with me as in times that are passed ; which, notwithstanding it is an involuntary effusion of cheerfulness, I cannot afterwards help considering with a kind of remorse. What will become of me I know not ; my afflictions are at times very great, the conflict of soul I suffer excessive. I sometimes think my heart is more corrupted and my temper more depressed than any other person's, but I hope I shall not utterly fall— rather than I may,—that the time of my probation may be shortened, and that I may soon go down to the chambers of the grave —is my prayer, and I hope will also be thine for

Thy very affectionate friend.

Extract of a letter to JOHN MACCAPPEN, *dated* *January 17th,* 1765.

After informing his friend that he had sent him a copy of "Locke on St. Paul's Epistles," and of "Law's Letters," he adds :—"It is some time since I read the latter, but I remember that (a few passages excepted,) I approved it much, as it strongly inculcates the necessity of a change being wrought in the heart —a renovation—a being born again, as the Scriptures express it, and that without this being experienced, all outward performances, the use of outward means and all religious ceremonies avail nothing."

To JOHN MACCAPPEN.

Coalbrookdale, 2nd of Sixth Month, 1766.

MY DEAR FRIEND,

Although I am not in a humour for writing a long letter, yet having half-an-hour to spare, I thought I would just inform thee of my return from London, whither I went from Bristol, and that I shall be very glad if this finds thee in health, disposed and at leisure to pay us a visit at the Dale. I hope this wet weather will not continue much longer, and yet if it does, I fancy

8

if we were together, we could find means to make staying within
doors agreeable ; however, I wish thou would come and try, not
that it can be reasonably supposed there will not be some inter-
vals proper for walking at this time of the year.   I spent an hour
or two with ———— at Bristol.   He complained of thy letting
him have but little of thy company.   I recollected then, and have
since reflected on the many agreeable hours we have passed together, but on none with more pleasure than those which are
distinguished by their having been devoted to mutual excitements
to religion and virtue.   It is true there were few such, and yet
I rejoice with a degree of humble thankfulness, there were a *few*
——those with the rest are fled, are gone for ever !   May the consideration that the present *now* is instantly on the wing to join
them, strongly engage us to be instant in prayer to Him, without
whom we can do nothing, for assistance to devote it to his service
in the way of his requirings, how much soever in the cross to
our natural wills—then shall we look backward with pleasure,
and forward with hope, which is the greatest happiness this state
of probation admits of.

Thy truly affectionate friend.

To JOHN MACCAPPEN.

23rd of Seventh Month, 1767.

MY DEAR FRIEND,

————I lately had an opportunity of spending a few hours in
the late Shenstone's walks at a place called the Leasowes, near
Hales Owen, and not many miles from Hagley. * * * It would
give me great pleasure to spend a couple of days at both places
with thee, and if it will also be agreeable to thee, I will endeavour to meet thee any day thou wilt appoint after the first week
in the next month.   I think it not only lawful but expedient to
cultivate a disposition to be pleased with the beauties of nature,
by frequent indulgences for that purpose.   The mind, by being
continually applied to the consideration of ways and means to
gain money, contracts an indifferency or at least an insensibility

to the profusion of beauties which the benevolent Creator has impressed upon every part of the material creation. A sordid love of gold, or what the possession of gold can purchase, the reputation of being rich, has so depraved the finer feelings of some men, that they pass through the most delightful grove, filled with the united melody of the winged inhabitants, and the various murmurings of the brook in the valley, with as little pleasure, with no more of the vernal delight which Milton mentions, than they feel in passing through some obscure alley in the town. Nobody, I believe, thinks me too indifferent about getting money, but I believe too, very few endeavour more to make the most advantageous use of those means of happiness which are independent of riches. Few are better pleased with a beautiful prospect, few contemplate the delicate or the bold, the gay or the awful of nature with more complacency, or a higher relish. It is true I have not the taste which some men have, but I endeavour to be as happy as I can, and I think anything which increases the number of the means of procuring happiness, is worth endeavouring after.

Coalbrook Dale, 20th of the First Month, 1768.

I find myself a little under the influence of that dejection of mind to which I am at times subject, but I will endeavour to rouse myself therefrom by a recollection of the many blessings I enjoy, and though thy apparent neglect has a little affected me, I will not doubt the continuance of thy regard, but account it a principal cause of thankfulness that I am blessed with a friend that will pity a casual imbecility of mind, which I believe is constitutional, and the effect of a particular temperament of body, sensible too that I have *in general* a disposition to enjoy those pleasures which are adapted to, or resulting from, my rank in the animal or intellectual world,—that the beauties of Nature are not wholly lost upon me, nor the powers of reflection and contemplation entirely withheld. Though I raise not the dust by the rapid whirl of the wheels of a chariot, nor am ever the object of popular applause, I repeat with thankfulness to the Giver of all things good—.

> "Mine are retirements; silent joys,
>   And all the soft engaging ties
>   Of still domestic life."

I have been, and how many *now* are, confined to the bed of sickness or of pain? How many feel the immediate want of food and raiment, or the equally dreadful certain apprehension of it, not confined to their own persons only, but involving the wife of their bosom—the children of their love. These are far removed from me. I have all things and abound, and, for this I desire to be thankful to Him who alone worketh in us, both to will and to do every thing that is good. I also am blessed with the inclination, and the means in some measure, to alleviate the distresses of others,—this is a source of pleasure unpossessed by many. My dear friend will excuse my inserting a verse I just now recollect from an hymn to benevolence—

> "Hail source of transport! ever new,
>   Whilst pleased thy dictates I pursue—
>   I taste a joy sincere:
>   Too great for little minds to know,
>   Who on themselves alone bestow
>   Their wishes and their care."

Thou probably will remark the same quickness of transition, not to say incoherent rambling, in this letter, which thou may have observed in some others of mine, but I need not trouble myself about order in writing to thee. I think I find the beneficial effects of my attempt already. I will mention one more cause of thankfulness. Some perhaps are sunk in despair—it is possible some may have sinned out their day, that the visitation of a gracious God so frequently slighted, will never be repeated to them. I shudder at the thought. I too have sinned, have frequently and grievously offended, and yet I hope. May a just sense of long continued mercy engage me to make such returns, as will be well pleasing to Him to whom I owe so much; may I love much, and manifest that love by keeping his commandments. Upon the whole I find I have abundant cause to be humble and thankful, none to be dejected or discontented.

To George Harrison.*

Ketley, 23rd of Sixth Month, 1769.

Esteemed Friend,

I duly received thy letter of the 3rd instant, and take kindly thy so soon complying with my request to let me hear from thee. I was at that other exhibition, and saw the piece thou mentions, and though I guess partly the subject, I doubt not if thou had been with me to have told me the history it represented, it would have heightened my satisfaction in looking at it. Our little tour was as pleasant as I expected it would be, and a strict adherence to the resolution I had taken not to be hurried, prevented my brother Darby's desire to be soon at home from lessening my enjoyment much. I think Greenwich Park and Kensington Gardens the pleasantest places near London; the latter especially is a place which, as it is within reach, and the continued noise and hurry of the city would certainly make solitude and rural retirement pleasant to a person less naturally disposed to enjoy them than thou art, I cannot but recommend to thee. The admission is easy, the walks extensive, various, and calculated for those who are disposed, as I think somebody expresses it, "to woo lone quiet in her silent walks;" and as I doubt not thy being sometimes in the disposition Young was, when he exclaimed—

"O! lost to virtue, lost to manly thought,
Lost to the noblest sallies of the soul,
Who think it solitude to be alone—"

I dare say thou would like the place. If I had not apprehended the four next lines would have made the division in so short a sentence too wide, I should have added them; and yet I think them so good, and my letter likely to be so much in want of enrichments, that I will give them a place.

"Communion sweet! communion large and high!
Our reason, guardian angel, and our God!
Then nearest these, when others most remote,
And all, ere long, shall be remote, but these."

8 *   * Private tutor to Richard Reynolds's eldest son.

But to return. The morning after we were there, we came by Kew to Richmond. Whilst the rest of the company went to look at the outside of the king's house—for the family being there, they could not be admitted into it—I spent the time till dinner very agreeably upon the hill, regretting, though, that I had not "Thomson's Seasons" with me, whose animated descriptions of the prospects to be seen therefrom, would have increased my satisfaction. After dining and drinking tea there, we had a very pleasant ride to Twickenham, which we could not pass without thinking on Pope, and inquiring which was his house. Bushy Park, in which were a large number of chestnut trees and hawthorns, both in full bloom, with much deer, and a very fine evening, made our next stage to Hampton Court seem a short one. The seeing the house and gardens, the wilderness and labyrinth, took up the next forenoon, and occasioned us to have a very late dinner at Windsor. We came through the park and by the lodge. It was as much as we could compass that evening to see the castle, and take a turn or two upon the terrace, which I have always thought the grandest walk I have seen, and the prospect it commands a very fine one. We repeated it in the morning, and from the fineness of the weather, for the evening was but moderate, to great advantage. After staying two meetings there, we reached West Wycombe that evening, time enough to see a handsome church upon the top of a steep hill, and a spacious cemetery, or rather cenotaph, adjoining, both built by Lord Le Despencer, formerly Sir Francis Dashwood; whose house, though small, is, I think, the highest finished I have been at, not excepting Lord Littleton's at Hagley. I have heard much of Earl Tilney's house on Epping Forest, but was never there. I confess I am not so much pleased with superb edifices, as the gay or the grand, the bold or the delicate of nature; nay, I think I can go so far as to say with Scott—

"The grassy lane, the wood surrounded field,
    The rude stone fence, with fragrant wall-flow'rs gay,
    The clay built cot, to me more pleasure yield,
    Than all the pomp imperial domes display."

We spent the next forenoon in seeing the house and gardens and being upon the water, and should have repeated the latter part of our entertainment had not the thunder and the rain prevented. We came to Stowe next morning to breakfast. Lord Temple's house and gardens there, though they were the last that we saw, were not the least pleasing. I am not capable of giving thee a description of them; but was I, a printed account with engravings of the remarkables therein, which is to be bought there, and I presume in London also, renders it unnecessary. I shall only add on this subject that we came through Banbury, Warwick, and Birmingham, home; and through mercy found all my family well, who generally made affectionate inquiries after thee, especially Billy, who desires his dear love to thee, and is much obliged for thy letter and thy book. I have now wrote a pretty long letter, and yet am not willing to close it, without inserting my sincere wishes for thy preservation from the evils which are in the world, and that as thy situation and uncommon acquirements will make thy company and conversation much sought for, thou may be enabled to stand against those temptations, to which in consequence thereof thou will be in a particular manner exposed. May all thy abilities be exerted, as often as occasion shall require, in the cause of virtue and Christianity, and may we never be ashamed nor afraid of testifying our obedience to the cross of Christ, or of acknowledging the truth which we have professed, though it may be in the midst of a perverse and gainsaying generation. Sensible of my inferiority, I presume not to dictate; but I trust thou will not take amiss my thus expressing my good wishes for thee, and joining thee with myself in desiring that our conduct may be such as from my own small experience, and the ample testimonies of others, I am sure will be productive of pleasantness and peace. Farewell—I shall always be happy to hear from thee, and am truly,

Thy obliged and affectionate friend.

R. R.

To George Harrison.

Ketley, 30th of Ninth Month, 1769.

Esteemed Friend,

——It affords me pleasure to observe, that the hope I have conceived of my son's acquiring a power of application, as he advances in years, is consistent with thy apprehensions concerning him. I am thankful I have no greater faults to condemn or more vicious dispositions to lament in him, and can with great truth repeat, that I much more ardently desire his advancement in virtue than in learning, and that if he lives, he may merit imitation as a good man, rather than be admired as a great scholar; and yet I flatter myself that my conduct towards him will sufficiently evince the favourable opinion I entertain of the advantages resulting from science, whether considered as conducing to the good of the community, or the enjoyments of the individual.

I was at Manchester whilst I was out, and at the house of Ashton Lever, Esq., about six miles beyond, who has a pretty large collection, consisting of curious birds, beasts, reptiles, shells, petrifactions, fossils, &c. &c. We went to the Duke of Bridgewater's coalworks, and came along the side of the navigation as far as it extends towards Warrington, which is, I think, within two or three miles. There have been frequently published in the newspapers descriptions of the works and navigations, but I shall only say, I never read one which gave me an adequate idea of the performances; they are really amazing, and greater, I believe, than were ever before attempted, much less achieved by an individual and a subject.

We returned to Liverpool, where I was very agreeably entertained. I love to be so far idle as to have no part to act in the midst of hurry and bustle, but to have the mind engaged in the observations and reflections which occur from the sight of such a seaport as Liverpool. The "Adventures of Telemachus," and "Nature Displayed," furnish me with as many pleasing sentiments on such an occasion as any books I have read. From this busy scene—to take a solitary walk along the sea-shore, to survey the broad expanse, to listen to the sound of the waves, sometimes from their rushing with impetuosity, as it were awfully shouting, sometimes from their running faintly over the sands, gradually dying away on the wings of the passing breeze. The "Spectators" on the "Pleasures of the Imagination," which I dare say thou hast or wilt read with attention and pleasure, account very rationally for the delight which the sight of the sea or extensive prospects from hills or mountains give us, and I will add that my disposition to enjoy them has not been lessened by the remark that they have the sanction of the practice of our Saviour, who spent much of his time by the sea-side, on mountains and in desert places; nor will the enjoyment of them, either present or in retrospection, be impaired by remembering the use which he is recorded (and I believe in more places than one,) to have made of them, and which our circumstances render more than equally necessary to us.

I hope thou wilt always believe, without my repeating it in every letter, that I shall always be glad to hear from thee, and that I am with much respect and esteem,

Thy affectionate friend,

R. R.

To George Harrison.

Ketley, 20th of Eleventh Month, 1769.

Esteemed Friend,

I received thy acceptable letter of the 16th ultimo, the morning I set out on a visit to my father at Bath. I left him this day fortnight, and though not likely, in my apprehension, to continue a great while, I yet thought it probable he might live longer than, from an account I received last night, I now fear he will; however, I have the satisfaction of *believing* with him that he has lived long enough for the greatest purpose of life—the being fitted for the enjoyment of a blissful eternity—as well as of *knowing* that he has for all the desirable secondary considerations. He has been enabled to discharge every relative duty, to make sufficient provision for his children, and to see them all settled to his mind. *   *   *   *   *   *   *

The apology thou makes for using the word Mooreish would not have been wanting, had I not been very dull. I join with thee as to the propriety of its application. I agree too with thee that the difficulty we meet with in expressing *viva voce* what we easily conceive in the mind, would be lessened by our being obliged in our youth to make frequent extempore dissertations under the direction of a proper person, and also that a facility of writing might reasonably be expected from a similar practice upon paper. I can conceive, too, that it is possible for thee on thy own account to wish that the former had been thy practice, but I really know not how to think the latter can be the object of a wish to thee. For me, I am sensible it may be *desirable*, but I am not willing to think it of consequence enough to justify the use of the word *necessary;* for if I did, how much more reason than thou should I have to lament " the deficiency of my own acquirements, and be disgusted with my own ignorance." I have looked over the list of books recommended by James Beesly in the " Cambridge Magazine." If it is correctly copied from the "Public Ledger," I shall only say, I should have expected from him something more highly finished than the Introduction, and the few remarks upon the books he recommends, appears to me to be. I have a good esteem for the young man (as he is, I believe, younger than I am, I hope I may call him so without offence,) and would wish him now to avoid everything he shall hereafter wish he had avoided. Of many of the books I *am* no judge, of many I *can* be no judge, and of the few with which I am or have been a little acquainted, I cannot approve of all. I cannot think all his poetical authors likely to promote that purity of heart, nor all his speculative ones that humility of soul, which I wish for every friend of mine, and for myself. I should have thought the number of dictionaries, and of books upon the same subject or science enough for a compiler, and more than enough for the man who reads only for his own information or amusement. As impartial-

ity is the alleged plea for his introducing to his friend the oppo-
sers of Christianity, and amongst others, Shaftesbury; I am
surprised he should omit the "Essay upon Characteristics," by
J. Brown, a book which I will venture to recommend as abundantly capable of affording a high entertainment to the liberal
unshackled mind, or, to adopt J. B.'s divine character to a
gentleman, according to Sir Richard Steele's definition of a
gentleman.   The author appears to me to be perfectly well
acquainted with the powers of the human mind, with a discrimination of them superior to most I have met with, and his execution
as a writer, if I may be allowed the expression, has all the force,
the perspicuity, the elegance of a master—in short, however
redoubtable the noble writer may have appeared in the view of
his admirers, in my opinion, he is a mere puppet in the hands
of the author of the Essay upon the Characteristics.   Thou wilt
perceive I am not deterred by the fear of exposing myself, from
writing my opinion freely; however, I will just add, that whatever
I may say now, or at any other time, of the merits of books, is
only advanced as *my opinion*, and not absolute, as though I
deemed myself capable of pronouncing thereon; no, no,—for a
person to commence critic without understanding any one language grammatically would be an absurdity of which I hope not
to be guilty.   I only speak of books and other productions of
genius, as I do of wines—calling those good which I relish.   In
a former letter I recommended Lefevre's letters to thee—hast
thou seen them?   Billy wrote in Latin whilst I was from home.
I hope his letter has been received.   I expect an opportunity of
having the drawings Dr. Bell was so kind as to promise him, with
some prints from London, soon.   *   *   *   *   *

To GEORGE HARRISON.

Ketley, 2nd of Twelfth Month, 1769.

ESTEEMED FRIEND,

I am at present troubled with a violent fit of the headache, which makes writing rather troublesome to me; but I am not willing thou shouldst see my brother Darby without a written acknowledgment from me of the receipt of thy favour of the 25th ultimo.

Excuse me if I cannot think the want of a truly catholic spirit characteristic of J. Lefevre's letters. Whether it is that my being so much pleased with them prevents my observing imperfections which are really to be found in them, or it is that bigotry and a want of charity are utterly incompatible with such attainments as I think he had experienced, they appear to me remarkable rather for a universal love and cordial desire for the happiness of mankind, as well as a belief that a capacity for the attainment of it is not confined to any particular sect, or insured by the performance of any particular ceremonies.

I believe I can form pretty adequate ideas of thy occasional mental feelings and the consequential alteration in the Index; but whether I am right in conjecturing that the first part of the paragraph may have reference to persons whose intellectual capacity has not appeared to any disadvantage, from their outward circumstances, and the latter part to one whose superior discernment has not been lessened by a want of respect or esteem in thy own mind, thou knowest best; but I believe from my own experience that we never fear nor scarce ever suspect a superior discernment of our own mental weaknesses in those of whose esteem we do not wish to enjoy a considerable share; for our own mental weaknesses and imperfections are naturally best known and most intimately felt by ourselves, and when I observe a person uncommonly apprehensive of the superior discernment of another, I generally suppose he thinks that other possessed of many other excellencies besides *superior discernment.* I could strengthen what I have written by Locke's definition of shame—"that it is an uneasiness of the mind upon the thought of having done something that is indecent, or will lessen the valued esteem which others have for us ;" and if I am not mistaken, and thou wilt be honest, I am partial enough to myself to conclude, that what I have written will be no discredit to my own *superior discernment.*

Thy observations upon the difference between wisdom and learning are undoubtedly just; but however nearly thy equal thou may allow me to be in one, I cannot at times help regretting there is so great disparity between us in the other. To write to the learned with the pen of the learned, must never be expected by me; but I am thankful I have a mind so well disposed to be happy in the enjoyment of the pleasures within its reach.

If I do not soon mention what I intended most particularly to do when I began to write, I foresee I shall not do it at all in this letter, already much longer than I expected it would be, and that is, that as I take copies of the letters I write to my particular friends, the sending of my letters to them, and theirs to me now and then, appears to me in some sort entering into conversation with them; but, then, to keep up that idea, it is necessary the several letters should be regular, and as much as is consistent with freedom, circumstantial answers to the several observations or remarks made in the preceding, or a free communication or exchange of sentiments upon the same subject. Considered in that light, I cannot think thy last letter, however valuable and pleasing it is to me, is a full answer to my last; but if thou hast not been accustomed to consider an epistolary correspondence in this light, perhaps the remark will give thee no greater an opinion of my wisdom than thou must have of my learning: however, look upon it as the effect of the freedom resulting from friendship, in which too I have made my remarks upon what thou calls "the vagaries of thy thoughts," and with which I subscribe myself most truly,   Thy affectionate friend,

R. R.

To S. LLOYD.

Ketley, 19th of First Month, 1770.

—— I duly received thy affectionate letter of the 20th ult., at my brother Cowle's, at Bristol. The part thou art pleased to take, and the sympathy thou expresses on the sorrowful occasion of my father's death, is consistent with that friendship which I believed thou hast entertained for me, and to which, notwithstanding, give me leave to say, mine for thee is at least equal. I wish not for many friends, nor to be the friend of many; but I would have my friends more eminent for their virtue than understanding; for understanding than wealth; and rich, so far as riches may contribute to their advancement in either virtue or understanding; and so far, and no further, may I be rich myself.

The death of my father did affect me a good deal; but I have so frequently considered, and according to my degree experienced, the instability of the most desirable enjoyments in this world— the frequent sudden abrupt transitions from earth's happiest lot— the possibility of a life of misery—the danger to which we are exposed, and the infinite consequences of a miscarriage—that I soon acknowledged, as I had many times before confessed, in the words of John, the Divine, "Blessed are the dead who die in the Lord." And, with respect to my father, he had lived to discharge every duty to his children, and to see that his care and prayers for them had not been altogether in vain—he was favoured with an evidence of his acceptance with God. Surely then, with respect to my father, justly might his death be considered as a blessing.

Our youngest son was taken with the small-pox while I was from home, though I did not know it when I wrote to thy brother N——. He has them very thick, and was so ill, on Second-day, that my wife began to think more favourably of inoculation than she had done before. He is better since, but the disorder is scarcely at the highest yet. Billy, as soon as they appeared, went down to his grandmother's at the Dale, with a resolution to be inoculated, and is now under preparation there. I am glad he determined without my interposing; for though I much approve of the practice, I was afraid of saying much to him in favour of it, as he expressed an aversion thereto. I wish every body who is against inoculation could see our poor baby, and know what it suffers. To relieve, or prevent it, if that were all, would justify inoculation; and this consideration seems to weigh more with my wife, taken separately, than connected with the probability of preserving life. The considerations I have mentioned as sufficient to reconcile me to the death of my father, would, I doubt not, be equally effectual, should one of our dear innocents be taken from us, after our having made use of all the means in our power to preserve its life: and how far inoculation should be considered as a means of preserving life—and, consequently, how far it may or ought to be practised, must be left to every parent's own determination; but I think the natural affection and concomitant apprehension of the parent, will prevent its being done in the hasty forwardness of our own wills, and though we justly conclude, that "giving a blessing even to life, is only in the hand of the Almighty"—I do not see that the inoculating of children lessens the necessity of their or our dependence upon him for a blessing, even to life itself. In short, it appears to me a subject that will not bear reasoning upon; but if any say they have not freedom in their minds to do it—that it is matter of conscience to them—far be it from me to judge them; to their own Master they stand or fall—"Let every man be fully persuaded in his own mind; and happy is he that condemneth not himself in that thing which he alloweth."

To George Harrison.

Ketley, 8th of Twelfth Month, 1770.

Esteemed Friend,

Since the receipt of thine of the 26th ult., I have looked into the account of the Society, in *Randal's System of Geography.* For the reason thou mentions, it certainly would not be advisable to transmit it in the form it bears in that book; but, as I know not the size of the work now under hand, nor the proportion the abovementioned account will bear to the whole performance, I know not that the *size* would be equally objectable; however, if no one is able and willing to send such an *original* sketch of our principles as is wanted upon the present occasion, I think a tolerable one might be compiled from the above account, as readily as from any other book that occurs to me at present. Whilst I am writing the wind is very high, and frequently has been so of late. It has brought to my remembrance a storm which blew down a part of the booth that was then building at Wellington, on occasion of the Welch Yearly Meeting. I fancy thou remembers it; but perhaps thou dost not remember a remark, which, if I am not mistaken, occasioned thee to observe, that the Greek words, which in the common translation of the 2nd chapter of St. Paul's Epistle to the Ephesians, are rendered, "the prince of the power of the *air*," might have been more properly rendered by some other; was it not *darkness?* I have looked to see what Anthony Purver makes of it in his translation; but, fond as he is of differing from the vulgar, even though it be in expression only, and that not always for the better, he retains the words, "prince of the power of the *air*," but in his note says, "the evil spirits there—but not as having power over the air;" which he corroborates by a reference to the 22nd verse of the 14th chapter of Jeremiah. I suppose the passage, as it stands in the Ephesians, has occasioned the notion which the common people entertain, of the evil spirits having a peculiar influence, or rather dominion in that element; and thou, I doubt not, hast remarked their application of it at the times of the assises, which, from the seasons of the year they are usually held at, are frequently attended with high winds; for, was I to judge by my own feelings, and suppose those of other people are similar, I must conclude it could not be from their sensations the common people suppose that the winds, these especially which usually blow about the time of the vernal and autumnal equinoxes, are the effects of a malign spirit. I well remember that, even when I was a child, the wind blowing from the west, or the south-west, though ever so high, had an exhilarating effect upon my spirits, and seemed to inspire a lively vigour that disposed me to rove through the fields and the woods, amongst rocks, or along the brook-side, with a joy and satisfaction which I still recollect, with a kind of pleasure that I cannot easily describe; but thou will perhaps have a pretty just idea of it by thinking upon some long past scenes of rapturous enjoyment, and innocent as joyful, and which, therefore, are more frequent in the early part of youth than afterwards. Nor am I yet insensible to the sprightly influence of the cheerful south-west: I know not if that particular point of the compass has ever been personified, or I should have been disposed to have closed that period with his name; but either Zephyr or Favonius, though not exactly south-west, seems to me tolerably expressive—that is, according to the idea I have annexed to it, without understanding Latin. Thou knowest my ignorance, and therefore I scruple the less to write that, at a venture to thee, whether right or wrong, that I should not to some others, lest they should suppose I understood Latin when I do not, which would be bad; or that I would wish to have them think so, which would be worse.

I little thought when I began to write that the blowing of the wind would have carried my pen so near to the end of my paper, before I had thanked thee for the trouble thou hast taken to execute my trifling commissions. Thomas Hatton desired me to let thee know how much he was obliged to thee. The maps are come to R. P.'s this morning. The Josephus may, if thou please,

9 *

be sent by the wagon to his house. I bought Prideaux's Connection some time since for my wife, who had read part of it formerly, but I have not yet read it. I think it most likely he should borrow pretty largely from Josephus; but, from the opinion I have conceived of the Dean's honesty, I conclude he would take care to acknowledge the debt, which is equivalent, in my opinion, to a receipt in full, in trade and business. Ramsden is very remiss—but I am in no haste about the globes. I would not have thee by any means risk thy health by going after them. I have seen a biographical chart by Dr. Priestley, and, I think, a topographical one also. Thou will further oblige me, by procuring one of each, pasted on canvass, with rollers, to hang up in my study, as I call it. I will let thee know, in a future letter, how to send them to

Thine, &c.,
RICHARD REYNOLDS.

To George Harrison.

Ketley, 27th of Second Month, 1771.

——I have not seen Beattie's treatise, but shall procure it from thy recommendation of it. I find thou hast not read Hume; think not I should draw any conclusions to thy prejudice, if thou had told me thou had read his writings, or those of any other deistical author. I cannot say I have been much, if at all, hurt by what I have read of that sort. I think Christianity nas been more ably defended than attacked; and well, perhaps, it may have been for some, that the refuting the objections and silencing the cavils of sophistical infidelity, has been undertaken by those who, though they could not have acknowledged the truth of the gospel or the doctrines of Christianity with greater sincerity than myself, have possessed a power of investigating and discussing a concatenation of arguments, involved as well as abstracted, which I shall never attain. I have been long accustomed to consider Christianity as supported by two kinds of proofs, external and internal; by the external consisting of miracles, &c., the relation whereof has all the proofs of authenticity of which such kind of writing, and such accounts are capable; by the internal, which I may perhaps think the strongest as well as most necessary, by reason of its having been most frequently the object of my consideration, I mean the superior excellency of its precepts and doctrines. These appear to my mind with such force of conviction (not to say demonstration), that, though a professed disputant might possibly raise objections which I could not answer, yet I should not be moved thereby from my own persuasions, or rather feelings; and however deficient I may be, as deficient I confess I am, in the practical part of my duty, my disobedience neither is, nor will be, the effect of a disbelief in the authority of the Lawgiver, or proceed from an unconsciousness of the propriety of his injunctions. Since I wrote last, I have read Robertson's *History of Scotland*. His style pleases me much, and, from its perspicuity and strength, is well adapted to history. I was carried along, as it were, by a majestically flowing river, through a country abounding with differing prospects, pleasing though rude, and as a vessel that, favoured by a propitious gale, moves over the heaving surface of the ocean with a kind of dignity and triumph. The history is like those gleams of sunshine which, from the course of the clouds, appear to move over a tract of ground in a pleasing but swift progression, beautifying as well as rendering conspicuous those fields, and other objects over which the irradiation passes, and extending some degree of illumination to those adjacent. Still more just is the simile, if the duration of the improvement I make be likened to those fleeting glories of the sunshine. As the fields smile during the transient brightness, whilst its effects upon vegetation are inconsiderable; so, though I highly enjoy the instant satisfaction, the traces made upon my memory are slight and evanescent from what was chiefly addressed to my imagination. And this I attribute partly to my being necessarily engaged, the most of my time, in the employments resulting from my station in life, and partly to my having indulged in a vague and desultory manner of reading.

If the length of this letter, instead of being tedious, atones for my apparent remissness, indulge me with one as long when it suits thee to write; for I assure thee with truth, great is the satisfaction thy letters afford to

Thy affectionate friend,

R. R.

To GEORGE HARRISON.

Ketley, 4th of Fifth Month, 1771.

ESTEEMED FRIEND,

I duly received thy favour of the 6th ult., and also of the 23rd; but have been prevented from replying sooner, by an attendance upon the Northern and Welch Yearly Meetings. The former was held at Chester, and as there were several Friends from Kendal, I thought of thee with a wish for thy company, apprehending it would have given thee pleasure to meet so many of thy old acquaintance upon that occasion. The Welch Yearly Meeting was held at Ludlow last week.

—— Since my last, I have run through Robertson's *History of Charles the Fifth;* being straitened for time, I was obliged to content myself with a cursory reading. I think, from the extent, as well as the importance of the transactions of that interesting period, their great variety and unavoidable complication, it required a clear head and extensively comprehensive eye to conduct the relation of them with so much perspicuity, and at the same time so well connected as our author has done; and though I join with thee in preferring the style of his *History of Scotland* as more strong, warm, and animated, I consider the other's being less impetuous and commanding, as an unavoidable consequence of the more widely diffused stream of the narration.

Thou will perceive I have not attributed the freedom of thy remarks to a want of sincerity, and I am pleased that thou so cordially accedes to my proposal of unlimited freedom in all our future communications. Instead of complimenting thee, or speaking as I think of thy mental acquisitions, I will only take the liberty of differing from thee in opinion, and of thinking that a proper arrangement and discrimination of the furniture of thy mind, will not prove such an Augean task, as to require an effort beyond thy powers. Time does much for us; and in the particular I am writing about, a degree of adjustment and regulation is effected thereby, without our attending to it; or is there an effect similar to that produced by attraction in matter, whereby our notions and ideas consort in proportion to their congruity? Give me leave here, however abruptly, to remark the distinction I make between notions and ideas, which by some have been, and I believe by some yet are, used as synonymous terms. By notion, I mean my opinion or sentiment of or about any matter or thing, which may consist or be made up of many separate and distinct ideas, of which, perhaps, some are simple and some complex, as a constellation includes divers stars, and of different magnitudes. But to return: I was going to say, I remember a certain author advises the youth to make reading one of their chief amusements, and says that, though they may not perfectly comprehend the whole drift of an author, or that their conceptions in some cases may be crude, time, with reflection and observation, will meliorate and bring into order those stores of the mind which may have been accumulated before the judgment was mature.

It seems strange to me, that thou hast occasion to lament thy not having opportunity of associating with those whose conversation, though not absolutely necessary to thee for the attainment of the power of understanding clearly, thinking justly, and judging accurately, would, nevertheless, be assistant thereto, as well as a high entertainment at the time. I thought that, as well as every other advantage, was to be had at London; and have considered it as one of the chief reasons for preferring a residence in town to living in the country, that a man might there have such company, as well as as much or little of it as he chose. * *

I have received the map, charts, and Æolian harp. I am pleased with them all. The latter exceeds my expectations. Though it has great compass and variety of notes, I have not remarked anything like light fantastic tunes; from the irregular motion of the wind, I should have expected something of that sort; but it has been either solemn, soft, or sweet, and most naturally brought those lines of Milton's to my mind, where Adam speaks thus to Eve :—

>   * * *   " How often from the steep
> Of echoing hill or thicket have we heard
> Celestial voices to the midnight air,
> Sole, or responsive each to other's note,
> Singing their great Creator? Oft in bands
> While they keep watch, or nightly rounding walk,
> With heavenly touch of instrumental sounds
> In full harmonic number join'd, their songs
> Divide the night, and lift our thoughts to heaven."

The extract is from one of the most amiable scenes in the poem. Thou wilt read or recollect the whole with pleasure, but, perhaps, will be ready to sigh, as the poet does, at the conclusion of another highly-finished picture of conjugal felicity :—

>   * * *   " O, when meet now
> Such pairs in love and mutual honour join'd !"

If thou can write in the course of next week, I shall be glad to hear from thee, and very glad to meet thee at the Star at Hockliff, on Fifth-day, the 16th inst.

I am truly,

Thy affectionate friend,

R. R.

To. S. LLOYD.

Ketley, 25th of Ninth Month, 1771.

To be considered by thee as thy friend, in the most intimate and endeared sense of the word, gives me particular satisfaction.

The warmth and cordiality of the assurances in thy last letter, as well as in many others, have excited congenial sentiments in my breast. My constitutional ardour, together with my having pretty early in life formed to myself very exalted, not to say romantic ideas, of friendship, as well as of some other affections of the mind, if it has sometimes subjected me to disappointments and chagrin, it also insures to those who merit and engage my regards, a warm and more than equal return of affection, for all the love they bestow upon me.

Perhaps some might think that the expressions *more than equal*, should have been qualified by an occasional exception; and it may be, was I writing to some people, I might have said, in *general more than equal;* but to thee, whom I consider as more happily and more temperately constituted, whose passions burn with a mild lambent flame, compared with the vehement ardent blaze of mine—I think I safely say, thou may assure thyself of a more than equal return to thy friendly regards. If my expressions of regard have not been equal to my conceptions, they have been sincere. Convinced of the justness of the sentiment, I have remembered the expressions of Young to Lorenzo upon this subject, and endeavoured to be to my friend such as I would have him be to me.—

> " Lorenzo! pride repress, nor hope to find
> A friend, but who has found a friend in thee."

Shall I add, without censure—

> " All like the purchase, few the price will pay,
> And that makes friends such miracles below."

If I do not express myself exactly as thou hast done, on the notion that matches in friendship, as well as in love, are made in heaven, I am sure thou wilt join me in hoping, that whether or not ours was made in heaven, it may at least be admitted there. I so far agree in the notion, that I consider a faithful friend as a blessing from the Almighty, if not the greatest blessing we can here enjoy. Friendship, including true religion, and a proper subordination of our affections, from the Author and object of love in heaven, down to the subjects of it among our fellow-creatures, as certainly tends to insure celestial happiness, as it constitutes the greatest part of mundane felicity. But I confess with thee, that among our numerous acquaintance, though mine may not be equal to thine, I have not many friends, in the sense of the word in which I use it—when I call thee mine, or myself thy friend; nor shall I scruple to add, I wish not for many. There is something of peculiarity or appropriation in my idea of friendship, which though not confined to absolute unity, precludes a promiscuous indulgence or indiscriminate effusion, without prejudice to that universal philanthropy which considers all mankind as children of one family. Our relative connections, though equally near in consanguinity, admit of a diversity in the mode or degree of our affection. And though we cannot doubt that all the *twelve*, while faithful, were objects of our Saviour's affectionate regard, one of them is emphatically distinguished as that disciple whom Jesus loved. This, if I am happy enough in exemplification, will illustrate my apprehensions of friendship, as well as it suggests the supplicatory wish that his blessing may accompany our friendly regards for each other; then will our love increase in this world, and perhaps in the next with an enlargement of capacity. Our advancement in love, as in bliss, may only be bounded by eternity. ———

To George Harrison.

Ketley, 8th of Tenth Month, 1771.

Esteemed Friend,

Let me repeat it gives me pleasure to correspond with thee—a pleasure which is increased by the reflection that my letters are acceptable to thee. If, indeed, they contribute to thy improvement, it is the most adequate reason for thy being pleased with them; and be assured, that the pleasure I receive from thine has not the superficial foundation of mere amusement only.

If I have lived longest in the world, and, from my intercommunications with its inhabitants in the course of trade and business, am more hackneyed in the ways of men, thou possessest a greater share of erudition, and mutual advantage may therefore be reasonably expected; but I will venture to advance it as a general rule, liable to very few if any exceptions, that he who improves another benefits himself; or, in the words of Young,

> " Thought, when delivered, is the more possest,
> Teaching, we learn, and giving we retain
> The births of intellect."

I write thus, that thou may not think I consider as compliments thy honest declarations of apprehended advantages by our correspondence, and would return them in kind. If Young reasons justly, my general rule must be good, and we are both improved, as well by the letters we send as by those we receive.

Thou should not indulge the thought, though suggested by a delicacy of sentiment too seldom met with, that thou dost too little when thou doest all thou art engaged to do, which is abundantly manifested by the solicitations for thy continuance; nor, when the value of thy services is estimated by the importance of the trust, canst thou deem thyself a useless or supernumerary member in the community. But I do not mean that these considerations, though sufficient to reconcile thee to thy present situation, and to justify thy availing thyself of all its advantages, should conclude against thy embracing any proper opportunity of putting thyself in a capacity to entertain thy own friend in thy own house; and it would increase my happiness did I possess the power of advancing thine, to exert it in the manner most agreeable to thy wishes. We went upon the Wrekin sooner than usual this year, that my children might partake of the pleasure. The weather was pleasant, though rather windy. From the top of that hill the prospect is so rich, so extensive, and so various, that, considered as a landscape only, it beggars all description; and yet I cannot forbear, as thou desirest it, mentioning the tufted trees in the adjoining woods, upon which, occasioned perhaps by the uncommonness of the scene, I always *look down* with a particular pleasure, as well as survey those more distant, which are interspersed amongst the corn-fields and meadows, contrasted with the new ploughed fallow-grounds and pastures with cattle; the towns and villages, gentlemen's seats and farm-houses, enrich and diversify the prospect, whilst the various companies of harvest-men in the different farms within view enliven the scene. Nor are the rivers that glitter amongst the laughing meadows, or the stupendous mountains which, though distant, appear awfully dreary without their effect considered as a part of the landscape only. But not to confine the entertainment to visual enjoyment, what an intellectual feast does the prospect from that hill afford when beheld, "or with the curious or the pious eye." Is not infinite power exerted, and infinite goodness displayed, in the various as well as plentiful provision for our several wants. Should not the consideration expand our hearts with desires to contribute to the relief of those whose indigence, excluding them from an equal participation of the general feast, is for a trial of their faith and patience, and of our gratitude and obedience? Whilst with an appropriation of sentiment which receives propriety from the consciousness of our own unworthiness, we substitute a particular for the general exclamation of humble admiration, in the words of the Psalmist, "Lord, what is man that thou art mindful of him, or the son of man that thou (thus) visitest him."

The romantic scenes of Bentall Edge; its rocks and precipices, its sides and top covered with wood; the navigable Severn, in which its feet are immersed; the populousness of the opposite shore; the motion, noise, and life on the river; the adjoining wharfs and manufactories, are capable of affording an high entertainment; and I should willingly devote one day in the year to a repetition of the enjoyment of the pleasures I have heretofore received from them; but though equally near, and equally desirable, a jaunt to Bentall Edge is not equally facile with one to the Wrekin. It seems more out of my province.

I am pretty much a stranger to the controversy begun by J. Beesly with Doctor Formey, and continued between J. Phipps and Newton, a dissenting minister at Norwich; but conjecturing from the little thou mentions, that it is chiefly about matters of opinion, and the different apprehensions of different men concerning notions of little or no consequence, (for such I deem all of little or no practical inference,) and perhaps for that reason uncertain, I am inclined to wish that it had not been begun, or that it may be speedily concluded; for contention about trifles is frequently productive of evils of infinitely more consequence than even a mistake would be in what occasioned the dispute, as must be allowed to be the case when charity and brotherly love are gradually eradicated by an acrimonious contention about modes of faith, or what is, if possible, of still less importance, modes of opinion.

Thy affectionate friend,

R. R.

To GEORGE HARRISON.

Ketley, 24th of Fourth Month, 1772.

(EXTRACT.)

Reflecting lately upon the distressed condition of some individuals, I recollected the poor man for whom thy friend Lanthoine solicited, and whom as I remember he represented as a foreigner in jail, in consequence of his being bound, or making himself accountable for a countryman in distress.

As I do not know that he is *not* a good Christian, I will suppose that *he is,* however he may differ in sentiment from ourselves, and then, as a disciple of Jesus Christ, most if not all the calamities enumerated by our Saviour as affording an opportunity for the diversified exercise of that species of charity that consisteth in doing good to his little ones, seems to be accumulated in him; hungry, thirsty and a stranger, naked, sick and in prison. Who that has any feeling, but must pity the object of such complicated distress? who that is able, would not be willing to contribute towards the alleviation of such aggravated misery? Even if his misfortunes were the consequence of attempts in trade that prudence could not justify, or he had been the victim of disappointed dependence upon the promises of the rich or the great, who would not cheerfully assist him? But when our unfortunate fellow-creature is deprived of that participation of free air and sunshine, subjected to pain, poverty, and confinement, far from his friends and native land, not for a crime committed, but for an incautious act of benevolence and friendship, in becoming responsible for the debts of a stranger like himself; I believe many would rejoice to be informed of such an opportunity of applying a small part of the abundance with which they are blessed in a manner that their benefactor has told them he would consider as done to himself; but if *he is not*, as I have supposed him, a disciple of the holy Jesus, *if we are* we shall not forget that he has enjoined us to be mindful to such, thereby approving ourselves the children of our Father which is in heaven; for " he maketh the sun to shine on the evil and on the good, and sendeth rain on the just, and on the unjust." Lanthoine had some thoughts of an address to the public by an advertisement in the newspaper. I doubt not of a proper representation of the case producing a considerable effect. I shall willingly contribute my mite as soon as I know the sum wanted, or if it should have happened that, since I was in town, the object of our present consideration has been released by friends or by death, it is too likely there are others in similar circumstances for whom Lanthoine's humanity will equally interest him, and who are equally welcome to my mite.

I did not expect to have written half so much upon this subject, but I must add to it, by desiring that if anything be done in consequence of it, it may not be known it was at my instance, nor my name mentioned upon the occasion, either as a contributor or otherwise. Thy strict care in this respect will oblige me.

Ketley, 2nd of Eleventh Month, 1772.

ESTEEMED FRIEND,

A journey into Wales is the principal reason I have to assign for my not having sooner replied to thy favour of the 22nd ultimo. I am much pleased with the agreeable continuation of thy narrative. Thy descriptions of the places and manners of the inhabitants are sufficiently explicit to convey a complete idea, and thy account of and reflections upon the effects of superstition and arbitrary government in thy abovesaid are sufficient, though brief, to make me thankful that I possess in *so great a* degree mental and corporal liberty, the freedom of thinking and an unrestrained power of communicating my thoughts. I say *so great a degree*, because I believe every mind, even in this land and day of liberty, is more or less shackled by the prejudices of education and the conduct biased by early example.

The conclusion of thy letter was particularly acceptable to me, and together with a letter I have received from S. L., has nearly removed from my mind the painful apprehension which distressed me when I wrote last. The wound may be healed, but the scar will remain—to remember or forget depends not upon the will; but though I cannot forget, I can remember without resentment. The impression was too deep to be immediately erased, but whilst it continues it will continue to remind me of the sincerity of thy friendship as well as to excite the endeavour in myself, not to furnish occasion for apprehensions so different from my intentions. It was a conduct so much the object of my contempt, and for which some who have had many other valuable qualities have been the subjects of my pity, mentally and verbally, that it hurt me exceedingly to think I should be, not thought but reported, not suspected but accused, of meanness and ingratitude by those whose candour and veracity would be undoubted, and instanced towards those who I valued chiefly for being of a temper as much the reverse of such a disposition as I knew my own was—to them especially.

10 *

It is high time I should resume and conclude the account of my journey to Kendal. It happened to be the time of the races when we were at Lancaster, which made it rather unpleasant at the inns. As a town, it equalled my expectation; as a seaport, it fell very far short of it. I thought from what I had heard, it must be somewhat like Liverpool, or Bristol at least; but though there is a spacious quay and a custom-house as remarkable for its neatness as its size, the number of vessels bore no proportion to either: instead of a forest of masts and the strand swarming with the children of commerce and of labour, the few separate vessels were like single trees upon a plain, and the silent solitary quays revived in my remembrance, however remote the allusion, the predicted desolation of Tyre and Sidon. It is likely there are sometimes more vessels than were there at that time, for I believe there were not six in all. The men I suppose were all upon the horse-course. I was acquainted with but one friend in the town, but the generous hospitality of William Dilworth would have rendered a further acquaintance unnecessary if we had not chosen to be at an inn. We were at their week-day meeting, and from the number then assembled I suppose there is a pretty large body of Friends in the town. If thou art not acquainted with John Bradford, I wish thou wast. Though I had not seen him before, I was much *pleased* with spending a few minutes at his house. If the word was not generally confined to devotional performances, I should have said *edified*; for certainly there was something very propitious to virtuous resolves in the amiable simplicity and cheerful innocency of the good old man. We staid and dined at William Dilworth's, drank tea at Burton, and came to Kendal about seven o'clock. The next day we went to meeting in the forenoon; Rachel Wilson and her daughters—for Isaac was from home—took a walk with us to the top of Fellside, &c. in the afternoon, and went from one Friend's house to another, finishing the evening at her daughter Braithwaite's, for *her* husband was also abroad. The next day thy father was so kind as to accompany us with Molly and Betsy Wilson, the three Masters and Thomas Crewdson, to Winander Water. We could scarcely have had a worse day. It rained very hard all the time we were there, and all the way back. The young women could not go upon the water. The Masters, Billy and I, went over to the island; and, as I expected to see the proprietor in London that day two weeks, I took of the soil and the produce with an intent to carry to him—for he has never seen either—but unluckily left it in Shropshire at last.

Though I think Kendal a pleasant place, the surrounding mountains, the clear river, and the adjoining enclosures, adding considerably to the town, of itself very agreeable; yet I must say I like the people still better than the place. I was about to mention the names of some to whom I thought myself much obliged for their civilities, but I have not room to enumerate half, so shall only say that for hospitality towards strangers, love and unity among each other, and universal good will to their neighbours, I never saw the place whose inhabitants appeared to equal the Friends at Kendal.

I am, thy obliged and affectionate friend,

R. R. ·

To HIS DAUGHTER,

(Then about twelve years old.)

Ketley, 7th of Second Month, 1778.

DEAR HANNAH,

I have intended many times since I saw thee to write to thee, but have still been prevented, and now take up my pen at an unusual time to inform thee of the continuance of our health, and to inquire after thine, of which I should have been glad to have heard by letters from thee oftener than we have, for I think we have received but one letter since I left Bristol. I hope it will not be long before I receive copies of those papers I saw when with thee—I mean some expressions of a child of John Gurney's—a testimony concerning her sister Corkfield by M.

Ash, and I think there was another, the title of which I have forgotten. I hope thou readest frequently in the "Dying Sayings" as well as other good books, but above all and most frequently in the New Testament. The Old Testament contains many instructive and edifying accounts of good men and women, as well as many relations of the just judgments of the Lord upon the wicked and disobedient, and may most certainly be read to great advantage; but our duty as Christians, and the glorious hopes of immortality and eternal life, are more immediately revealed in the New Testament: there we read of what our Saviour did and suffered for us, as well as of the doctrines he taught and the duties he requires of those who would receive the advantages of his coming by becoming his disciples and followers—and these are in an especial manner comprised in his sermon on the mount, which thou hast been taught, and I hope wilt never forget. If thou rememberest it, and thy conduct is influenced by the precepts it contains " of doing good and bearing ill," thou wilt be as happy in this world as is consistent with the nature of our existence in it, and inconceivably happy in the next, where neither our own infirmities nor those of others will prevent the completion of that bliss which is perfect in its degree as well as endless in its duration; and after such momentous incentives to a life of religion and holiness, let me add (and that with good hope of its having some weight with my dear daughter) that it will be as a cordial to the hearts of her father and mother, who love thee with a sincere affection, to see thee dedicate thy early years to him that hath promised that those who so seek him shall find Him; and then it will be a pleasure to us to make thy passage through life as pleasant to thee as we can; but nothing we can do for thee (were we ever so able and ever so willing) will be sufficient without it is accompanied by the blessing of the Almighty, which I therefore hope thou wilt be most concerned to seek after. I lately heard from thy grandmother of thy being a good scholar with thy needle. I am glad of it. I wish thy progress in writing and arithmetic may enable me to bring thee home for good before it be long. Joe gives his dear love to thee, in which he is joined by thy mother and cousin Sukey, and thy very affectionate father,

R. REYNOLDS.

I heard from Billy lately that he was well and had written two letters to thee, but had received only one from thee. He loves thee—write to him again. Give my kind respects to thy mistress, &c.

Ketley, 26th of Second Month, 1773.

ESTEEMED FRIEND,

I have to acknowledge the receipt of thy very acceptable favour of the 18th instant, which confirms the opinion I entertained before from some hints I had heard, even from Blakey himself, of the detestable habits of the French. Their want of cleanliness is incompatible with their acknowledged politeness, at least in my apprehension. I should have expected a refinedness of manners and an abhorrence of filth would be as necessarily connected, as sordid customs with a savage heart. Thy description of the city and public buildings is entertaining, and rendered still more intelligible to me by some views of them by Perelle, which I happen to have among my prints. The public gardens, or rather those of the king and the nobility which are of public access, the paintings in the churches, convents, and palaces, would have frequently attracted my feet and my eyes; and though the sight of a library can give no great pleasure when one has not time to avail oneself of the stores of information it contains, I think I should have endeavoured to have seen at least what English authors they admitted, especially on politics, and whether heretical writers of polemic divinity were allowed a place among the avowed champions for papistic orthodoxy. I join heartily in thy ardent wish that mankind might more generally be able to distinguish between religion and superstition, Christianity and idolatry. One of the good effects of travelling must be (I think) an enlargement of the heart as well as of the mind, an increase of the benevolent affections as well as an increase of knowledge, demonstrated by the effective wish for the happiness of all mankind in *this world*, as well as by the belief of the possibility of it in *the next*. Reading the histories of different countries may have the same effect in degree, but not so extensively as residing in them; if, indeed, there is not a possibility, not to say a danger, of a person's losing the belief of the truth itself by a residence in the regions of error. This thought occurred to me as I was reading Alexander Dow's dissertation on the religion and philosophy of the Hindoos, prefixed to his *History of Hindostan,* and his Introduction to that history. Perhaps a rigid belief of the Hebrew cosmogony and the earlier historical part of the Old Testament, may be dispensed with, in those who pretty early in life remove into a country possessed of records of equal authority among the natives, whose confident claim to an antiquity inconsistent with the relation before mentioned may well be supposed to relax *their* opinion of the literal authenticity of the latter, who have not been accustomed to consider it as a dogma in divinity; but I should have thought the belief of the truth of the gospel effectually secured by the superior strength of its internal evidence. As it is common for the historians of kingdoms and governments, as well as biographical writers, to say the best they can of their respective subjects, so I can suppose the above-mentioned author, willing to give his history as much consequence as possible, has represented the religion and philosophy of the Brahmins in the most favourable point of view, not suspecting that it was as likely he would thereby prejudice his own judgment as that of his reader; and perhaps that will be the most charitable method, if not the most just, of accounting for the preference he seems to give even to the Mahometan religion before the Christian in the following paragraph :—

"Should we judge of the truth of a religion from the success of those who profess it, the pretended revelation of Mahomet might be justly thought divine. By annexing judiciously a martial spirit to the enthusiasm which he inspired by his religious tenets, he laid a *solid* foundation for that greatness at which his followers soon after arrived. The passive humility in-

culcated by Christianity is much more fit for philosophical retirement than for those active and daring enterprises, which animate individuals, and render a nation powerful and *glorious*.
We accordingly find that the spirit and power, and, we may say,
even the virtue of the Romans declined with the introduction of
a new religion among them; while the Arabians, in the space
of a few years after the promulgation of the faith of Mahomet,
rose to the summit of all human greatness."

I believe some of the advocates for Christianity may have
mentioned the rapid success of its promulgation, without external
compulsion, as a circumstance in favour of its truth, but I do not
know that any have alleged it as a proof of it; and yet, when we
consider the very different weapons therein exercised, as distinguished by the Apostle in his Second Epistle to the Corinthians,
from those employed by Mahomet and his party, it concludes perhaps the stronger in its favour that it made such a progress in
the minds of mankind, at that time as contrarily disposed, by
the subtleties and refinements of worldly wisdom, philosophy
and taste, as they were disposed to receive the religion propa-
gated by the sword of Mahomet and his followers at a time when,
as the author informs us, "all manly spirit was extinguished by
despotism, and excess of villainy was the only proof given of
parts." I can attribute it to nothing less than a prejudiced
judgment, occasioned, as I have before supposed, that the
author does not see that the obligations of Christianity are to
the practice of those virtues which are essential to the happiness
of mankind—that granting the greatest degree of happiness of
the individuals is the greatest degree of glory to the whole, it is
most rationally to be expected from the influence of that religion
which enjoins, with at least equal rigour, active benevolence as
" passive humility"—which, connecting the adoration of the
Almighty with the discharge of the relative and moral duties
to our fellow creatures, exhibits, in the emphatic language of
the gospel, "Glory to God in the highest, and on the earth
peace and good-will to men." My paper will not admit, and in
writing to thee it would be superfluous to be diffusive in further

remarks upon the quotation; yet let me add, that it must be a false glory that is acquired by the slaughter of mankind, as it is an abuse of the word to call that *virtue* which can "animate individuals" to attempt the acquisition of power and greatness at the expense of their humanity. If, on the contrary, the author would have us understand by *virtue*, moral goodness, the declension of it among any people was never occasioned by the introduction of the religion he styles *new to the Romans*, but by their accounting the cross of Christ foolishness, because inconsistent with their false notions of greatness and glory. And if "*human greatness*," as the author uses the word, implies nothing more than mere extent of empire, did not the Romans—and if it includes also the more glorious enlargement of the mind, did not the Grecians—did not both, in literature, in every science and every art that adds to the "pleasure, elegance, and grace" of human life, surpass the Arabians, when, the author affirms, "(in the space of a few years after the promulgation of the faith of Mahomet) they were risen to the summit of all *human greatness*."

The book thou hast bought for me at the instance of J. B. was recommended by a person whose judgment I esteem, but I have never seen it. J. B. has obliged me by a very kind letter; perhaps I may take the liberty of writing to him again. If Robert Barclay is gone, I wish him a good voyage and a safe return; if he is not gone, he has my good wishes, wherever he is or shall be. I hope to hear from thee again soon, and am

Thy very affectionate friend,

R. R.

To R. REYNOLDS.

17th of Sixth Month, 1773.

MY DEAR WIFE,

—— I hear nothing but bad accounts, (as they are generally called) respecting the pig-iron trade, and predictions of its being still worse. I am thankful I can say I am at all times enabled to consider the things of this life in that degree of subordination

and inferiority to the concerns of the next, that whether an increase or a decrease of outward riches seems most probable is
matter of great indifferency to me, and when I consider further
the ill effects riches frequently have upon the mind, especially
of young people, together with the remembrance that where there
is but little given there is but little required, and where there is
much given there is much required, I am inclined to contemplate
a state of inferiority to former expectations, if not with a positive
desire for it, at least with a cheerful acquiescence in it. If I attain to purity of heart and meekness of temper, how little of
worldly riches will be sufficient, and if either one or the other
of the former will be prevented by my having even so much as
I have of the latter, may I be deprived of it. This I can truly
say has been the desire of my mind many times, and especially
of late, and when I have considered the probability of losing
much in London and elsewhere, the hope that it might have that
effect has made the apprehension more tolerable; but I know
that purity of heart and meekness of temper are not the *necessary*
consequences of outward poverty, and that in every state and in
every station sufficient assistance will be afforded, if properly applied for and properly used for the discharge of all that is required of us; but, my Rebecca, it is difficult, when surrounded
with outward besetments as well as inward, to keep the eye of
the mind singly and steadily to the divine Leader into purity and
humility, and I long for the return of the time when retirement
and quiet from the continual hurry I have lately been in, will
afford opportunities for that recollection of mind so necessary to
one of my natural activity of spirit, and abounding with so many
and so various concerns in trade and business.

11

To S. Lloyd.

Ketley, 3rd of Twelfth Month, 1774.

——However much one virtue may be supposed to differ from another, in kind or degree, it is our duty to practise them all as necessities or occasions present. The injunctions of honour or of gratitude, as well as the laws of justice and equity, are of eternal obligation: perhaps their greatest difference may be occasioned by the latter being so cognizable by a human judicature, and the former necessarily unamenable to any other bar than that of conscience here, and of Divine justice hereafter. I wish this consideration may have an influence proportionate to its truth and importance upon all our transactions with our fellow-creatures, however different they may be in outward circumstances.

I sympathize with thee under every disappointment; but as disappointment is only the frustration of hope, and more properly a negative than a positive loss, instead of attempting to suggest alleviating considerations, let me inform thee, that under a recent positive loss of many hundreds, and a probability, next to assurance, of a still greater, I endeavour to reconcile myself to what I cannot avoid, not only by remembering the important truth thou mentions, "That trial, and even adversity, is best for us," but also by considering that the real goods of life are to be purchased for less money than I shall have left at last. That what I have lost if not absolutely superfluous, was not absolutely necessary; but which, notwithstanding, would have increased my duties and my dangers. That the happiness resulting from the gratifications of sense or of intellect, is as much within my power as if I had not met with the loss. Most, if not all the former, result from habit, the effect of custom, and require circumstances to which abundance and money is not always propitious. In general the peasant enjoys his coarse fare with a higher relish than the peer his costly viands, and I drink ale equal in colour and brilliancy to wine with superior satisfaction, though at a sixth of the price. If *this sense* can be gratified as fully and as exquisitely by a man in moderate circumstances as by the rich, *the others* are, if possible, still less dependent on wéalth—*Feeling* not at all—*Smelling* very little—*Hearing* as much as any ; but *that*, perhaps, with *Seeing*, may, with almost equal propriety, be considered either as a faculty or a sense. However that may be, I have been very apt to consider the two last different, at least in degree, from the three former, partaking more of the soul than the body, and contributing little to our pleasures, but as they administer to mental gratifications by interesting or employing the intellect. I confess that a disposition to be pleased with modulated sound is natural, and manifested as early as most others that have not a nearer relation to the preservation of life; and I conceive it is not a proof of a depraved taste, or a mean understanding, if—at a time of life when we readily incline to reason from effects to causes, and to follow from link to link that great connecting chain through the amazing variety of its grad-ations—if, then, the melody of birds, the voice of winds and of waters, from the whispering of the breeze to the shouting of the storm ; from the tinkling of the rill to the roar of the ocean, and the still more awful thunder ; if these are then listened to with greater satisfaction than more artificial sounds, I conceive it is no impeachment of the understanding; and to enjoy these it is not necessary to be very rich. What music *can do*, it is not to be expected that I *can* pronounce; but if as a science it is capable of pleasing. I conjecture it must be by the discovery of the relation, dependencies, and connection of its several intri-cacies and involutions, by

" —— untwisting all the chords that tie
   The hidden soul of harmony,"

and that is more properly the object of intelligence than of sense. Great effects have been attributed to music. I do not forget those which it is recorded to have had upon Elisha and upon Saul. It is *not said* the minstrel accompanied his harp with his voice; but as from all accounts of those men in ancient as well as later days, their practice was to rehearse suitably to the occasion, accom-

panying their verses with their music, or as Homer, a cotemporary
with Elisha, describes it:

> " The heavenly minstrel taught to sing
> High notes responsive to the trembling string."

So, in the latter case especially, I think it may be inferred, that
as the *sweet singer of Israel* was not less likely to excel in poetry
than in playing, the change in Saul's mind is most feasibly
accounted for, not by attributing it to the sound of the harp only,
but to the powers of music united to poetry, or in the language
of Milton, "married to immortal verse."   I would not be understood to exclude, in either case, the subserviency of natural causes
to the divine will, or to attribute that to inferior powers, which
can only be effected by the supreme.   On the contrary, as it is
the Almighty who has established certain laws in nature, which
operate uniformly, except he is pleased to suspend them ; so I
consider every display of human genius as the effect of delegated
power from the Divine origin of all things, and only wrong when
perverted or misapplied by us.   And though, under the present
dispensation of superior light, the doctrine of sounds is unconnected or opposite to the nature of that worship which is required
of us; under the Mosaic, the proper application thereof was
acceptable to God and beneficial to men.   The late J. Brown,
author of the Essay upon the Characteristics, a book I very much
admire and approve, wrote on the cure of Saul, or the power of
music : I have not yet seen it, if I had, it is likely thou would
not receive this rambling scrawl, which may well be thought too
little connected with the subject upon which I was writing; but
after having supposed all the other senses may be gratified as well
with a moderate share of wealth as with a superabundance, I
think the sight, as still more immediately subservient to the
intellect, and furnishing the mind with more ideas than all the
rest, is capable of ample gratification as independently of riches
as any other.   Music without poetry can afford a rational entertainment to very few, but ideas the most sublime, as well as the
most tender, may, since the invention of writing, be excited in

the minds of most by the visual faculty. The grandeur of the scenery of the visible creation, the immense ocean,

"The pomps of groves, the garniture of fields,
And all the dread magnificence of heaven,"

these, through the goodness of the great Creator, who makes that which is most valuable the most common; these are offered, not to say obtruded, upon the sight of all men; and well might the author last quoted consider it as a degree of impiety, to sacrifice the beneficial effects of a proper survey of the charms of nature to the lust of wealth. What then have the rich that we have not? The finest productions of the chisel or the pencil are only valuable as they approach to a just representation of nature. "The human face divine," that "index of the soul,"—how varying—how expressive ! We admire a faithful delineation of one passion, or still more of such a complication as occupies the countenance at one instant; but no copy can equal the original : how quick are the transitions and varied the combinations in the same subject at different times, observable in real life, and equally obvious to me as to a greater man.

To his Daughter.

Ketley, 6th of Seventh Month, 1776.

Dear Hannah,

I fully intended to have written a long letter to thee by this post; but the same reason that prevented my writing at all, will prevent my writing much by this, (I fear); but thou must not judge of the strength of my love and affection for thee by the length of my letters to thee. I wish thy happiness as I do my own, and knowing how much it depends upon humility and meekness, I am earnest in my recommendation of those virtues—we have them not naturally—but God is the giver of every good and every perfect gift. If we ask them of him with sincerity, and evince our sincerity by taking up our daily cross and denying

11 *

ourselves, we shall find, through the operation of his divine Spirit, that alteration and change in our natural dispositions which is meant by being born again, and without which, our Saviour assures us, we cannot see the kingdom of God. What have we experienced of this change? Another change approaches certainly, perhaps suddenly, and assuredly final, as to our happiness or misery. I write in haste, and these are only broken hints; thy own reflections upon them will probably be more serviceable than the additions I might make if I had more leisure. * * * I meet with many disagreeable occurrences, and some from unexpected quarters. Next to the peace of God in my own breast, which I desire in the first place, the greatest alleviation I experience is the hope I entertain of my children's growing in grace as they grow in age. Continue, my dear, by increasing in humility, meekness and self-denial, to increase thy own happiness, and thereby that of thy affectionate father,

R. R.

To his Daughter.
Bridgwater, 10th of Sixth Month, 1777.

—— I am not willing to close this letter without mentioning the desire that oftener than the day has been in my heart, that my dear children may live in the fear of the Lord, and die in his favour; particularly that my only and beloved daughter may like her dear departed mother, know the power of the cross in her youth—that, if length of days should not be her portion she may also experience the happy effects of an early obedience to the Divine requirings. It is only by the power of the cross we can experience a being crucified to the world, the love of and conformity to which brings death to that life which consists of happiness and *peace.* Let not, my dear Hannah, the example of others, who may be ashamed of the cross and of the plainness and simplicity which we profess, influence thy conduct; nor the levity of heart incident to youth prevent thy seriously and frequently reflecting on the shortness and uncertainty of this life, and the continuance of the next, as well as of the infinity of the consequences of our present conduct. We are advised to pass the time of our sojourning here *in fear*:—how different is the conduct of the world. It ridicules or despises that fear in which is true safety and real wisdom. But let us rather be the companions of the despised followers of a despised and crucified Saviour, in meekness and lowliness of mind, than grieve them, and injure our own souls, by conforming to the world and the fashions and practices of it. If thou knew or could conceive how much my happiness (at least in this world) depends upon thy being good, because I know thine entirely depends on it both here and hereafter, I believe it would—nay I believe it will—have great influence with thee.

I am, and desire to be still more humble and thankful to the Almighty that he has blessed me with children so affectionate and dutiful. Be assured I wish nothing more ardently respecting you than to contribute all in my power to your happiness, and consider me as a friend to whom thou may with confidence communicate everything that concerns thee, and grieve me not by discovering a distrust of my being at all times and on all occasions,

Thy most affectionate father,

RICHARD REYNOLDS.

Ketley, 6th of Eleventh Month, 1777.

—— I received thy short letter at Stourbridge, and that of the 31st ultimo since, and am obliged to thee for both. I shall be very glad to hear thy anxiety on account of thy little daughter is converted into thankfulness by her perfect restoration to health. The uncertain tenure by which we hold this life, and all its connections, justifies our endeavouring to sit as loose to them as their nature admits, as well as endeavouring with superior ardour primarily to seek the kingdom of God, and his righteousness, the which if we attain we shall cheerfully leave it to

him, to add or to resume so much or so many of the good
things of this life, as in his wisdom and providence he shall see
best for us and for them, and be enabled equally in his giving
or taking away to bless the name of the Lord. I can truly sympathise with thee, and join in lamenting that our advancement is so
slow in the heavenly race; but I trust we do not so absolutely
stand still as to be carried towards the confines of this world by
the current of time, without also in some degree experiencing our
salvation to be nearer than when we might reasonably expect our
exit to be more distant. I should not be just to the unmerited mercy
of God, if I did not acknowledge with the deepest gratitude my
hope that, through the assistance of his grace, I have experienced
a small degree of deliverance from the sins that did most easily beset
me; but at the same time I must as freely confess that if I had
been more obedient and more watchful, had made use of all the
assistance that has been held out to me, I might have witnessed
a much greater advancement; and that I have not is cause of
sorrow of heart unto me, and oh, that it may continually operate to
the quickening my desires and prayers for perfect redemption
from the power of sin, as well as from condemnation for past
transgressions, whether by commission or omission.

Thy father expressed a wish to have the enclosed list of the
places at which the yearly meetings for Wales have been held.
I hoped to have had it ready to have given or sent to him at
quarter-day last.*   Please to present it to him, and with it my
dear love, for I have a very great respect for him, and sincerely
wish that, as some of his predecessors were eminently serviceable
to their companions and fellow-labourers in those days, and upon some of those occasions, so his descendants may be concerned
to cultivate the same field, and like himself, as a shock of corn
that cometh in in its season, be gathered at the great harvest
into the garner of eternal life. I sometimes reflect upon those
former days and former worthies, as we read of them in the accounts by our ancient Friends and in their dying sayings. What
zeal and love animated them, what running to and fro that the

* The Quarterly Meeting of Ironmasters.—Ed.

knowledge of the principles which they through faith and obedience had experienced to deliver them, might be attained by
others. How constant in their attendance, and diligent in their
meetings for worship and discipline—how careful out of them ;
I long to be like them—I desire to be redeemed from the world
and everything in it. To be what the Lord would have me to
be, whether anything or nothing, is the first and most frequent
wish of my heart, and the hope of witnessing his peace in good
meetings or out of them, the greatest source of enjoyment to
me. * * *

To. S. Lloyd.

Ketley, 17th of Twelfth Month, 1777.

—— Thou asks me "how I feel myself as to the late news
from America." I do feel and sympathise with our suffering
friends on that continent, and am sorry for the effusion of blood
the contest occasions ; but with respect to the political justness
or injustice of either party, I do not feel about it. My opinion,
were I capable of forming a right one, would have no influence,
and as consistently with my profession I can do nothing, I think
it is best to say nothing. Were I a man of fighting principles,
perhaps I might both say and do, at least I should think it right
to support the cause I espoused mediately or immediately, by
acting myself, or hiring others to act; but as I trust I have been
favoured to have a sight, if not an experience, of a state in which
there can be no wars or fightings, so I think it my duty to pity
and pray for those I believe to be wrong, and to acquiesce in
every dispensation of Providence, with a steady belief that all
things will work together for good to those who love God, with
an earnest endeavour to evince my love to him, by keeping his
commandments, and in particular the new commandment of loving
one another. The lukewarmness and indifferency, the love of
the world, and consequent degeneracy of our Society, has been
long loudly and justly matter of complaint; perhaps sufferings

may be necessary, in a Society capacity : I wish the present may be effectual ; if not I might be allowed to say in general, what I have often secretly said for myself in particular, that if nothing but sufferings would make me perfect, may I experience them in the kind, number and degree, the Lord should see meet for that purpose, and so still prays,

Thy affectionate friend.

Ketley, 25th of Twelfth Month, 1778

MY DEAR DAUGHTER,

While I was last from home it was frequently in my mind to write to thee, and that I did not, gave me some uneasiness. Now thy absence revives the disposition ; and though, from having much to do in a little time, together with my mind being less qualified than at some seasons that are past, I apprehend that I shall do still less justice to the strong desire I have to promote thy happiness, I am induced to avail myself of the present opportunity, lest a better should not be afforded me.

I have sometimes considered how much we are disposed, especially in what may be called the spring-time of life, to indulge the wanderings of the mind in the flowery regions of imagination, and, untaught by experience, to suppose the gay visions are representations of scenes as real as they are pleasing. Hence in part, proceeds in after life, disappointment and chagrin, indisposing for the enjoyment of happiness ourselves, or contributing to it in others; but, why not come to the point at once? The truth is, what I have spoken of as cause and effect are properly both effects, or rather, the one natural effect of our depraved condition ; assuredly evidenced, if we were told nothing of its origin or introduction, by our constantly seeking happiness in subjects not adequate, till reiterated disappointment wrings the frequent sigh under a sense of the necessity of that reformation or change of heart which our Saviour calls our being born again; but to which nature is repugnant, because it is only effected by the inward crucifixion or death of the vain mind, and manifested outwardly by a denial of the vanities and follies, as well as of the impieties of a wicked world. Hence appears the danger of reading books that tend to increase the activity and extend the influence of the passions at the same time that they represent the beauties of the mind as possessed or attainable in a state of nature; "but all is false and hollow."

When, by sickness, the *awful* future is brought near, or by the immediate visitations of Divine mercy the illuminations of truth are strong in the soul, and we see all things as they will *then* appear, or when we advert to the degree of estimation in which the objects of sense or refined imagination have been held by our great Pattern, and those who we believe have followed him the nearest, the insignificancy and emptiness of the poet's visions, the tender or the pathetic descriptions of ideal happiness or misery which agitate the distempered mind, appear as they really are—as much beneath our notice as the empty toys of our childhood.

The most earnest wish in my heart for my dear Hannah, as for myself is, that by a constant earnest attention, and faithful obedience to the inspeaking word of Divine grace, we may, in the Lord's due time, experience that change. Great would be the advantage even in this life; the truly happy are the truly religious, who having known, in their measure, a death to sin and a new birth to righteousness, love God above all, while in a due subordination to him they are more susceptible of pure impressions, and better qualified for the endearing connections of affection and friendship than those whose licentious passions are not regulated by the salutary restraint of religion.

I doubt not thy admitting the truth of what I have written: the assent of the understanding is readily obtained; but to have the heart replenished with the holy preserving fear of the Lord does not at all times depend upon the will of the individual, much less upon that of another. There are seasons of grace, times when the Divine visitation is extended in an especial manner; may we wait for it with more ardent breathings of soul than for every other blessing, and, by giving way to its leavening influences, experience that meekness, patience, true charity, and self-denial wrought in us, which, and than which nothing else, will make us happy in ourselves and a blessing to others.

I love thy brother as I love thee, and equally desire his happiness with thine. Knowledge is not wanting to any of us, and oh! that obedience may not be! Give my dear love to him, and let him remember—let us all remember—God sees the heart; if our professed desires to grow in grace are sincere, they will be heard and answered. To the protection and preservation of the Almighty arm in every season of danger and difficulty I desire to commit you both with my own soul.

To S. LLOYD.

Ketley, 29th of Third Month, 1779.

—— The occasion upon which I am going from home now, and went to Birmingham last, as well as to some other places lately, has excited in my mind a consideration how far my conduct has suited these occasions, which I think may be compared to the solemn assemblies of the Jews formerly, when I presume their minds were occupied on sacred subjects, to the exclusion of secular concerns. Perhaps it may not be necessary to some, (as I think I heard thee once express it) to have the ark always upon their shoulders; but for my own part, so easily do my feet slip and my attention relax, I have more reason to fear a getting from under the burden or weight of the word, (if I may use that expression) too soon, than bearing it too long. And I think, too, the generality of mankind are most likely to miss their way on the same hand. When I consider William Penn's description of us as a people, in his account of our rise and progress to his day—when they were in conversation innocent, serious and weighty, their wills and affections bowed and brought into subjection; and that nothing could draw them from this retired, inward, watchful frame, and compare it with the present state of our Society, or indeed my own, need I scruple to acknowledge and lament the disparity—to admire, in his own words, "the humility and chaste zeal of that day?—how constant at meetings! how retired in them! how firm to truth's life, as well as truth's principles! how entire and united in their communion?" Ah! my friend, how are we now? But, instead of ineffectual bewailings and fruitless comparisons, let us, through the assistance and divine help of the Holy Arm, which supported them in that day, and which is equally ready to lead us in the same path, let us endeavour after a reformation in ourselves, let us walk by the same rule, let us mind the same things, and following them, as they followed Christ, be qualified to be examples to others in the same way. The state of the Society, of our own families, the glory of God, and our own happiness, —everything unites to excite us to watchfulness and to constant prayer; and may we be thereto so excited, so wisheth

Thy affectionate friend.

Extract of a Letter to A FRIEND, *who was a member of the same Monthly Meeting, and the mother of a large family.*

Ketley, 1st of Fifth Month, 1783.

——— When I was sitting with thee and thy children, in company with the Friends concerned to pay you a religious visit, certain considerations occurred to my mind, which my unwillingness to prevent such advice as they might have to give, and a hope that their observations might supersede the necessity of my making any, together with the thought that if they did not, I could adopt this method of communicating them to thee, occasioned me to omit mentioning them at the time; and may be considered as the reasons for my addressing this letter to thee; and as I have no motive to do it that is not consistent with sincere desires for thy own peace and thy children's welfare, I hope thou will receive it in the love in which it is written. It became

12

the subject of my considerations, of how great importance is the trust committed to a parent of children and the mistress of a family. That duties and obligations which exist not in a single state arise. from the relation in which we stand to our offspring, who we ought to believe are entrusted to our care by the Almighty—that every additional child is an additional charge, which enlarges the account we shall have to give for our conduct to them, and before them; and also adds to our obligation to train them up in the nurture and admonition of the Lord, were it only for this reason,—that the consequent good example of the elder will make it more easy to manage and bring up the younger in like manner. When I consider how much thy husband is abroad, and when at home, how much his engagements in business oblige him to be absent from his family, it appears to me thy duty increases with the increased necessity there is for thy exertion in well ordering thy children, and more especially while their tender age renders them susceptible of the *authority*, as it subjects them more immediately to the *care* of a mother: I might add, too, how desirable it must be to a father, after a long and close attention to business, for the maintenance of his wife and numerous tender offspring, to have a comfortable, well-regulated family, to sit down with at his meals, and to retire to in an evening. What a pity would it be, if through a want of timely exertion on thy part, ill habits, which are too readily as well as too early contracted, should acquire such strength with increase of age, as to be unconquerable by all the endeavours thou can use; and how would it add to thy compunction and sorrow to reflect that much less reprehension and restraint, laid on them in early life, might have prevented their too-late lamented defection from the right path. Or, supposing it should not, it will be some consolation to thee, as it has been to others, to be able to say, thou wast clear of them—thou had restrained them from evil while they were under thy power, and when their age exempted, or their distance removed them from it, they could have no more from thee than thy example, thy prayers, and thy occasional advice; and all these I sincerely desire they may always have, and in future always observe.

I remembered the exhortation was not only "be sober," but also "be vigilant"—that it is not only our duty to be watchful to foresee, but also diligent to prevent occasions of blame in our children: and shall we, through indolence, through a want of that vigilance and diligence, which the importance of our trust, the safety of our children and our own peace should inspire, suffer them to contract habits of inattention and rudeness, even in their very tender age, and when most easily governed? What, then, is to be expected when increasing years shall give the elder greater strength, and the younger have the influence of their example, superadded to the propensity which thy children, in common with all others, have to do wrong. Children soon grow too old and too strong for a mother's government; but, till a certain age at least, the mother has the greatest part, if not all the care of their conduct, as well as of their health; and the success of their father's or master's endeavours afterwards, in their learning and deportment depends much upon the mother's previous good management.

When I again assure thee I have nothing but love and good-will in my heart to thee and thy children, I hope thou will excuse the freedom of the preceding remarks, and one other hint, with which I shall conclude an epistle already longer than I expected it would have been,—and that is, concerning thy well-ordering thy children on the First-day. It is to be desired that the *frequent* reading of the Holy Scriptures mentioned in our queries, should be understood by us to mean oftener than on one day in the week, and I hope it is recommended and practised by some accordingly; but on that day especially, it should not be *neglected*; and as, from the many engagements so numerous a family of little ones as thine must furnish, it is not to be expected thou can have many opportunities for reading, I have not a doubt, if thou set thy children to read them, with sincere desires for their and thy own benefit, it would prove as much to thy edification and comfort as if thou read them thyself, as well as it might be the means of preventing them from mixing in company and conversation with the many rude children which, on that day especially, are to be met with; and as there is then

the greatest danger, they should be particularly restrained from
it, by being kept with their parents, or other suitable company;
for as six days are sufficient for labour or learning, they should
be also for play and amusement.

Ketley, 17th of Second Month, 1784.

DEAR NEPHEW,

The perusal of thy first letter above mentioned revives in my
mind a consideration that has many times employed it.   Can thou
tell me why a sentiment not more justly conceived, nor always
more happily expressed, is, notwithstanding, better remembered
and more willingly quoted from a heathen philosopher, than from
a Christian apostle,—from the writings of the Greeks and Romans,
than from the Old or New Testament?   Thy adducing as an
instance of public virtue in the Romans, their applauding this
line of their poet,—

   " Homo sum, nihil humani a me alienum puto,"

furnishes me with the occasion to remark in the first place that
there is a material difference between entertaining just apprehensions of moral obligations and acting conformably to them, as
was observed of the Athenians.   Thou will readily suppose I
allude to the contrast between their behaviour and that of the
less refined Spartans, to the old gentleman, which occasioned him
to exclaim, " The Athenians *know* what is becoming, the Spartans
practise it;" and let me observe the latter only is public virtue.
I admit the beauty of the sentiment, as thou perhaps will that
of a modern poet, who, after recommending to his pupil the
observance of the nearer relative duties by an affectionate regard
to his parents, &c., enjoins an unlimited interest in the concerns
of his fellow-creatures :

   " All human weal or woe
   Learn thou to make thine own."

But in what does that differ from the Christian injunction,

"Rejoice with those who do rejoice, and weep with those who weep;" or is the Roman's language more animated than the Apostle's, "Who is weak, and I am not weak? who is offended, and I burn not?" Where will thou find tender sympathy and ardent love more strongly recommended, more cogently enforced, or more conspicuously exhibited, than in the language of the New Testament and the example of the Apostles, for I would not on the present occasion mention their Divine Master? "Love as brethren; be pitiful, be courteous." "Remember them that are in bonds, as bound with them, and them that suffer adversity, as being yourselves in the body." "Look not every man at his own things, but every man also on the things of others;" and, says the Apostle, when imprisoned at Rome, to those whom he had converted by the preaching of the gospel at Philippi, "Yea, and if I be offered upon the sacrifice and service of your faith, I joy and rejoice with you all." I have set down such passages as occur to me at the instant, neither believing they are the best, nor by many the only ones, which would be found for my present purpose: on the contrary, I apprehend neither this sheet, nor another with it, would contain every correspondent injunction, or similar declaration. I have wished somebody capable of doing the subject justice, would collect the most celebrated sentiments of ancient and modern philosophers and poets, and contrast them with parallel passages from the Bible, especially the New Testament: being of opinion, so far as my contracted reading and observation enables me to form one, that there is nothing truly valuable in either of the former, that is not to be found more simply and intelligibly expressed, as well as more strictly enjoined, by the precepts, and more powerfully recommended by the examples, recorded in the latter. I am also of opinion that the light estimation in which the Scriptures are held by too many, is in some degree occasioned by the *manner* in which they now peruse them, as that perhaps may be owing to the manner in which, by the general mode of education, they were subjected to their perusal in early life; and my inducement to say so much upon the occasion which I hope thou will at least excuse, is the wish that a frequent and attentive reading of them, may not only make them acquainted with and relish their beauties, but what I believe is a certain consequence, conduce to the practice of the virtues they recommend, and thereby procure that happiness which can be obtained by no other means. ——

To THE REV. THEOPHILUS HOULBROOKE.

21st of Fourth Month, 1784.

—— I have always maintained a firm belief in a particular, as well as a very extensive belief in a general Providence; I think I am justified in it by experience and observation, as well as warranted by the doctrine of the Gospel and the declaration of our Saviour. If our solicitudes respecting the necessary supplies of food and clothing are obviated by an appeal to the providence of God manifest by his *care* for the inferior part of his creation, ought we not much more to believe, in an affair whereon so much of our happiness in this life depends, and that has so great an influence on our conduct, that the Lord whom we are taught to supplicate as our Father who is in heaven, has an especial regard to us in so interesting a conjuncture, and that every circumstance, however fortuitous in appearance, will be found to have been controlled, if I say not adapted, by a wisdom and direction superior to our own contrivance, as well as, perhaps, contrary to our own intention, and at the same time perfectly consistent with the benevolence of a tender Father to his dependent children. It is not only best but easiest to me to adopt these lines:

> "All nature is but art unknown to Thee,
> All chance, direction which Thou canst not see."

on the principles of Christianity: and I account it an happiness that, not having learning sufficient or a capacity equal to it, I have not attempted to reconcile the difficulties that occur, whether in the intellectual or moral system, by philosophy. We seem

to be placed here rather to act than to speculate, to be per-
fected in love than in knowledge. The prime instructor in religious and civil duties, I believe consistently with the profession of the Society of which I am a member, is that portion
of Divine grace which is communicated to every one, or as the
Scriptures and our primitive Friends affected to express it, the
Light, that enlighteneth every man who cometh into the world
—the grace of God that bringeth salvation to those who are
taught by it, as the Apostle describes its effects; and the next
and only inferior as the mediate manifestation of it, the holy
Scripture of the New Testament, without excluding the old Bible;
and so far as I may be permitted to form an opinion, it is, that
every excellency in every system of ethics taught by all the
philosophers before or since the promulgation of the Gospel, is
included in it, and surpassed by it; that every man who reads it
with simplicity of intention, and sincerity of desire to be benefited by it, will, through the assistance and illumination of the
same Spirit by which the holy men who wrote it were inspired,
be enabled to read it to advantage, and with sufficient information
for present duty and final acceptance with God, so far as either
depends thereupon. He will, *too*, I think, be convinced that the
world is infatuated, and that the generality even of professed
Christians, are unacquainted with the privileges of the Gospel,
the victory to be obtained over the guilt and the power of sin
through faith and obedience, and the deliverance from the fear
of death, to which they must otherwise live in continual bondage;
and the wonder is, that truths so important, so alarming, or so
animating, as are those exhibited in the sacred volumes, should
so generally and so long escape their attention. But what am I
writing? where, in the words of the poet, "where falls this censure? it o'erwhelms myself." I am far, very far, short of the
attainment I might and ought to have experienced, and would
have this apply rather as an incitement to further diligence in
myself, than be considered as needless declamation to another.
But it is time to check my pen, which has run on further
and faster than I either expected or intended, and yet, though I

sincerely believe I have said nothing which thou did not know before and better, I will make no other apology for writing it.

To the Rev. Theophilus Houlbrooke.

Bridgwater, 28th of Seventh Month, 1784.

My dear Friend,

I thought the time long before I received thy letter of the 23rd instant; and yet I had no reason to expect it much sooner. We were gone from Bristol before it came there, and they lost no time in sending it hither, for I had it last night. I was so sensible of the state of thy mind the last evening we spent together, as well as the next morning, that I regretted I had at all urged thy coming down at a time when, if thy inclination did not lead thee another way, it certainly did not appear to tend towards the Dale. But I did not suppose, nor can I yet conceive, from any outward circumstances that have come to my knowledge, there was any reason for thy being, and consequently that thou would be, so uncommonly depressed; for to a man of sense—I had like to have said to a philosopher, but I will rather say, to a Christian—possessed of the favour of God, of the love of the object of his tenderest affections, and of the esteem of his friends, what should prevent his enjoying such blessings, in the manner that inspires the disposition of mind which the Apostle intends when he exhorts to constant rejoicing? But though I cannot account for it from any outward circumstance, yet, as I can conceive from experience of my own, as well as thy account, the reality of such a state of mind, it must, I think, be attributed to other influences, which I shall not attempt to discriminate or define. As a simple man—and God knows I am a very simple one—it seems more my business to make the proper improvement of such seasons, than to attempt to discover whether they are most justly to be accounted for by the action of matter upon spirit, or of spirit upon matter, by bodily temperament or extraneous influence; and yet (that I may not use another word that would imply a capability at some time to discuss such a subject) if I had leisure, and was, or rather only was, as much disposed thereto as I have been, I think I could assign what would appear, at least, not contradictory to Scripture nor inconsistent with reason, in support of what thou art pleased to call my hypothesis—if, indeed, I rightly apprehend thy intention in thy present application of the word.

But not to forget what would be of most consequence to myself, and if I could suppose anything I wrote could be of consequence to thee, I would mention that the most natural, because most profitable, effect of such seasons of desertion and spiritual desolation seems to me, consistently with thy practice upon the occasion, to be the taking refuge, or, which is the same thing, the desire to take refuge, under the wings of the Almighty, the God and Father of all our mercies, equally infinite in goodness as in power, and who is justly called a God hearing prayer.

If anything can make us happy in this world, it must be the same that is to constitute our happiness in the next; and that is an abiding sense of his favour: but as the present is only a state of probation and refinement, and which, from our belief in God and his above-mentioned attributes, we must conclude necessarily involves a vicissitude in the state of our minds as of the seasons; so to pray without ceasing is the most safe, and I believe the most pleasing employment of a truly devout soul, and not only completely consistent with, but immediately conducive to that love and joy and peace, that sunshine of the soul which inspires the constant rejoicing and thankful acquiescence with every dispensation of Providence, so much the duty and interest of every one, though so little the experience of many and of myself. Even while I am writing, the consciousness of my own deficiencies would deter me from describing what I really believe to be attainable and intended for all Christians, because it is really only ideal or notional in myself, did I not hope thou would not only read it with the candour and allowances of friendship, but also consider it as the strongest proof I can give of a confidence which friendship only can inspire; for to very, very few others in the world could I say the same thing. But I will further add, that being firm in the belief that such a state is attainable, and was intended for all, I do at times, and I hope with sincerity and earnestness, desire to experience it, and thereby to have cause of rejoicing in myself, and that all mine, from the same experience, may give me the same reason to rejoice in them also. I have written so much, and I had like to have said so differently from what I intended,—but I really began without any specific intention, only to answer thy letter as it should happen; but it has happened so as I did not expect it would; and I had a passing thought of the propriety of sending it; but such are my sentiments. If I conceal them from thee, I could not call thee *my friend*, as I now mean it, and if I disguised them to thee, I should not deserve to be called *thy friend*, as I have desired it; so I shall let it go, and abide the consequences.

That I think egotisms as admissible in correspondence between friends as thou dost, my practice will demonstrate; nay, I think it cannot subsist without them. Thou can write to me on no other subject half so interesting; but thou will understand me (as our friends sometimes express it of a man and his wife) to include *thy whole self*, and I will include my Hannah with myself. We went to Ford yesterday. The pleasure ground is laid out very agreeably; but the house, at an expense of time, labour, and materials sufficient to have built a complete dwelling, is so void of elegancy, and even of conveniency, which I think may well exist in the same structure, that to avoid being vexed myself, or vexing those who did for the best, I think I shall go there but seldom, if I go there at all; and yet it is the place I most peculiarly intended for Hannah. ——

To J. PHILLIPS.

Ketley, 24th of Eighth Month, 1784.

—— I spent a week at Bristol. One day I went to the woods on the other side of the river, and opposite to the hot wells; the scene pleases me better, though it is adapted more to the pencil of a Salvator than a Claude. The pomp of groves and savage grandeur of the rocks, the awful aspect of the genius of the place, (if I may use such a figure,) and which was scarcely to be contemplated without a mixture of terror, naturally tended to inspire that sense of the presence of Almighty power and our own insignificancy which produces humility and thankfulness, a rejoicing in a consciousness of his presence and protection, and acknowledging our own unworthiness; to which kind of devotion in the soul, the gloom and silence of the grove, into which one immediately enters, upon turning round, was also exceedingly propitious. Though I do not adopt all the notions, and cannot receive all the relations of Swedenborg, I have always believed that the spiritual world is nearer to us than many suppose, and that our communications with it would be more frequent than many of us experience, did we attain to that degree of purity of heart, and abstraction from worldly thoughts and worldly tempers, which qualifies for such communion or intercourse.

We confer with each other through the medium of our organs, being in the body; but that the Supreme Intelligence communicates of his will concerning us, and of the comforts of his Holy Spirit to us; that we hear his voice, saying, "This is the way, walk in it," when we would turn to the right hand or to the left, and that we are conscious of the renewals of his love and of strength to our souls, without the medium of external language, our own experience, I trust, convinces, as well as the Holy Scriptures assure us.— I believe in the ubiquity of the Almighty; that "God is ever present, in the void waste, as in the city full;" but whether it is that I am constitutionally weaker than some others, as well as that I am far behind them in attainments, I confess

I find myself not equally capable of introversion or abstraction of mind in all places, and therefore I think it allowable to avail myself of such retirements as often as I can; which practice, as I once observed to another friend, has the sanction of our Saviour's example, who so frequently resorted to the sea-side, to the tops of mountains, and to desert places, that I believe it is mentioned or referred to more than thirty times by the different Evangelists; and I repeat the wish, that my practice on such occasions may be consonant to his, inasmuch as we stand in greater need of Divine assistance, and we are exhorted to continue instant in prayer.

LETTER SOLICITING A CONTRIBUTION TO A CHARITY.

6th of the Ninth Month, 1784.

That ———, as well as thou and I, have more than is necessary for our own use, will be readily allowed, and I hope we shall as readily acknowledge, that we are but stewards for the overplus, as that we have not merited the abundance any more than many who stand in need of our assistance; and, in short, that as we must render an account of our stewardships, the abundance is only a trust, or rather a trial, which will prove a blessing to us, or otherwise, accordingly as we acquit ourselves under it. It has been justly observed, that a bequest by will is rather obliging our heirs to be liberal than being liberal ourselves. While we could keep it we did not give it, and when we can keep it no longer, we direct them to apply to charitable purposes that which, if not so applied, would have come to them, and which therefore seems more properly to be considered as theirs than ours, and consequently is more properly to the credit of their stewardship account than ours. I would not be understood to discourage all charitable legacies; those who have only enough to support them comfortably and properly through life, give it as soon as they can spare it when life is over; but we who have every year more coming in than we can properly spend, besides accumulated savings already at interest, may very properly, and I hope profitably, revolve in our minds the foregoing considerations, with many others which might be mentioned, and which I doubt not will be brought to our remembrance, if our minds are rightly applied; but I will add, without any comment, a passage of Scripture, which has appeared to me awful, and particularly applicable to the present purpose—" We must all appear before the judgment-seat of Christ, that every one may receive the things *done in his body*, according to that he hath *done*, whether it be good or evil."——

To S. Lloyd.

Ketley, 16th of Eleventh Month, 1784.

—— I have for some time past intended to address a letter to thee upon a particular occasion; but a variety of engagements, and thy absence from home, have hitherto prevented me. Understanding by thy letter last night, that thou art returned from London, I take the liberty of applying to thee for thy assistance towards the establishment of a fund for a charitable purpose, and which I flatter myself the long subsisting friendship between us authorizes me to do without apology—nay, rather, that thou will consider it as the fruit of genuine affection and that I shall be entitled to thy thanks for presenting thee so fair an opportunity of contributing to an establishment productive of consequences pleasing to every benevolent mind, but applying most forcibly to thy feelings as a parent, and thou hast heard I presume of the abundant success of the charitable endeavours of the Friends in Ireland for raising a fund to give portions, according to the exigencies of the case, to young persons of exemplary conduct, upon their marriage. A consideration of the state of the Society in Wales, has inspired the wish that something of like kind could be effected here, and something has been done by way of beginning. The share thou permittest me to hold in thy friendship, together with a superior propriety from certain peculiar circumstances, induces me to give thee a

13

preference of application, with an assurance of success greater than I should have from some others. When I inform thee that in all North Wales, (unless I should except ———— Clerk at ———— who has a wife and three children, and who may have saved rather more than is absolutely necessary for them,) there is not one person whose situation in life or abilities would justify his or her giving on such an occasion ; thou will perceive and admit the reason for my applying elsewhere.

The reduced scattered state of the Society in Wales with respect to property, but more especially with respect to numbers, cannot fail of exciting the pity and sympathy of every tender feeling mind who knows and considers it. From the accounts in print and in manuscript, as well as by tradition, we learn not only how much more numerous they were in North Wales, but also the countenance and support they received from the example, the labours, the charity and hospitality, of thy worthy ancestors, who it is probable gave and spent more in the service and for the spreading of the truth, and to the honest though poor and simple professors of it, in one year, than has been required from their descendants in seven. The consideration too, of their sufferings, in property as well as person, during their imprisonment for the testimony of a good conscience towards God, has often occurred to my mind ; and shall not we, whom the good providence of the Almighty hath exempted from such sufferings, be willing to devote a little of that abundance, which might have been taken from us by the hand of persecution, to Him, and for his sake, who giveth us so plentifully of all things richly to enjoy ? The loss the Society and individuals have sustained by mixed marriages, is universally admitted and lamented ; and though I should not think it right to bribe or hire mere nominal professors to continue in it, yet, when we reflect on the exposed situation of the children of very poor parents, (perhaps the orphan children of such,) in very small meetings, secluded thereby from the company and countenance of Friends, will it not give a pleasure not otherwise to be purchased, to reflect that there is some provision made for the comfortable settlement of such pitiable objects, and who will not be the less likely to be *deserving* of it, by knowing *that only* will entitle them to it. There is a poor Friend, and I believe as simple and honest as any one in North Wales, who has several small children, I believe six, and who may have as many more, whose earnings as a mason do not exceed two shillings a-day in summer, not amounting to eighteen-pence a-day all the year round: let us put ourselves and our children in the place of him and his children—and who hath made us to differ from him?—and why? With what comfort should we reflect on an establishment furnishing motives to our children to an orderly conduct, even in the means of a comfortable, though little provision, when it should be desirable to them to settle in the world, and which it was so far from being in our power to give them, that our present earnings, with some occasional assistance, was barely sufficient to provide them with present necessaries. Considering it in this light, and certainly this is the right light in which to consider it, the number of our children furnishes so many additional inducements to our liberality, and I think, were I in thy place, I should be very willing to give every little child I had at least a couple of guineas to contribute, considering it as a part of their portions, and believing they would never be the poorer, but either have more, or want less, for it as long as they lived; for faithful are the promises of the Lord, He will fulfil them.

My pen has run on longer than I expected; I have said what I did not expect to say, and have omitted what I first thought of. But I will now be as brief as I can, and leave it to thee to make such a comment as shall arise in thy own mind. I thought of the superiority of Evangelical to moral righteousness, of the precepts of the Gospel to the obligations of the Law. The latter enjoined the appropriation of the tenth of the increase, to the retainers of the temple, the stranger and the poor, besides many other sacrifices and offerings. Under the Gospel no specific proportion of our substance is mentioned, but we are to consider ourselves as children of one family, and manifest our love to God the Father of all, by a love of our brethren, or how dwelleth the love of God in us?   I do not say every one is to give a tenth; but it may be well for us to consider what we have given, and I desire for myself and for my friend, that through the influence of Divine Grace, our righteousness may exceed the righteousness of the Scribes and Pharisees. ——

Ketley, 12th of First Month, 1785.

If my advancement in a fitness for a *better* was in proportion to the declension of my attachment or liking to *this life*, its cares and concerns, I sometimes think I should have much more cause to rejoice under the frequent remindings of futurity, which advancing age and declining health administer; but though my lot has been cast among scenes of worldly care, and continued from early manhood—may I not say to this very day?—whereby secular concerns have employed the greater part of my time and my faculties; still I have loved and wished Godspeed to those who have been better employed; and if I at all know my own heart, my most earnest desires are to be with and to be like them.   And if I have any inducement to look forward to the possibility of continuing a few years longer in this world, it is from the hope of greater liberty for that retirement from the busy scenes of it, which, if not absolutely necessary to so weak a mind, is at least, with submission to the ordering of an all-wise Providence, desirable, as likely to be conducive to that preparation of heart which qualifies either for solitude or service, as the great Master of all shall permit or require.   Continue thy prayers for me, as a poor, weak, unworthy creature, but who loves thee with an affection not founded on worldly considerations, or of which the merely worldly-minded have any conception; and may the Shepherd of Israel, who hath hitherto led and fed and preserved us, have us and ours in his holy keeping and protection in every difficulty and under every besetment, while we pass along through the vicissitudes of time to an unchangeable blessed eternity.

EXTRACT.

2nd of Eleventh Month, 1786.

I admit with thee, "there is nothing amiable in melancholy;" yet it is the tincture of my soul—"that there is no virtue in closing the avenues of the heart to innocent pleasure." *I* will go further, and say this is a crime. Can we then suppose we comply with the dying injunctions of our departed Saints, manifest a respect for their memory, and insure our blissful meeting again hereafter, by a temper unlovely, and a conduct criminal? That they do communicate with our spirits, and that our felicity is consistent with theirs; that it is increased by our taking those steps which lead to our present and future happiness, and that we may be therein assisted by their ministration, is a thought I have often indulged with delight, if I say not with advantage; and I could enlarge upon it with pleasure, did time and opportunity permit, but can now only say, it doth not appear to me inconsistent with reason, or unwarranted by Scripture; and after mentioning the one text that hath most forcibly affected my mind at this time, I will request thee to let me know how many others may be adduced in further confirmation of an opinion so soothing to those who, with all the helps they can draw both from Scripture and reason, cannot be insensible of the loss they have sustained; though the happiness of those they have loved, or thought they have loved, better than themselves, has been increased by their removal to scenes

"From sin, and pain, and death, for ever free."

I said *thought* they loved better than themselves; for if we did, should we not, on such occasions, rejoice rather than mourn? But I *feel,* and God and they *know,* the weakness of human nature; and that they are not indifferent to our highest interests is fairly to be inferred from the text to which I before alluded, and which informs us there is joy in heaven over the repenting sinner.

13 *

EXTRACT OF A LETTER TO R. D.

Ketley, 28th of Fourth Month, 1787.

I send herewith a New Testament, in which I have marked some texts that directly assert, or manifestly imply, the immediate or present deliverance from the guilt of sin, of which we spoke: or, in the words of one of them, "the forgiveness of sins that are past."

This hath long appeared to me most essential to our present happiness, as being the only means to deliver us from that bondage, to which without it we must, through fear of death, be all our lifetime subjected : and it hath been occasion of thoughtfulness to me that so glorious a truth, and which is so clearly, so strongly asserted, in the places I have marked, and doubtless in many more in the book I have sent; a truth so comfortable to us, so consistent with the goodness of God, and the practice, (if I may use that expression,) as well as the doctrine, of our Saviour, should be so seldom proclaimed, or the experience of it declared, by those who are called to the work of the ministry—the preaching of the glad tidings of the Gospel among us, even deliverance to the captives, and the opening of the prison doors to them that are bound. I have wondered at it the more, because they have boldly and frequently asserted a doctrine which I admit to be equally glorious, though not more than equally true, but harmonizing most perfectly with it, and that is, not only the possibility, but the necessity of Christian perfection, of manifesting our being born of God, by living without sin; which I apprehend will justify the appropriation of the texts I have marked by those who have attained to it, and that if, by the effectual assistance of the grace of God, we are delivered from the present power of sin, we are also through the mercy of God in Christ Jesus discharged from the guilt of sins that are past; or as it is expressed in the text, "There is now no condemnation to them who are in Christ Jesus," (that is) to them, "who walk not after the flesh but after the Spirit." I have no doubt, from what I recollect of the writings of our ancient Friends, their testimonies were as ample to the one as to the other of these great and glorious truths of the gospel, and if my leisure admitted, I should gladly look over the few I have, with reference to them. I think the time would be well employed. But my dear friend, may we never believe we are justified while we are not sanctified, or fancy we can be free from the guilt while we are willingly subjected to the power of sin; but by walking in the fear of the Lord may we experience the comfort of the Holy Ghost, and know the Spirit itself to bear witness with our spirits, that we are the children of God. This I believe was the experience of those to whom the apostle then wrote, and that it was equally intended to be the privilege and experience of Christians in every succeeding age—that it may be ours, is the fervent prayer of

R. R.

To D. DARBY.

Ketley, 30th of Seventh Month, 1787.

—— I know not what others may expect from me—perhaps, I know not my own heart; I believe, in its natural state, mine is no better than my fellow-creatures; but if I have at all known the changing power of redeeming grace, if I at all know its present desires, it forms no wish so frequent or so strong, as that I may be and do what the Lord would have me—that he would create a clean heart, and renew a right spirit within me. Not having nor expecting any great or lasting satisfaction from the enjoyments of this world, possessed of enough of its treasure, and withdrawing from its cares, grieved by the evil that is in it, and by the ingratitude of too many of its inhabitants, I sigh for peace and perfect redemption; and desirous of obtaining the former by experiencing the latter, I often look forward to a time, which I hope is not far distant, when removing from these scenes of business, where I am and shall be liable to be called to take a part in engagements of a more public or of a private nature, I may be in a situation more favourable to that advancement I wish.

* * * * * * * * * * *

I often look round me, and often consider if I have anything
to do; I am willing to spend or to be spent, but afraid and unwilling to engage where I am not employed. Those who staid
latest, but could give as a reason—"because no man hath hired
us"—were employed, when the Lord of the vineyard bade them
go, and received their penny when the even was come. If in
some instances I have not been altogether idle; if at present I
appear so to others and do indeed stand still, I can truly say, I
am not hired, and I hope as truly, that I desire to be as ready,
under the same qualifications, as he who said, "Here am I, send
me."   *   *   *   *

I do not envy the advancement of others, I am glad of it. I
heartily bid them Godspeed, and rejoice in the success of their
labours. I wish to be like them, and am willing, nay, rather
desirous, to be employed with them—further I dare not go; and
finding myself, still so poor, so barren and so desolate, I ask myself is there not a cause? my unworthiness presents itself; but, if
I was not afraid that my heart retained some secret impediment,
unknown to myself, I should adopt the language of Peter, and
say, "Lord, thou knowest all things: thou knowest that I love
Thee," and the consciousness, that if I do not love him above all
things, I do desire to do so, is my only support under that withdrawing of light and sense of Divine requirings which I so frequently experience, and which I sometimes fear will continue
till perfect light and love shall exclude all doubt and darkness
in the life to come; for under all, I am enabled to hope I shall
be saved at last with an everlasting salvation.

To SARAH TRIMMER.

Ketley, near Shifnal, Shropshire,
4th of Second Month, 1788.

RESPECTED FRIEND,

I duly received thy favour of the 15th of last month, that of
the 25th was mis-sent to Stourbridge. It is now also mine, and

I am much obliged by the attention thou hast been pleased to bestow on the hint suggested in the letter which I took the liberty of addressing to thee, on the 11th ultimo. But permit me to say, if my expressions did admit of such a construction, it was not in my idea that a petition to Parliament should even be signed, much less be presented, by women : the most I could desire or expect was, that they would publicly and in print declare their abhorrence of the inhuman traffic, and their wish that the measures pursuing for the abolition of it might be successful, confirmed by a small subscription annexed to their names, for defraying, in concert with that already begun, the expenses attending the efforts now making for that purpose; to which I doubt not would have been added, their private and personal influence and interest with those who are most capable of giving effect to the benevolent attempt, whether of the nobility, clergy, or members of Parliament. Perhaps even this was more than I should have expected; or, if I had known much of the world, should have proposed. My ignorance and my motive will be my apology, or rather will render one unnecessary to thee.

I wish to have reason to think well of everybody, but especially of those of whom I had formed, from whatever circumstance, an opinion higher than common. I admire the bright qualities of the head, but I love the good ones of the heart. I was sorry that anything, whether I know its name or not, should prevent H. M. from cordially uniting with thee on the present occasion ; but I hope that will not prevent thee from using thy pen if it appears necessary, not doubting thy acting with caution, or fearing the cause will suffer by thy injudiciously attempting to serve it. I hope too, for her own sake as well as the poor Africans, her extensive influence among the great, and all the powers of her genius will be exerted ; and am confident we shall both rejoice in the accomplishment of our wishes, by whatever means it is effected.

As to the money, it has touched the altar—has been appropriated to a charitable purpose. Thou will admit it cannot be so properly applied to any other: be pleased to pay to the Humane Society — pounds, *from a friend unknown*; and if thou will direct thy bookseller to send for me twenty of thy *Economy of Charity*, neatly bound in calf and lettered, to James Phillips, he will convey them to me, and I will distribute them in the best manner I can, to promote thy benevolent intention in publishing them; the remainder be pleased to apply to thy school, or such other purpose as thou shalt think best. Thy mentioning thy hopes of conveying to the hands of the Queen, whom I believe everybody honours and loves, the late publications on the slave-trade, induced the thought of my sending to thee a copy of an address to her by Anthony Benezet, whose name thou will have seen among those who have written on the subject, and whose address appears to have been accompanied with his books. I do not know how they were received; but as a matter of curiosity at least—thou will accept it, as thou also will excuse my wishing thee to peruse a book of the life and writings of John Woolman, who was one of our Society in America, the first I believe and most eminent, or at least with Anthony Benezet, an eminent instrument in the commencement of the concern for the relief of the slaves on that continent. The simplicity of his manner and some peculiarities as one of our Society, will not I am persuaded prejudice thee against the writer, nor prevent thy uniting with his most tender concern for the distresses of mankind of whatever colour or station. I have taken the liberty to desire James Phillips to send the book, which I hope thou will condescend to accept as a small token of the esteem and regard with which I am

Thy obliged and respectful friend,

RICHARD REYNOLDS.

P. S. Pray hast thou seen a book entitled *An Introduction to the Reading of the Holy Bible*, particularly adapted for the use of Sunday Schools? Those I have were printed at Birmingham, and are pretty well executed and bound, at 22s. 6d. per score. I do not like it the less for having been written by a lady in Poland.

EXTRACT FROM A LETTER TO THE REV. THEOPHILUS HOULBROOKE.

6th of Tenth Month, 1788.

I feel for thee and with thee—that is, for myself—on thy bemoaning the days that have passed without benefit to ourselves or to others, and the opportunities of spiritual improvement that have been neglected. May my desires be equally ardent and my endeavours equally strenuous to redeem the time, fully expecting, if they are not, that the days I have to come in this world will be, as the Patriarch said his had been—few and evil. Fewer and worse than those that are past they must be by the course of nature; but if I am enabled, or rather, if I avail myself of the help that is graciously provided for those who want and ask it, an irradiation from the glory which shall be revealed, will gild the gloom of darkening days—of those of which I should otherwise have so much reason to say, I have no pleasure in them.

I, too, have made the same humiliating comparison of the superior dedication of heart, and devotion of powers, that thou so justly remarked in the amiable young woman thou saw at our house: the expression of all the meek virtues which soften without weakening, and distinguish the Christian character with a lustre no other religion can give, was not more conspicuous in her countenance than their influence was real on her conduct. I had many opportunities, and became intimately acquainted with her. The more I knew of her, the more I approved and the better I loved her. I hope and I expect a friendship between her and ——— will be productive of advantage—to one at least, and satisfaction to both, when, if I am sensible of it at all, I shall partake, in common with the spirits of the just made perfect, of

the joy they receive, from the advancement of others, by an increase in their virtues toward the same blissful communion.

I must as readily, and with equal grief at least, admit to thee
that those of our Society do not generally exhibit such proofs of
the efficacy of the principles we profess; but while I acknowledge and lament our defections, permit me to suppose others are
not less culpable because they profess less. On the contrary, from
the baptismal engagements of the national church, and many parts
of its service and prayers, it should seem the composers of them had
as high a sense of the Christian duties as we have; and though it is
true the mode of education, and in some, though too few instances,
the influence of example among us, may give some of our youth
advantages that some others have not, yet it ought to be remembered ours are by nature "children of wrath, even as
others;" that religion and virtue are not by inheritable descent;
the same aversion to restraint, the same propensity to evil, the
same reluctance to the cross and self-denial, is inherent in them
as in the rest of the descendants of Adam; and if these considerations obtain in mitigation of defects in other professors of
Christianity, I presume they will not be considered as aggrava-
tions in the failings of ours; but I wish not to justify or palliate
the wrong in any. I lament it in myself and in them, earnestly
desiring it may not terminate in unavailing acknowledgments
and ineffectual bemoanings; but that animated by the promises
and privileges of the gospel, we may let the time that is past of
our life, wherein we have walked according to the course of this
world, suffice, and considering that the end of all things is at
hand, we may be sober, watching unto prayer, and above all
things, have fervent charity among ourselves!

I concur in general with thy remarks and reflections on the
Spirit of God as given to men for a guide and leader. Indeed it
is the fundamental principle of the religion I profess; but
neither my time, nor my paper, and I might say my abilities,
admit of my saying much on the subject; nor would it be
necessary, were I ever so well qualified in every respect. I believe thou art already in possession of my sentiments concerning

human literature. I am not capable of appreciating its merits accurately; but I do not think so much of it, as thou says, is necessary; for the examination of the external evidences of Christianity can be obtained by the generality of the professors of it. I have been long of opinion that the internal evidences,—and to the consideration of them every rational mind is competent,—are abundantly sufficient to satisfy such a mind; but even that consideration abstractedly may not be practised, nor is necessary to many. A simple Christian, who attends diligently to that Spirit of Truth, which is given to every man, and will lead into all truth, will find as little difficulty in comprehending his duty as he that hears a voice behind him, when he turneth to the right hand, and when he turneth to the left, saying, "This is the way, walk in it."

To the Bishop of Bath and Wells.

Bath, 7th of Eleventh Month, 1788.

The condescension with which thou permitted my friend and thy tenant, John Thomas, to mention his conscientious scruple to the terms made use of as thy designation in a deed to which he was to be a party, was very sensibly felt, and will be always gratefully acknowledged by him. But as thou did not conclude to give the solicited direction to thy steward, but wast pleased to say thou would consider of it before thou went to Wells, and to recommend my friend to do the same, with which I doubt not he will comply; permit me to mention a few particulars, should they only go to show that the alleged scruple is so far from being as thou seemed to think, altogether unfounded, that it is supported by reasons that appear, to us at least, conclusive; but which could not be urged at that interview without trespassing too long on the attendance of others; and this I shall attempt with the same attention to the value of thy time, as well as with that respect and deference that is due to thy age and rank, and under a lively impression of thy late courteous attention to those, whose station in life and mean acquirements, would be supposed by some men to give them but little claim to such

14

indulgence. I apprehend, the form or style of the designation of a bishop of the Church of England, as by law established, is, the Right Reverend Father in God, by Divine permission, Lord Bishop of ———. As we have conscientiously withdrawn from the national worship, and are considered as one sect, among the others of Protestant dissenters,—can it appear strange, that those who think the legal ecclesiastical Establishment incompatible with the freedom of the ministry of the gospel, as well as that the gospel itself forbids the application of such epithets to any man, should object to the use of them? Christ hath said, "Call no man your father upon the earth, for one is your Father, which is in heaven; and ye are all brethren." As this cannot apply to our natural parents, I think it must have a spiritual and religious intendment; and hope it will be allowed sufficient to furnish a scruple to a tender mind, and therefore obtain that consideration thou kindly professed a willingness to indulge to such minds.

However justly the preceding words, "right reverend," may apply to thy deportment and conduct, their connection, in the present instance, will, I persuade myself, warrant their omission without impeachment. The words, "by Divine permission," are so convertible, so equally applicable to opposite circumstances and characters, that, as they may be admitted in any case, the recital of them doth not seem essential in the present. But if they must be understood to imply an appointment commanding obedience, our being dissenters supplies a reason for their being omitted. And as to the title of *Lord* Bishop, let it not offend, that we, who cannot admit the established hierarchy, who have different ideas of a gospel ministry than that it can be *constituted* or *limited* by human authority, or ought to be supported by compulsory exactions, though sanctioned by acts of parliament, that we scruple to acknowledge under our hands and seals, an appropriation of terms, inconsistent, in our apprehension, with the office of a Christian bishop, as well as forbidden to be applied, by thy Lord and ours, to any man upon the earth.

I do not forget that it was urged there was as much reason to object to the terms *sacred majesty* as applied to the person, and *the grace of God* as applied to the office of the king, *the worship-*

ful as applied to magistrates, &c. All this we admit. And may I be permitted to observe, that producing a variety of similar objections is not likely to weaken or do away the one alleged by us. But we, as a people, do not apply those titles, so justly said to be equally objectable. Our addresses to the king have been favourably received, though expressed with our wonted simplicity, as I presume thou may have remarked. And I hope thou will be equally condescending to the tender conscience of an aged man, as have other dignitaries in the national church to others of our friends, who have permitted them to give the bonds for duly administering under wills, and I believe to renew leases also, without the epithets which they were not easy to subscribe, and very much to the credit of their humanity and Christian charity.

Thou remarked that thou had granted leases to.some of our profession who had not scrupled thy customary designation; but, if that was occasioned by their not having adverted to the preceding objections, or others that might be made, let me hope the proof it also furnishes that my friend's scruple is not borrowed from others, but the result of mature consideration, will prevail with thee to give directions to thy steward to leave out the words objected to in the deed to be signed by him, and such others of our profession who have the same scruple. If such omission was to invalidate or weaken the lease, the loss would be theirs who pay the fine: but I am as certain it will not, as I wish thee to be assured it would not be requested by him or by me, if we thought it could operate to thy injury in the remotest degree. I will only add, to an address already longer than I expected it would have been, by desiring that what I have written may not be considered as intended to oppugn the doctrines or practices of the church of England,—but so far only as to account for the conscientious scruple alleged by my friend, which the time did not admit of his doing himself: and that thou will permit me to subscribe myself, though so little known, with much respect,

Thy Christian friend,

RICHARD REYNOLDS.

To SARAH TRIMMER.

Bath, 12th of Eleventh Month, 1788.

RESPECTED FRIEND,

Of avocations so numerous and important as are those that engage thy attention, and employ thy time, I must have a very inadequate opinion; as well as of my own claim to thy notice, could I think the bare mentioning of them was not a more than sufficient apology for the protraction of thy reply to my last letter; but I should not have thus long delayed my acknowledgment of it, if I had not been very busy after my excursion to *Bridgwater*, previously to my leaving home to make a trial of the water at this place, which my friends and the faculty have recommended, with more kindness and expectation on their part than hope on mine; but that doth not prevent me from concluding to give them a full trial, for which purpose I shall be likely to stay a month or six weeks longer, having been here a fortnight already, and I shall gladly hear from thee at No. 11, in the Grove, if thy better employments admit of thy favouring me with a letter.

I wish our school at Ketley was the only one that has suffered and will suffer for want of regular and properly qualified visitants —with us it seems irremediable, there not being a sufficient number in the vicinity, but I regret it the more in cities and towns, where there are many capable but few willing. The decrease of the numbers in some schools, and of schools in one city, are sorrowfully affecting. I really fear the consequences will be fatal in some places, and discouraging to those who are meditating the extension of the benevolent undertaking to others, where the establishment is most apparently wanting. I rejoice in thy account of the success of your school of industry, and shall thankfully accept the lady's account of that so well conducted by her, and adapted to retired villages, hoping to profit by the communication in an attempt, or at least a proposal, for something of that kind in our neighbourhood.

It is now my turn to be very sorry if I have given thee reason to suppose I was displeased with thee for thy manner of introducing the *advice to parents* into thy magazine. I only meant to express my apprehension that an inference might be drawn from it, as inconsistent with my attainments as opposite to my inclination, but I doubt not, the notice taken of it in the number for the succeeding month, though I have not seen it, has done away the occasion.

I expected when I wrote, to have built *seven* habitations, but the plan was so altered as to admit only of *six*. If the letter is still in existence, I wish the number might be altered to *six*. I am glad to find thou will give *Turford's grounds of a Holy Life*, a further consideration with reference to the introduction of an abstract from it into thy magazine. I thought it well calculated for the class of readers intended to be benefited by that publication; and without referring to the hint I ventured to suggest, as furnishing the reason for such an opinion, I may mention the great success that has attended a mode of instructing young children by a pious gentlewoman in the parish of Madely, who has favoured me with a short sketch or specimen of her manner —the questions she asks the children, &c., and which, if I thought it would be acceptable, I would send to thee, as little doubting thy considering it with the same candour and charitable allowance as if it was written by

Thy very respectful friend,

RICHARD REYNOLDS.

21st of Eleventh Month, 1788.

—— The morning was serene as my placid companion—the western breeze rather breathed than blowed, and as we gained the gradual ascent at Ford and moved slowly, very slowly indeed, along the broad back of Cockhill, our eyes wandered over the recognized scenes and delightful prospects with a pleasure softened by the recollection of former days and absent friends. The sun

14 *

that had been up nearly two hours, shed a mild lustre through
the thin mist that mellowed the uniting hills and bended skies,
which bounded the charming horizon; the scattered herds on
Sedgemoor; the recumbent flocks on the green sides of Socum;
if they did not really enjoy the scene they might be fancied to
be contemplating or reflecting on what they had before enjoyed,
added to the beauty of our present views without embittering our
retrospect on the past. Never did I experience a completer
harmony,—the weather—the scene—the beholders, were in perfect unison,—our enjoyment was as exquisite as we could wish
it; nor was it I trust, without a degree of that reference to the
Dispenser of all things good, which consecrates every place, and
sanctions every enjoyment   *   *   *   *

I trace in idea again and again the varied picture; some of the
trees still retained a part of their leaves, but *tinged* with autumn's
dying *breath*, and some despoiled of all, would have made us
think winter was indeed arrived, had not the late rain, succeeded
by uncommonly warm weather, given the meadows a verdure,
more frequently the livery of a spring than a winter month,
while the mild effulgence of the sun, the balmy freshness of the
air, and the accordant wood-lark's sweet note, diffused a tranquillity
not often experienced at any season of the year.

To the Rev. Theophilus Houlbrooke.

29th of Eleventh Month, 1788.

—— Intellectual pleasures depend but little on pecuniary resources—indeed, some of the most sublime and refined entertain-
ments that we receive through our bodily organs, are the effects
of the works of nature, or rather of the God of nature, and
therefore depend little on an abundance of wealth. I have
passed "my flowery spring—my summer's ardent strength"—
and "sober autumn *fast* fading into age," is now my time of life—it
is therefore no virtue and confers no merit, that I consider death
as the termination of a state of existence, the protraction of
which could only be with a certainty of weakened powers and

increasing conflicts; but though I am thereby reconciled to the approach of death, I am contented—I ought to be more than contented—to live. I wish to be duly sensible of, and sufficiently thankful for, the many blessings with which the evening of my day is brightened. But there could be no enjoyment of them if there was not a belief in Him, who hath been to many and would be to all, a deliverer from the fear of death; which otherwise, by subjecting me to bondage all my life long, would mar every pleasure that this world could produce, or human nature admit. But in Him, we have pardon for the past, preservation for the present, and reliance for the future. He has not only made reconciliation for us, but is able to succour us when we are tempted. And, confiding in his mercy, I *am* sometimes enabled to consider with thankfulness the very many outward advantages I partake, more than I once expected, or ever deserved.

My endeavours, I hope I may say without boasting—my honest endeavours, in that station in which his providence placed me, have been sufficiently successful to enable me to retire to that shade and privacy which is most favourable to my time of life and temper of mind; and, if I mistake not, to my advancement in virtue, and, that with more than enough for all the accommodations which age or sickness shall make necessary—may the surplus be applied to alleviate the pains and supply the wants of those, whom in his wisdom and providence He may have seen fit to make the occasions for the exercise of our benevolence, as the medium by which to extend of his blessings to them also.

If I shall have health to enjoy them, many are the pleasures, that as the scene in which are exhibited manifestations of his power and wisdom, displayed with a goodness peculiarly and solely adapted to the rational part of his creation, the country will afford me. Nor is it the least of many favours, that He has endued me with a capacity to observe, and a disposition to enjoy, the beauties of "these his lower works"—but higher still should my gratitude arise for the more exquisite as well as more important advantages of virtuous friendship, which thou so truly defines, and so justly derives from God, as a kind and indulgent father to all his creatures and the dispenser to them, of all the good they can communicate to each other.

—— I am never so much in possession of myself, nor ever so capable of contemplating the face of nature, of attending to the music of the groves, or inspecting the peculiarities of colour and of shape that distinguish and beautify the different subjects of the vegetable kingdom, as when upon my feet. This makes summer so desirable to me—we can then move slowly, or sit still with safety and with ease. The present severity of the weather forbids our going out, or obliges me to walk so fast as to convert the excursion into mere bodily exercise, without much interesting the mind, or, at least, without that converse which converts a walk into a social entertainment. But, while we have spirits, from good health, and peace from a good conscience—

> " Every season with us suits—
> Spring has pleasant flowers,
> Summer shade, and autumn fruits,
> And winter, social hours."

It is time, however, to check the roving of my pen. I began this letter full of the idea of Susan Nicklin. I have again read her letters with satisfaction and pleasure, and hope she will excuse the liberty I have taken to make some extracts from them in my common-place book, so just do I esteem some of her opinions * * I rejoice thou art in the possession of a friend so much better qualified to administer to thy entertainment, though not more desirous of promoting thy happiness, than

Thy affectionate
RICHARD REYNOLDS.

EXTRACT OF A LETTER TO J. PHILLIPS.

Ketley, 17th of Second Month, 1789.

—— At the same time I must add, of however little consequence my letters are, it would be difficult, and I find the difficulty increase, as I grow older, and perhaps too as my leisure increases, to correspond with any body, but in certain relative proportions, or according to the laws of action and reaction. But if every instance of declension, reluctance, or abatement in my friends, has an irresistible, as well as a proportionate effect, I am at least equally susceptible of impressions, and subject to influence from the opposite exertions. Naturally diffident from early youth and always conscious of the little claim my education or acquirements in religion or science gave me to notice or confidence, my heart has glowed with gratitude, as well as exulted with pleasure, when I have shared the friendship of those who have been wiser or better than myself, and if I can boast of but few such friends, I am thankful for the few, and am glad I have never cultivated any other.   *   *   *   *

I shall now be at liberty to enjoy that relaxation of mind and freedom from care I have long desired, and which I found in the degree I experienced it last week, so soothing and grateful, when my health admitted of it, or perhaps conduced to it more than it doth at present, but whether it was the effect of the recent change, and total absence of all anxiety or solicitude about secular concerns, or is to be otherwise accounted for, I enjoyed better health as well as greater peace and tranquillity of mind, than I had for some time past experienced.

The first religious meeting I attended after I had quitted the trade, though small and silent as ours generally are, was a season of comfort and refreshment to me, and earnest were my desires that it might not only be a time of renewal of strength, but of renewal of covenant also, that now I was in one sense of the word become, more than before, my own freeman, I might be more than ever I had been a servant of Christ, of his church, and of his people. And one sweet week I passed—nor are I trust my desires weakened, though my abilities seem lessened, and my powers both of action and enjoyment reduced by a return of my complaint.

24th of Third Month, 1789.

I acknowledge I frequently have lamented—I have still too much reason to lament, my own languor in religious affections. I often contrast the lively zeal, the apparent heavenly-mindedness of some I know and love, with my own cool or constrained devotion; the difficulty with which I restrain, or rather attempt to restrain, my thoughts from wandering when in public worship or private retirement, is painful to me. It is the wish of my heart that every faculty may be engaged, may be absorbed, in the devout application of my soul to him who seeth in secret, and that under the influence of Divine assistance, I may acceptably worship and availingly supplicate the adorable object of all my hopes of happiness hereafter; a sense of whose present forgiveness and favour alone can convert the consciousness of former transgressions into an occasion of thankful acknowledgment of the mercy, and an increased desire for instant and future preservation. These are often my sentiments, and sometimes I trust, my experience; but alas! I want it to be the abiding, the habitual state of my mind, as of others who have appeared to me to possess that uninterrupted access, or at least that constant looking to the Lord, that is implied in its being as our meat and drink to do his will.

I believe "it is a faithful saying, and worthy of all acceptation, that Christ Jesus came into the world to save sinners," and as confidently trust in the efficacy as I am sensible of the need I have of his salvation, and am equally desirous of being delivered from the power as from the guilt of sin; still this appears to me at times more like a cool rational deduction from admitted premises, than an experimental knowledge in my own particular —though I admit and admire it in others—and more worthy. If the absolutely necessary change is effected in me, why do I ever find a reluctance to religious exercises? Why do I not always prefer books in proportion to their religious tendency, and discharge religious duties with an alacrity in proportion to their fitness to a redeemed state? I have often thought of one trait in *the widow* (Mary) Fletcher's delineation of her late husband's character, and I believe as true in him as it was striking to me; "he was," says she, "ever alive to Christ"—that is the state I wish to experience; but alas! if I am not dead, I fear I am too often less lively than I should be: still I desire with unceasing, though I doubt it will never be with unremitting ardour, to press toward the mark for the prize of the high calling of God in Christ Jesus, as the only means of attaining to that blessed assurance of perfect redemption and finished salvation, which thou admits some have enjoyed before they have been at the gates of death, and which if not absolutely necessary, is very desirable for all when they pass through them.

Green Bank, 4th of Seventh Month, 1789.

MY DEAR SON,

Thy brother's letter of the 29th past was very acceptable to me, and I desire thee to give my dear love to him, and tell him so. Thine of the same date gave me equal pleasure. I readily admit the reason thou alleges for its brevity—so long as you are well, and do well, I shall be happy in you, and thankful for you, however short or seldom I hear from you; and yet the more frequently I receive a letter from either of you, the more as well as the oftener shall I be gratified; but I do not forget your numerous and important engagements, nor desire or expect they should be sacrificed to inferior claims. It occurs to me while I am writing, as it did before I received your letters, that the quarterly meetings of the iron masters at Birmingham and Stourbridge, are in the course of next week. This has occasioned me to reflect on years that are past, and the sentiments that so prevailed in my mind before I went to them, as well as the reflections upon them after my return home. I will not say that the consideration of the dangers to which I was about to be exposed, and the desire that sometimes accompanied it for preservation from them, was always attended with that degree of watchfulness and circumspection which would have ensured the plaudits of my own conscience after it was over. For though I may say, with humble thankfulness, I hope my conduct did not bring any reproach on my religious profession—nor I trust, will my children have reason to blush when their father's name is mentioned—yet, when I reflected upon the levity of the conversation, (to speak of it in the mildest terms,) and how far I had contributed to it, or, at least, countenanced it, by sitting longer among them than was absolutely necessary, it has brought sorrow and condemnation on my mind. And earnest are my desires that my dear children may be wiser and better than their father has been. I know I allow for the influence, more especially at your time of life, of company, conversation and business. The season of the year will have its effect: but the more the occasions, and the greater the danger, the more necessary is watchfulness; and the more fervent are my prayers for you, as I hope yours will be for yourselves. Thy drinking water with thy food, will, I hope, not only conduce to thy health, but contribute to thy safety. I would recommend thee to drink some port wine after it, especially in this hot weather; and, as I am thankful to say, I have not had one uneasy hour on thy account, so, I hope, my dear son, thy conduct will continue to administer comfort and joy to thy parents and friends. And among them, I have reason to believe, no one will more sincerely rejoice than thy brother William, to whom, I trust, thou wilt be an useful assistant, and that he will be a good example and kind encourager of thee. But this I know; there are others who would triumph if they could lead thee, or any other sober young man, into excess or intemperance. And, strange as it may seem and sorrowful as it is, they are more zealous to make converts to the master they serve, than too many of us are to bear an open and decided testimony against their principles and practices. Of such may my dear children be aware: and may others who are looking up to you, and are influenced by your example, derive strength and encouragement from the consistency of your conduct to resist the temptations to which they are exposed in common with you.

I have thought of going to the Quarterly Meeting at Lancaster, which will be about the time you are attending one of a very different kind at Birmingham. I believe I shall think of you— and if you should, at that time, recollect your father's care for you, I think the remembrance of me will do you no harm. Thy mother continues very well, as is my sister—who both, as well as thy sister, join in dear love to thy brother and thyself, with

Thy affectionate father,
RICHARD REYNOLDS.

To P. H. GURNEY.

14th of Ninth Month, 1789.

—— I believe I am too apt, in referring to the communion of the highest nature and greatest importance, and to which all my hopes are founded on the unmerited mercy of the Lord, to be affected more by what I wish to enjoy than by what I ought to expect; consequently every withholding of light and comfort is, perhaps, too forcibly attributed to my own unworthiness; when alas! were that the alone cause, it would never be otherwise; for in me dwelleth, and from me can proceed, no good thing— all I have I have received; and all, if any I have done or should do, has been and must be as He shall see meet to work in me, and by me, of his own good pleasure; if I allow, and I will not deny, that He has committed to me a talent, or talents, though not such or so many as my too partial friend supposes, I am not conscious that any concurrence of circumstances "*dependent only on endeavours of my own,*" has prevented their full and due exertion. On the contrary, shall I confess to thee, in the confidence which only such a friendship as ours will justify or would inspire, that so far from it, I have rather sought than shunned such opportunities; that though I have been very often desirous above all things, and if I know my own heart at this instant, I still am so desirous, that I may be one of His flock and family, though it

15

should be the least in the one or the last in the other. I have
also at times been willing to run on His errands, and be employed
in his vineyard; nay, so earnest has been my desire for good, as
well as so great my poverty, that it has reminded me of the expressions, however foreign the occasion—"Put me, I pray
Thee, into the priest's office, that I may eat a piece of bread."
But yet whatever I may suffer, or whatever I want, I hope I shall
never presume to run where I am not sent, or intrude where I
am not called; and weak as I am compared with many, and
desirous as they can be to have me, of earning my own bread, and
if it might be to administer to others, it is the ardent prayer of
my soul—and will not she whose peace and preservation I covet
as my own, unite with me in it? that we may never suffer ourselves to be permitted to move in His work under any influence
but that of His Spirit, nor follow any call but that of His inspeaking word. Thou hast heard of impulsive and compulsive love :
I hope I shall be at least equally intelligible, if endeavouring
also to express my meaning in two words, I most earnestly desire
we may move and act in every religious duty rather by *incitement*
than excitement, by the requirings to service inwardly manifested,
than the desires and opinions of others, however superior their
qualifications, their love, or their zeal; for by patiently abiding
in quiet resignation to His will, as contented to be nothing, as
willing to be anything, we shall both do and prove our own work,
and then shall have rejoicing in ourselves, and not in another."

EXTRACT FROM A LETTER TO ONE OF HIS SONS.

Bath, 2nd of First Month, 1790.

I can very sensibly, as I do very affectionately, sympathise with
thee on thy present solitary and embarrassed situation at ———,
yet I can conceive the possibility of an aggravation, having experienced it; and as long as thou art exempted from *that,* thou wilt
not want an incitement to diligence, nor a consolation under thy
difficulties, if your affection is founded on virtue and supported

by religion. If you love God above all, and manifest it by a due discharge of your religious duties and conformity to the example of a crucified Saviour in bearing the cross and denying yourselves, you will be happy here and hereafter; but if you turn your backs on the straight and narrow way, and seek for happiness in the indulgence of the vain mind, in the spirit and friendship of the world, depend upon it you will soon or later find your mistake: the wish of my heart is, that it may be while it is retrievable, neither the will nor the power, any more than the time, being at our disposal. I little thought when I began to write, to have said any thing of this kind, and now I hardly know what I have said, having written in great haste, and not looked it over; but I know it is the effusion of a heart replete with desires for your happiness, and convinced it is only to be expected from a life of Christian holiness and self-denial.

To M. WRIGHT.

Coalbrook Dale, 14th of Sixth Month, 1790.

DEAR FRIEND,

I have this morning received a letter without a date from ——————, by thy desire, informing me that Lord Sheffield is nominated for a representative in parliament for the city of Bristol, and requesting my interest, &c. I never yet gave a vote for any man, and as I understand the party only propose one member, I hope there will not be a contest. I admit Friends, as well as any others, have a right to act for themselves on such occasions, but I think the more it is by themselves the better—much hurt has been sustained by some from taking too active a part in elections, and especially in contested elections, which I believe are always occasions of doings which no good Christian could countenance, nor any good citizen support. My retired situation exempts me from much danger; may those who are more exposed seek for and find in this instance, preservation by that fear which I desire may be mine and theirs, under every other trial and

from every other evil. From what I know of Lord Sheffield, I
believe him to be uncommonly well qualified, from his very extensive knowledge of the trade and manufactures of this kingdom
and of commerce in general, to be a proper representative of the
city of Bristol; but with this persuasion, and the personal respect I entertain for him, I fear his opinion and conduct with
reference to the Slave-trade, will put it out of my power to give
him a vote; for I am not free, and I wish nobody else may be
free, to vote for any person who is against the abolition of a
trade inconsistent with the freedom, as well as love of our fellow-
creatures, and repugnant to the spirit, as well as in opposition to
the injunctions of the gospel of Christ. I am with love to thy
wife,

Thy affectionate friend.

Liverpool, 4th of Fourth Month, 1791.

MY DEAR SON,

I fully intended to have written sooner, but one thing or
another has prevented me. But though I have omitted writing
to thee for so many days, I believe I may say that not one has
passed without my thinking of thee. I am not insensible of
the temptations to which youth is incident, or the dangers to
which thy situation exposes thee; and frequently have I rejoiced
with thankfulness to the Almighty preserver of men, that thou
hast been enabled to conduct thyself hitherto with so great a
degree of circumspection and plainness, consistent with the religious profession we are making, as well as reputably among men.
Swift are the approaches of old age upon thy parents: nor slight
the occasions of sorrow to which of late years they have been
subjected. As, next to their own conduct, the conduct of their
children must affect their happiness, so they cannot but regard
with tender anxiety every indication of increased danger, and
with painful apprehension every relaxation of essential duty. Connected with my remembrance of thee, before I set out, as well as

since I came here, has been the exhortation, accompanied with the promise of our Lord, "Seek *first* the kingdom of God, and his righteousness, and all these (necessary) things shall be added unto you"—and earnest are my prayers that such may be thy choice, that such may be thy experience—then will every duty, whether religious or civil, be duly performed; and that preference given to the highest, which its superior obligation requires and justifies, and our esteem and our practice of it be in proportion to its greater importance. As such, religious meetings as the means of obtaining the blessing of preservation, as well as an occasion of thankfulness for it, will be gladly as well as diligently attended, and an humble reverend exercise of spirit maintained in worshipping God, who is a Spirit, and who is mercifully attentive to such worshippers; or, as it is graciously expressed, "seeketh such to worship him." It was a disappointment to me that I did not see thee at our monthly meeting the day before we set out. I attributed the omission to some secular engagement, though thy brother did not know what particular business prevented thee. Let me caution thee against giving way in that particular: every omission of duty, as well as every commission of evil, not only increases the difficulty, but lessens our power in future; nor should we be unmindful of the influence of our example in faithfully bearing that testimony, as well as in supporting every other branch of our Christian profession. Besides its effect upon those who are younger, or in any manner dependent upon us, it is sometimes, perhaps often, of service to others, when we do not think of it ourselves. I have experienced the benefit of it from others formerly, and sometimes in my attendance of the quarterly meetings of the iron masters, which I have considered as times of peculiar trial, and have often gone to them with fear as well as dislike. But even there, the conduct of some who have kept their places and acted consistently, has done me good and been a comfort and strength unto me, as the contrary has sorrowfully affected me; the remembrance of which, and the expectation of thy being about to go to the same places on the same occasion, has, at this time, as before now, excited in

15 *

my heart strong desires for thy preservation. And, I trust, He who has hitherto preserved thee thus far as thou hast been preserved, will continue his protection and renew the visitation of his love to thee—and may thy obedience to every manifestation of his will concerning thee, however apparently small or trivial the requisition, increase thy peace, as it will also increase thy strength to perform, as well as capacity to understand, his law.

I have written quite as much as I expected or intended. I trust thou wilt accept it as proceeding from the most affectionate desire for thy happiness, which will be some consolation under afflictions that cannot be altogether unknown to thee, but can only be adequately conceived as they can only be so felt by a parent. May thou, my dear son, have the foundation for hoping for happiness in that relation (should it ever be thine) which is to be derived from contributing to ours by thy religious and circumspect conduct, as well as continued kind and dutiful deportment to us, and which has been some alleviation of the sorrows and some support to the weakness incident to the situation fast approaching old age, as well as of a mother who loves thee and unites in prayers to God for thee, as, in an especial manner, to those of

Thy affectionate father,

RICHARD REYNOLDS.

EXTRACT.

Coalbrook Dale, 26th of Seventh Month, 1792.

Let not a desire of pleasing some, or a fear of offending others, turn thee aside from the straight line of duty. As it was formerly, so at this time, the way is narrow and strait the gate that leads to life. The terms of discipleship and admittance to rest here, and to the kingdom of heaven hereafter, are not different from what they were when our Saviour prescribed self-denial and the daily cross—*this*, therefore, I hope thou will not shun, nor be ashamed of the simplicity or singularity into which it leads. The influence of thy example will not be lessened by thy youth, either among those of thy own age, or those who are older.

Let me repeat the recommendation I was so free as to give thee before, though I may hope thy experience of the advantage to be derived from it may have been sufficient to induce thee to continue the practice of waiting upon the Lord before thou enters upon the business of the day, for the blessing of his preserving fear through the course of it; and in perusing a portion of the holy scriptures, under the influence of that desire, which some have experienced to be very helpful to them, often furnishing, as it were, a watch-word for the day, to which some occurrence has given an unexpected propriety. Many, indeed, are the precepts for our information and government; and many the examples therein recorded for the encouragement of our efforts and the animation of our hopes, under the various trials and afflictions to which our nature, our different stations in life, and the dispensations of Providence, in unsearchable wisdom and consummate goodness, may subject us. Of the latter, that of Joseph occurs to me as very worthy of thy attentive perusal. Of the former, as comprehending all that can relate to, or affect a proper disposition of mind toward God, and of conduct toward men—I would recommend to more than an attentive perusal, to a learning by heart and a frequent recurrence of the mind, our Saviour's sermon on the mount, as recited in the fifth, sixth and seventh chapters of St. Matthew. A conformity in practice to the doctrines therein contained, will not only supersede the necessity of further advice, but will make thee happy in thyself, a comfort to thy parents, a blessing (as Joseph was to Pharaoh) to the family whose kindness and care merits the best return in thy power, and a cause of rejoicing to all who know and love thee, and in an especial manner to

Thy affectionate friend.

Coalbrook Dale, 1st of Eleventh Month, 1792.

As every civil compact depends upon the observation of certain conditions agreed to by the contracting parties, so the several members of every religious society, whether by birth or admission, are responsible to the body for the violation of the rules of such society; and besides some, peculiar to every different profession whereby they may be in an especial manner distinguished from others, I should have supposed that every one would have admitted, that every part of a man's conduct whereby the reputation of the religious society of which he was a member could be affected, and as such in a more especial manner his *moral and religious conduct,* was cognizable by and himself therefore responsible to, the society so affected by his violation of it. And as such, holding a tenet subversive of order, subordination and responsibility, is inconsistent with our principles, incompatible with our discipline, and would disqualify the avowed professor of such an opinion for membership with us.

I am unwilling to add unnecessarily to the length of this letter by quotations from the New Testament, to prove that every member of the Christian church was, as a part of the body, responsible for his conduct, and amenable to its rules; that so far from being indifferent to the concerns of each other, the primitive Christians were taught, not only by the precepts and example of our Saviour to love their enemies, but also by the doctrine and practice of the promulgators of his gospel, to consider each other as brethren—children of one family; or nearer, as members of one body, united under one head, and subject to his government, who hath dispensed a variety of gifts, and appointed a variety of officers for the edification of his body, the church. The process of discipline in gospel order, and the ultimate appeal to the body, is distinctly prescribed by the head of it in the 18th chapter of St. Matthew; consistently with which, are divers passages in St. Paul's Epistles; how often we are therein taught to consider ourselves as members of, and interested in the happiness of each other, I need not attempt to enumerate to thee; and how far the apostle was from regarding himself in the unconnected state that would render him as indifferent to the concerns, as independent on the support of others, may be inferred from his animated exclamation—"Who is weak, and I am not weak: who is offended, and I burn not." And consistent therewith is his generous exhortation—"Look not every man on his own things, but every man also on the things of others."

Accuracy and correct arrangement I do not attempt; to serve thee is my wish, and I have no other interest in it than that which arises from the conviction of the truths I have endeavoured, under the influence of gospel love, to communicate. The conclusion I would draw from what I have more properly referred to than quoted from the New Testament, is, that if every believer ought to exercise the offices of love and care toward every fellow professor, every particular member is at least equally responsible to the body for the consistency of his moral and religious conduct.

TO THE REV. THEOPHILUS HOULBROOKE.

Coalbrook Dale, 18th *of Sixth Month,* 1798.

MY DEAR FRIEND,

—— I never was at Plymouth; but if you go to Plymouth I can accompany you in idea. I attempted to go to the Eddystone Lighthouse, but though we approached near to it we were obliged to return without landing at it. It would be more desirable to me *now,* from Smeaton's account of its erection, which I have been reading; and I think the fear of French privateers would not prevent me from again attempting to see it, if I was at Plymouth.

—— I am obliged by the manner in which thou speaks of the few opportunities we had of being together in London, and for the pains thou took to give me those few. I can truly say, it has been cause of equal regret to me that my time admitted only

of my seeing thee so seldom and so transiently. I should have
had particular pleasure in going with thee to those places thou
so kindly wishes me to have seen, from the advantages I should
have received by thy information and strictures upon the
several subjects, and the execution of them. I have thought,
too, I should also have received much pleasure from reviewing
in thy company some scenes both down and up the river, that
were formerly familiar to me; and, among others, Greenwich
Park and Kensington Gardens, in which I believe a concatenation of ideas involving persons dead or absent, and circumstances
which at the time of their occurrence I deemed important, would
present itself—and clothing the various emotions in words as
the surrounding objects excited them in my mind, with the freedom and faithfulness which only friendship would induce or justify, might have afforded a pensive kind of gratification, more
congenial with the temper of my mind perhaps than any other;
inducing, as it doth at this instant, as well as the idea among
others of the dear friend to whom I am obliged for them, the
verses which begin with this stanza,—

> " What art thou, memory of former days,
> 　　That dost so subtly touch the feeling heart,
> 　　That knows such pleasing sadness to impart,'
> That does such thrilling dear ideas raise?
> Each wonted path, each once familiar place,
> Each object that at first but common seemed,
> Beheld again some sacredness has gain'd
> With fancy's hues inexplicably stain'd,
> And by remembrance venerable deem'd.—
>
> Hence recollection prompts unbidden tears"—

—— but of this enough—perhaps for either of us—and thou
can recollect more, nor would the places, which I hope thou would
see soon after thou receives this letter, less forcibly than any
other touch that string in my heart—I mean Sutton and Ford.*
There, I have enjoyed the company of those together whom I

* Sutton and Ford were two estates which he had purchased in Somersetshire.

shall never see together again. There, I have been with some who will never be there again. And, what at this instant affects me proportionably—there, thou wilt be without me, and I without a hope of ever being there with thee.

I expect thou wilt see both places to a disadvantage from their having been neglected; but thou wilt see that they *might* be made pleasant, especially Ford, to which my dearest daughter was very partial. I expect, with increasing solicitude, her approaching time of trial, and the more from some apprehensions (I would willingly believe them superstitious) entertained by herself; and which, in hours of weakness, and many such are mine, are aggravated, in my imagination, by a long remembered similar occurrence—but on this subject I dare not enlarge. I believe thou can conceive, as adequately as most who are not parents, what a conflict the hazard of losing such a daughter as few parents have and including such concomitant sufferers, must excite in the breast of one so weak, so dependent as I am. But I cannot write much more. I will hope in the mercy of God for her preservation, as I confide in it when I reflect upon the accelerated approach of that change which I doubt not will be glorious to our dear E. R., who has been, long as known, deservedly esteemed and beloved, by my poor Hannah, as well as by

Thy affectionate friend,
RICHARD REYNOLDS.

I hope I shall hear from thee again, and that I shall see thee on thy returning to Holly Grove. Farewell!

TO A BOY AT ACKWORTH SCHOOL.

Coalbrook Dale, Ninth Month, 1794.

DEAR JAMES,

I have often, since I was at Ackworth, reflected on the privileges of the children who partake daily of the benefit of the Institution, and of the masters who feel the weight of the charge with which they are entrusted, in a manner which the objects of their care do not at present fully comprehend; but I was glad to hear that many of them had so far considered it as to enter into engagements amongst themselves, to give their instructors and guardians the least possible trouble, as well as to example their schoolfellows in general, in love and good conduct. I gave thy parents (who with thy brothers and sisters are pretty well) an intimation to this purpose, agreeably with what I heard when I was with thee; and they hope thou wilt increase the pleasure they will have when they hear of thy health, by informing them more particularly, of the good resolutions and rules agreed to by so many; and not only agreed to, but adopted, and kept by all the rest as well as thyself.

But to tell thee all the truth, dear James, this is not my only inducement in writing to thee at this time. A thought, which occurred whilst I was there, has been so frequently revived in my recollection, since my departure, that I am willing to mention it in this manner to thee; hoping it will be received as proceeding from that love which desires thy happiness, as well as that of every other member of the numerous family at Ackworth School.

The general appearance and deportment of the children at the meetings for worship was unexceptionable; and I have no doubt, many of their minds were duly impressed with the truth of what they had been taught and believed, that God is a Spirit, and that they who worship him aright, must worship him in spirit and in truth; but whether the minds of all were so duly and deeply impressed, I presume may be questioned without breach of charity.

The painful appearance of drowsiness, which, as I understood, was unusual, requires no further animadversion. But, if we do not sleep, yet, if by an indolent manner of sitting, looking about, or by gestures and motions inconsistent with the solemnity of the occasion, we betray an unconcernedness of mind which might grieve the rightly exercised amongst those who behold us; or if, under an orderly outward appearance, we indulge thoughts on our outward engagements, (which might be proper and even necessary at another time) and much more, if we admit such as would be wrong at any time, we not only miss the benefit we might hope to receive, but we trespass against God, who seeth the heart, at a time when we profess to be worshipping him. What would be our feelings, if every thought we admitted, whilst we are sitting in silence, were to be uttered audibly to the whole congregation? Should we not blush with shame at their folly; or with guilt, if they were worse than foolish? And is not the God, before whom we present ourselves as his worshippers, a discerner of the thoughts and intents of the heart? yea, all that we think, is spoken in the ear of the Lord; and how awful is the consideration! Let it sink deep in thy heart, dear James; and forget it not, when thou art about to assemble with others in public or private worship, or in those more secret opportunities of retirement, which, I trust, thou seekest, at times when no human eye beholds thee. That God is ever present—and not only our words and our actions, but our most secret thoughts are manifest to, and constantly observed by him, are truths to which we cannot too often advert; and which, if rightly attended to, would have a salutary effect on our conduct, out of meetings as well as in them; and I hope thou wilt cordially accept this earnest and affectionate recommendation of them to thy frequent remembrance.

From thy true friend,

RICHARD REYNOLDS.

3rd of Eighth Month, 1795.

—— Thou should not apologize for any remark that may occur to thee to make, especially any that may excite me to a more cheerful or a more faithful discharge of my duty. The time when it will be said to me, "Give up thy stewardship, for thou shalt be no longer steward," is swiftly approaching; and though the talents committed to me are mostly of the inferior kind, yet a great degree of circumspection and vigilance is necessary to enable me to give in my account with joy. Let it continue to

16

be thy desire that I may—the desire of the heart is prayer; for I find (not I hope a greater reluctance to give or a stronger desire to acquire) but less ability, and I fear less inclination for exertion, whether of body or mind, than when I was younger; if it influenced me only in respect to the business and pleasures of this world, I should not, so far as I only am affected, much regret it; but I fear its inducing a kind of spiritual indolence, that may terminate in lukewarmness and indifferency towards my religious advancement, more to be deprecated than the most acute sense of spiritual want, or mourning under apprehended desertion.

The possibility of our expecting stronger degrees of conviction than may be consistent with the unimpeachable will of the Almighty; the promptitude of our obedience to his requirings, should not be proportioned to our estimate of the importance of them to our fellow-creatures, though perhaps the manifestation of them may be; and may not the want of a ready compliance with the whispers of " the still small voice," have induced a degree of doubtfulness and uncertainty, which a more simple following of the gentle leadings of that Spirit, which would guide us into all truth, would have prevented? It is by walking in the light we attain more light, and by obedience as in the day of small things, that greater discoveries are attained.

EXTRACT OF A LETTER TO J. C.

Coalbrook Dale, 28th of Tenth Month, 1795.

——— On concluding a remark on the inequality of the ecclesiastical emoluments, and the inconsistency of the established hierarchy with the government of Christ in his church, as uniting the civil power therewith, thou closed thy acknowledgment of it with saying, " It is very true; but it matters not, we are told if we believe and are baptised we shall be saved." Now supposing it had been then asked what belief and what baptism was so efficacious, would it have been said that an admission of the truth of the relation of the facts recorded in the New Testament, or an assent of the understanding to the propriety of the doctrines inculcated therein, is that belief? or the administration of water, whether by immersion or sprinkling, is that baptism? —Do we not see, nay do we not experience, that one may be admitted, and the other received, without any renovation of the heart or melioration of the temper! If, as saith the apostle, there is one Lord, one faith, and one baptism, can there be more than one of either. We all acknowledge but one Lord—and shall we not also acknowledge, that the one faith is that which overcometh the world, which worketh by the purifying of the heart? and that the one baptism is not an outward application of water— not the washing away the filth of the flesh—but the answer of a good conscience toward God."

28th of Tenth Month, 1795.

RESPECTED FRIEND,

If the numerous and important avocations resulting from thy station, have prevented thy often remembering the writer of this letter, and those more worthy, whom he attended on their religious visit to the Isle of Man, permit me to assure thee that both they and myself, frequently reflected with gratitude and satisfaction on the general cordiality of their reception. And if it will not be thought too presuming, I may profess my peculiar personal regard, and the interest I take in the prosperity and the happiness of thyself and thy family, inspired by the condescension and candour with which thou wast pleased to communicate of the circumstances attending a life of important and arduous employment, which issued—however beneficially to those who have the advantage of thy abilities and thy experience, under thy government—less to thy own emolument than thy services would warrant, or thy friends would wish.

Disappointments are not always evils: if we are taught by the ingratitude of our fellow-creatures to estimate the returns we have rendered for the benefits we have received from our Creator, perhaps the acuteness of our feeling of the former may be blunted, our dependence on the smiles of the world be lessened, and the favour of the Almighty cultivated with greater diligence and more success. I will not apologize to *thee* for this reflection, which I had no intention to make when I took up my pen to request thy acceptance, as a token of my respect and esteem, of the books this letter accompanies, with a hope that the perusal of them may more than amuse,—may employ and improve some of thy leisure hours, in the lengthened evenings of the present and approaching season. The apology for the principles which I profess, written by thy countryman Robert Barclay, contains, if I mistake not, sufficient to justify from the imputation of admitting without proof or believing without conviction, those who make the same religious profession. Of the more multifarious writings of William Penn, though some of them being occasional, are now less interesting than when they were first published, the principal correspond with the declaration of our Saviour, that if any man will be his disciple, he must deny himself and take up his cross daily; and his example, as exhibited in his life and conversation, evinced his sincerity by a compliance with the condition imposed, for the possession of the crown immortal; which is on no other terms to be obtained. Other parts do him credit as a good citizen, a politician, and a legislator; nor will a parent read with less pleasure, or his children, I trust, with less improvement, his letter to his wife and children, his "fruits of a father's love," addressed immediately to his own, with his "reflections and maxims," more just as well as more liberal and benevolent than some since published in France or Geneva. The latter being printed separately, I shall request each of thy children's acceptance of one of them, as soon as they are received from London, and if they do not come in time to be sent with the other books, I have desired my kinsman R. B. to forward them accordingly.

I duly received thy favour of the 22nd ultimo, and communicated the contents of it to our party, who were all gratefully sensible of thy kindness, and especially our ancient friend from America, who will not forget, if she is permitted to return to her husband

and friends at Philadelphia, the encouragement and comfort she derived from the countenance and notice of the governor of the Isle of Man, in her religious visit to the inhabitants.

If, in the uncertainty of future occurrences, any thing should bring thee into this part of England, I hope thou would not pass by without calling at my habitation, and partaking of such entertainment as it would afford with the heartiest welcome, and in the mean time I shall rejoice to hear of the health and happiness of thyself and thy family, if thou finds thyself disposed to communicate the acceptable intelligence by directing it to Coalbrook Dale, Shiffnal.

Thy very respectful and obliged friend.

Bridgewater, 25th of Eighth Month, 1796.

MY DEAR SON,

Strange as it may seem, it is nevertheless true, that as including health and leisure, with a capacity for writing, this is the first opportunity I have had to begin a letter to thee, with reasonable expectation of finishing it in time for the post; and even now, I am apprehensive, I shall give but little proof of my possessing the last of the three before-mentioned requisites. I think I may say I am never well at my first coming to this place, and my spirits seem as unfavourably affected as my health, so that I am as much without energy of mind as activity of body, to which, perhaps, the continued, and, as we think, excessively hot weather, contributes. But I assure thee, my dear Joe, nothing has prevented me from frequently reflecting on my own children in Shropshire, and their varied situations; nor has it been without peculiar satisfaction that I have remembered thy sympathy with thy brother, and the liberality of thy conduct as well as of thy sentiments towards him. Continue, my son, the like conduct, so long as his circumstances shall furnish the like occasion and opportunity. I feel, as well as thee, for him and thy sister, in the loss of his little daughter. We have each of

16 *

us a daughter, and by considering how their death would affect us, we are qualified to sympathise with them for their little Hannah. My sister has written to him, and I hope to do so soon; but give my dear love to him and his wife, and I persuade myself he will not attribute the delay to a want of the most affectionate sympathy with them as parents; though many considerations will present themselves to prevent their grieving long or immoderately for an event which, to the dear infant, must be an exemption from suffering and danger, of which painful proofs in the experience and often unexpected reverses of condition in others, not to mention our own, too frequently occur. I find more business to be done by me than I expected; the allotment of a part of Sedgmoor to the land I had at Sutton, though not a fourth part of the quantity I was told would belong to it, is to be allotted to the farms; and though they are but four in number, it requires much attention to do it fairly and satisfactorily to each of them; and then new terms are to be settled for their future rents, and covenants for their observance. Though not very well qualified for such negotiations, and as averse as ill qualified, yet thinking I have faithful and capable advisers in John Wood and Robert Anstice, I am willing to complete it, if possible, while I am in the country, were it only to save my successors trouble, and to be a faithful steward to my children; nor do I think there is likelihood of a more favourable time occurring in seven years, which is the term proposed for the leases; and which, though there is not, according to the best rules of calculation, a probability of my seeing the end of it, cannot lay a long restraint on those who come after me.

Thy mother was a little poorly a day or two, being uncommonly cold, though the weather was so remarkably hot; but she is now quite well again, and I am better than I was at first coming. The rest of our relations at this place are in usual health, and I had a comfortable letter from my son Rathbone last night. T. H. and the boys are returned from the Isle of Man. They go on, though slowly, safely with the iron bridge at this place.

Farewell, my son. I shall be glad to hear from thee, and hope thou wilt have to give me a good account of thy own health and comfort, as well as, or which indeed includes, thy dear wife and children, to whom and to thy sister Betsy give my dear love, in which thy mother joins, as she does in the same to thyself, with

Thy affectionate father,

RICHARD REYNOLDS.

Liverpool, 12th of Tenth Month, 1798.

—— On the subject of my refusal to pay the assessed taxes, I have only to allege my belief that all wars are inconsistent with Christianity, and if it shall appear that paying the assessed taxes is not inconsistent with a simple, faithful testimony against wars, I shall not continue to refuse to pay them. That I apprehend the *practice* of our Society, and as being uncensured by any I conclude our principles also, are not thoroughly consistent, is also true. But as thou dost not say we should shut our eyes to such prospects, so I as cordially admit it is consistent with our peace and our duty, " to study to be quiet." How far the acquisition of wealth, or the application of it, can be subjected to the rules or censures of our Society, [I do not at present consider that it may be so to its advice and admonition,] our epistles and minutes afford satisfactory proof, I wish I could add with more certainty, *effectual.* But without wishing to make thee uneasy, or to be so myself, what thinkest thou of our Society voting for members of parliament? A man comes to me, asks me for my vote, to be my *representative,* tells me beforehand he is a friend to the present constitution in church and state, will support the hierarchy, compel the payment of tithes, &c., maintain wars by impressing as well as voluntarily enlisting, will swear himself and enjoin oaths to others, with many other things which I conscientiously refuse; I have, therefore, dissented from the National Establishment of Church and State, and subjected myself to pains and penalties, to imprisonment, and loss of property—how, then, can *I* be represented by *him*; or if I consent, do I not awkwardly refuse to be bound by the act of him whom I have delegated to be my *representative*, to *act* for *me?* To me, at least, there appears an inconsistency in it; perhaps others may reconcile it to their conscience; but I believe many have not adverted to it. I am thankful I did not give a vote before I had considered of it. Now I trust I never shall; but in this and every other instance in which my opinion differs from the practice of others, and especially of our own Society, I desire to consider the *possibility* of my being mistaken: the *certainty* that, in the instances of those whom I justly prefer to myself for their experience and superior religious attainments, the same things do not all appear in the same light, and that we have no right to judge one another, inasmuch as that to his own Master every man standeth or falleth; and all these considerations concur in disposing me "to study to be quiet, and do my own business."

To SARAH ALLEN.

5th of Fourth Month, 1799.

—— Nor can it in the course of nature be long before I may hope to experience a reunion with some who are now inhabitants of a purer region, where none of them say, "I am sick;" and who I am as willing as thou seems reluctant to believe I shall recognise, and thereby increase my own and their happiness. For though I do not suppose the bliss of the blessed is incomplete or imperfect, I think it is not inconsistently admitted, that their capacity to receive, as well as their powers to be thankful, may increase with the boundless continuance of their existence — or, as the poet expresses it—

——"Where the mind
In endless growth and infinite ascent
Rises from state to state and world to world."

Or as, and perhaps more in point with our present subject, a more modern poetess has it:—

> "Then sweet remembrance wakes without regret,
> And back each human path they fondly trace,
> That led through steady wisdom's peaceful ways,
> To this blest paradise, this beamy crown,
> This cloudless day whose sun shall never set."

Nor doth it appear to me that when we come " to the general assembly and church of the first-born, to the spirits of just men made perfect," it must be in the land of forgetfulness where former associates will not be remembered by us, though a consciousness of having been united in sufferings on earth—perhaps of having been in the ordering of a merciful Providence, mutually instrumental to their present respective happiness—would not lessen their gratitude to God, or the joy of the individuals.

Dost thou think, my dear cousin, that because we are not explicitly informed there *will* be a recognition in heaven, it is heresy to suppose it? Had we been told the contrary, I should not have allowed myself to conjecture; and rather than offend those who cannot receive it, I would continue to confine my thoughts on the subject to my own breast, though to thee I risk them. I trust I am not presumptuous. I affirm nothing; but I have thought it allowable to admit the supposition, which is not likely to lessen my comfort in this life, nor make me less solicitous of happiness in the next.

If the angels interest themselves in human concerns, and rejoice in the repentance of a sinner on earth, may it not be believed they will rejoice with him in heaven? If the apostles were made a spectacle to angels as well as to men, and the cloud of witnesses referred to by St. Paul were those mentioned in the preceding chapter, is it unreasonable to suppose that the communion of spirits may be more perfect and more comprehensive when the vail of our flesh is removed from both parties, than while it circumscribes the powers of one? I acknowledge we are told, "eye hath not seen, nor ear heard, neither have entered

into the heart of man, the things which God hath prepared for
them that love him." But because we cannot conceive all the
things we shall enjoy, is it a crime to expect they will in part
consist of something soothing to the human mind in its present
associations, and which neither reason nor revelation precludes,
but, on the contrary, so far as they are adverted to in it, are
countenanced by the scripture.

, I do not think I have done my own opinion justice, or that I
have mentioned all the arguments that might be rationally employed, or drawn half the inferences in favour of it, that an attentive perusal of the scriptures, with a particular reference to
the subject, would admit. It is sufficient if it induces thee to
consider it in that point of view; and if from reason, or the scriptures, thou shalt obtain more ample satisfaction on either side
of the question, I shall be glad to have my speculation corrected
or confirmed by thee. For let it always be remembered, I
only speak of it as a conjecture, or at highest as an *opinion* to
which I attach no obligation, nor think the worse of those who
think differently from me, or who do not so much as entertain
an opinion about it. But I should be sorry that any, (if such
there are) who would deem such a speculation presumptuous,
should be grieved or offended, by knowing that I had indulged
the thought; though it doth not appear to me to be among the
profane or foolish and unlearned questions which Timothy was
told to shun or avoid. If this opinion, as well as some others
generally admitted by the primitive Christians, was entertained
by Plato and others, heathens, before the promulgation of the
gospel, and not being incompatible with the duties enjoined by
Christ, were not particularly noticed by him or his apostles, must
they be rejected by us, because they were received by those who
also admitted notions or opinions which superior light has since
discovered to be erroneous? May we not allow that such spec-
ulations as do not lessen the inducements, or weaken the obligations to a virtuous life, may be indulged; as well as that no
change of *old* for *new* opinions, is worth adopting, where the

latter are not more conducive to our present comfort, or do not brighten our prospect of the future? By this rule, I adhere to the old opinion, that the termination of this life is the commencement of a happier, in opposition to the more modern supposition, that we shall be insensible of existence, either past, present, or to come, until the day of judgment, the "time of restitution of all things." This appears to me a kind of scepticism, tending to infidelity—and infidelity, so far as I have known anything of it, has invariably a cold, comfortless, and discouraging effect upon the mind; and so long as our hopes and fears can be affected thereby, must proportionably influence our conduct. * *

EXTRACT FROM A LETTER TO HIS DAUGHTER.

24th of Tenth Month, 1799.

—— There seems too much reason to fear the accomplishment of the threatened calamities, if not staid by repentance and reformation; for my part, I think I cannot remember a more awful conjuncture—war, pestilence, and famine, may be considered as impending over this guilty, if not devoted, land. In divers parts of the earth they have been, perhaps I may say *are* at this instant felt—the failure of harvest, and of seed-time, probably entailing a greater scarcity on the coming year; the consequent rapid advance in the price of wheat, already with us from fourteen to sixteen shillings a bushel, and scarce even at *that;* the still more rapid advance in the price of oats, hay, and beans, will make it difficult to support the horses, and probably make butcher's meat dearer; the fruitless attempt of our troops and the Russians in Holland—the expense and waste incidental to transporting and maintaining such a number of men and horses, with the increased consumption at home of the additional Russians to be wintered in England; and a long winter it may be; will have a sensible effect in enhancing the price of provisions to the poor tradesmen and others in this country, from whom more will be claimed in consequence of the measures that lessen their ability to pay and increase their difficulties to maintain their families;

these are afflicting considerations, and are ready to suggest the humble expostulation, "Oh Lord, how long," &c. &c. Besides "the pestilence that walketh in darkness, and the destruction that wasteth at noon-day," which hath swept away so many in Barbary, we are told that lately a vessel arrived at Liverpool, bringing letters to the 10th of last month, that the yellow fever was raging at New York and Philadelphia, and that the number of deaths was as great as at any former period of the calamity. How desirable amidst it all, my H——, is it to be enabled to say with David in the Psalm to which I have referred, "I will say of the Lord he is my refuge and my fortress; my *God*, in him will I trust;" and so far as is consistent with his good providence and gracious designs towards us, to experience that preservation from such outward evils as are therein enumerated, or such a removal from them as may exempt us at once from danger and from suffering. To thee I write without premeditation, and hope it will be received in that love which alone will induce that freedom, and in which, without further addition, I remain

Thy very affectionate father.

To WILLIAM SAVERY, PHILADELPHIA.

Green Bank, 10th of Eighth Month, 1799.

—— I am induced to send with the enclosed a plan of the Stranger's Friend Society, to bring under thy notice a charitable institution in this land, with a hope that thou will employ thy influence and endeavours to establish something similar at Philadelphia, in which I trust thou will have many associates among other people, as well as among Friends. By the papers herewith sent, thou will see it commenced with the people called Methodists; and though some of the rules laid down by them for the qualifications of visitors, as well as some expressions in the address, &c., may be exceptionable, I doubt not but others, as well as thyself, will find no difficulty in making such allowances as shall be thought necessary, for expressions as well as sentiments, which they cannot adopt, or in framing such other rules for conducting the business of such an institution, as will secure the desired effect, and which a knowledge of local circumstances, varing in different places, will enable you to do with the greatest propriety, and yet though it may be unnecessary to suggest any thing on that head, I will just submit that some of the rules recited in the enclosed, appear to be so generally applicable, as to require only such addition as the peculiar or differing circumstances of Philadelphia may render necessary. The sudden departure of the " Perseverance," and of which I have been this instant informed, doth not allow me to enlarge upon the subject, and which indeed my knowledge of thy liberality and charity in every sense of the words renders unnecessary, and would even if I had more time; but I will just add, that I think the attempt so desirable, that I am willing to be an annual contributor for five years to come certainly, and I hope longer, if longer I live, and therefore if thy endeavours shall be at all successful, be pleased to draw upon —— for —— as soon, and at as short a date as you please. It appears from the annual sums in the reports, that many of the contributors are among the comparatively poor, perhaps of twopence or threepence a week each, and divers of the visitors have been from among that class; perhaps it did not succeed the worse from its commencing with the poor, and ascending to the rich, than if it had been the reverse. I love that such may have an opportunity to contribute their mite, and to impart their advice and their sympathy.

TO THE REV. T. HOULBROOKE.

Coalbrook Dale, 26th of Sixth Month, 1800.

MY DEAR FRIEND,

The next post, after I had written my letter of the 19th to my son Rathbone, I received thy very acceptable favour of the 14th, which, by the post-mark upon it, appears to have been sent from Liverpool, the 18th. Thou may justly think my

17

acknowledgment of it protracted as much beyond the time when gratitude and affection should have dispatched it, as thy account of your safe arrival at Liverpool appeared to my anxious expectation. But though a week has elapsed since it first excited my thankfulness for the comfort it afforded me on your account, and a letter from my son and daughter has also relieved me in a good degree from the solicitude thy account of my son's indisposition had inspired; I assure thee I have not had an opportunity of thanking thee or them for it till this instant, having had to attend meetings of one sort or other every day this week, and yesterday one at Shifnal; in consequence of which I presume my son Joseph has written to Rathbone, Hughes and Duncan, for forty barrels of rice. Sir Corbet Corbet was there. I did not ask him what were his expectations respecting his application to the county; but from what he said of Kynaston Powell's claim to the peerage being deferred, and the difficulty attending the prosecution of it, I infer Sir Corbet does not think it necessary to urge his wishes, as the Apostle advised Timothy, to preach the word—"instantly, in season, out of season;" for he said not a word on the subject, though it might have been (considering the occasion of our meeting) rather in season than out of season. Thou will probably conjecture, from this light, not to say trifling way of writing, that my heart is relieved from the load which oppressed it, and to which thy pious suggestions, as opportunely as affectionately urged, were so well adapted to induce submission without repining; while they afforded all the assistance to bear the inevitable affliction which friendship and sympathy could contribute. I am thankful, if not in proportion to the blessings received from the Giver of all things good, yet, I trust, according to the capacity of my poor stupid heart, that my prospect, as referring to others near and dear to me, is less gloomy, though yet far from bright.

My health and spirits are much improved since last week, both, perhaps, most in consequence of the alteration last mentioned; but the latter especially, by the company and conversation of my cousin, Sarah Allen who has been with us three weeks, and will stay till we go to Bristol, in our way to Bridgewater. I think thou art not acquainted with her. If thou wast, and with her friendship, I might say her affection for me, thou would not be surprised I should be so much the better for the attentions which that has procured me, and my circumstances continue to render so desirable.

I rejoice with thee in thy favourable accounts from America: especially that the good fortune and success of thy nephew is accompanied with a continued attachment to the substance, as well as to the forms of religion. My acquaintance with him, if indeed I am warranted to use even that word on the occasion, is too slender to justify my sending a congratulatory message to him on the birth of his daughter, (Susan.) But his relation to thee, and my knowledge of the virtues and endowments of the estimable woman whose name she inherits, prompts the wish that her acquiring the same qualifications for living, if her life be continued, or preparation for an early departure, as was her aunt's, if such shall be her's, may make her a joy to her parents while she lives, or console them when she dies.

I condole very sincerely with Sophia Phillips. The sympathy of her near and numerous relations, her own good sense, still more her pious resignation; and more than all, the gracious assistance of the Father of mercies, the God of all comfort, by the influence of his Holy Spirit, which under every dispensation of afflictive providence, is most truly, as most emphatically, the Comforter, renders it as unnecessary as I am incapable to add more than the hope I indulge, that she will continue to remember me, as one sincerely desirous of her happiness in time and in eternity.

I anticipate, with thee, the return of thy friend, Guilemard, from America, and hope, besides the pleasure of his conversation and general information, he will continue and confirm the good account of thy relations and friends on that continent.

The parcel sent by my daughter is received and forwarded in a box, with some clothes of mine, to Bridgewater. The two handkerchiefs came safe, and have increased my obligations to thee, by enabling me to gratify two worthy women, whom I wished to please. My sister, Darby, went for Bath this morning. I expect to go into Somersetshire about the 9th or 10th of next month, but hope to write to my daughter, as well as to hear again from you both before I leave this place—and am, in the meantime, with dear love to her and my son, the children and thyself, in which my wife joins,

Thy affectionate friend,

RICHARD REYNOLDS.

Coalbrook Dale, 3rd of Third Month, 1802.

MY DEAR FRIEND,

I shall now reply to the latter, and as I truly said, in my last, the most interesting part of thy favour of the 11th of last month, hoping the reasons assigned in mine of the 25th were sufficient satisfactorily to account for my not writing sooner. The retrospect of nearly twenty years, and the particular instances which thy advertence forcibly revives in my remembrance, bring with them a comparison of the past with the present, which not only makes me sensible, and may it be profitably so, of the lapse of time and the account to be rendered for the actions of so long a portion of my life, but excites with the interesting recollection, an increase of consideration for those who so long since, and especially the few who also ever since, have been the sympathisers in my affections, the promoters of my comfort, the friends of my heart; nor can I number one of equal standing, therefore more justly dear to me than thyself. I never had many friends even at that time of life, when experience had not damped the ardour of expectation, and the unsuspecting heart readily attached itself to congenial dispositions and paid a willing deference to superior virtue and greater knowledge; the few whom my situation permitted me to know and love as such, are mostly dead; the two or three left are separated by distance and engaged in different pursuits. Our intercourse has gradually, and I trust without much blame to either party, declined. The bands that now connect us are so slender, that the event which will speedily and finally loosen them, will not be thereby made painful; though at times it is not unpleasant to remember that such were once my friends.

I have endeavoured to recollect the poets I had been pleased with, and thou disapproved, and the prose writers that I still thought might instruct me; but I believe few were then named, and thy dislike was expressed in general terms, rather than in particular objections, only I think thou said " there was little genuine or original poetry of late years, there were the same thoughts a little differently expressed, and one who had read the ancients would find little new." I think thou excepted Churchill. It would be very difficult for me of the very few I have read, to mention *one* poet, whose writings I *wholly* approve, nor of them can I name *one totally exceptionable.* I believe every body is pleased with writings adapted to their respective capacities, and that both in nature and in art, the pleasure as well as the excitement is in proportion to the competency of the beholders; and as the productions of a mediocrity of genius and the simpler or inferior ones of nature, are most numerous and easily obtained and better calculated for the meridian of common understandings, the possessors of such have a better chance for enjoyment than those of more enlarged capacities and refined taste, who would perhaps be disgusted by that which would delight their simpler neighbour: a reference to the imitative arts will illustrate my meaning. Suppose a rustic youth, who had never heard, not of Phidias or Apelles, but of statuary or painting, should find a barber's block in the pit he was sinking, or the ground he was ploughing; would not his admiration, his pleasure, be exquisite, while he contemplated his discovery and marked the striking resemblance to a man's head—" the human face divine?" " Look," says he, " here's his eyes—and here's his nose and mouth, for all the world like a man's." I think he would not be proportionably more highly gratified when, by a possible reverse of fortune and cultivation of latent genius himself become an adept, astonished if not ashamed that he could once have admired the rude performance of the blockmaker, he surveys with rapture the *chef d'œuvres* of the chisel or the pencil. So also of poetry and other kinds of literature. He is most likely to be pleased, whose understanding or whose taste is rather inferior than superior to the author whose productions he reads. I need not be ashamed to acknowledge what my whole life has evinced. I was never calculated for great things. Some men of bolder darings would perhaps, even with the opportunities I have had, have acquired celebrity as iron masters, as mineralogists, or metallurgists; but I was always so much without ambition, or more properly, genius, that I could not aspire beyond the contracted sphere allotted to my movements, and proportioned to my powers. I am of opinion with Cowper, a favourite poet of mine though a modern, and what if I say confirmed by experience and observation, that " God gives to every man—

> " The virtue, temper, understanding, taste,
> That lifts him into life; and lets him fall
> Just in the niche he was ordained to fill."

And happy those, so far as worldly success can make them, who risk not their safety by rushing from it. Will it be presumption in me to think God also gave

> " To me an unambitious mind, content
> In the low vale of life, that early felt
> A wish for ease and leisure, and at length
> Found here that leisure and that ease I wished;"

that is, so far as the latter consists with those relative dependencies that Cowper never knew; "but I am growing garrulous."

How has my pen run on! I have written not as I intended, for I did not think of making myself the subject of my letter.

Thou told me of the effects of approaching age. I can, by continuing my egotisms, tell thee of the effect of old age arrived. And, whether or not it will prove me silly as well as again childish, I am not sorry that I find the continuance, if not the increase, of a disposition which I felt in early life, to be pleased with those things in nature and in art, so far as I am thereunto liable, which are most obvious and most easily obtained; at least I am not much disposed to seek, nor at all to regret that I possess not a capacity for the enjoyment or the means of obtaining, the sublime acquisitions of science, or the exquisite productions of art. I could say formerly, and I can repeat it with undiminished complacency—

> " The grassy lane, the wood-surrounded field,
> The rude stone fence with fragrant wall-flowers gay,
> The clay built cot, to me more pleasure yield,
> Than all the pomp imperial domes display."

Not that, properly speaking, I have so much pleasure in these as less desire for the others; my inclination even for the allowable enjoyment of this transitory scene abates with my powers, and the attachment to life weakens as that shortens. May my fitness for the next world increase with my indifference to this! then will the gracious purpose of the Author of my existence be accomplished in my present acquiescence with his dispensations, and the future and endless happiness of

Thy affectionate friend,

RICHARD REYNOLDS.

Bristol, 12th of Fifth Month, 1804.

MY DEAR SON,

I am very glad to hear, by thy favour of the 10th instant, that thou found thy dear children pretty well, after thy having accompanied thy mother-in-law to London. It would have added to my satisfaction if thou had informed me of the state of thy own health, and that of thy sisters who are with thee, though I do not know which of them went with her mother, and who, as thou says nothing to the contrary, I hope thou left well with her there.

I take kindly the regret thou expresses at the consequences of my removal, as preventing the interviews that we might have had, and the delay the distance occasions in the information thou can receive of any illness to which I may be subjected. It applies respecting thyself and thy children with equal effect, and therefore I request that whenever thou writes thou will mention it particularly; and I hope thou will soon have leisure to write more frequently, as well as more circumstantially, than has been the case since our separation; nor will thou, I trust, have any reason to complain of the *delay*, whatever thou may have of the importance of my answers. If thy aunts should decline to purchase upon the terms I have offered to them, I think the expedient thou hast proposed so very eligible, and the reasons thou assigns as affecting thy brother's children, and your determinations respecting Ketley Coal-works, Wombridge, and Wrockwardine, so very conclusive, that I hope by some means or other, it will be brought under thy aunt's consideration before the pending treaty is concluded, especially if they will not purchase.

I have received a letter from John Prichard, of Brosely, inquiring for a certain deed which my friend Richard Hill's attorney supposes to have been, by mistake, placed among those which I left in thy possession, in the box No. 2, as by the list drawn up by Jos. Shipton. I have referred him to thee for an answer. I shall be glad to hear from Edward Simkin the expense of the late M. Bladen's funeral. Please to give my love to him and his wife, and with much to thyself, and the dear children, &c. I remain

Thy affectionate Father,
RICHARD REYNOLDS.

To his Daughter.

Bristol, 12th of Eleventh Month, 1805.

—— I also, my dear Hannah, have been longer than I intended to have been, or than is pleasant to me, in acknowledging the receipt of thy acceptable letter of the 30th of the last month; but I will not occupy thy time or my own in reciting the many occurrences that have contributed to prevent me, nor even by referring to my increased unaptness for this kind of employment. I hope this will find thee and my son Rathbone safely returned from a satisfactory visit with your sister Benson, to her children at Manchester, and that they, as well as those at home, will continue to justify her considering them as friends and supports in her declining age. Such, I also hope, will your's prove; nor is there, I trust, more than the possibility common to you with others, to induce the particular wish that the elder of them may be in the place of parents to their younger brothers. If, " as long as thou can suppose one human being is in any way pleased or benefited by this existence, it will be a sufficient reason for thy thankfulness in its continuance;" those who love thee most and most desire thy life, need not wish it to be longer: and if thy happiness is as much promoted by their regard as theirs is by thine, thou may reasonably expect as much as can result from the intercourse, affection and friendship, so long as love and gratitude shall influence those on whom thy conduct has established thy claim to both.

I can sympathize with thee especially in the declension of thy sight, though I apprehend mothers frequently experience its commencement sooner than others, and that with them it does not rapidly increase, but is rather stationary for some years, glasses of the same magnifying powers continuing equally useful to them. How it may be with the faculties of the mind in general, which certainly are affected by the weakness of the bodily organs, I know not; of the failure of the memory I have remarked a pretty general and a pretty early complaint; but mine, of late, declines

so very fast, especially of persons' names, that I sometimes think
if I remember my own and my children's, with a very few others,
that will be all. Were I to tell thee some instances that have
recently occurred, thou would be surprised, if not grieved; and
yet, my having this day completed my seventieth year, furnishes
abundant cause of thankfulness, that after such a series or succession of conflict, care and sorrow, on a frame never very strong
and a mind always very weak, I possess so much health of body
and mental ability, as is mercifully continued to me: but, my
dearest daughter, if " a consciousness that the gift of life has
not been improved as it ought to have been," necessarily pre-
cluded hope of succeeding happiness, how miserable must have
been thy father! No, though far, very far, short of the improvement I might and ought to have made, I am not without hope.
I believe that unless a man be born again, he cannot see the
kingdom of God, and that his grace operates as the leaven in
the meal till the whole be leavened; yet, incomplete as is my
experience, I derive some comfort and some support from the
consideration, that the new birth doth not imply an immediate
attainment unto the measure of the stature of a perfect man in
Christ Jesus, and that the operation of the sanctifying influence
of Divine grace is progressive. Nor need our consciousness of
past offences prevent our hope of future happiness. Believing
the divine authority of the New Testament, and that the gracious
promises and assurances contained therein are addressed to all
the descendants from Adam, I conclude they are as much mine
as any of my fellow-creatures, without presuming to pronounce
upon the incomprehensible economy (if I may use such an expression,) of the Almighty, or attempting to apprehend the
mysterious process of human redemption, I thankfully admit
that it is a faithful saying and worthy of all acceptation, that
Christ Jesus came into the world to save sinners; that God hath
set him forth to be a propitiation for the sins of the world, and
through faith in his blood we obtain remission of sins that are
past. I observe that the promises and the attainments are spoken
of in the present tense to those to whom they are addressed;

that is, according to my understanding of them as above expressed
to me and to my daughter. Are we sensible of having been, of
our being sinners? Such Christ came to call to repentance;
such had present salvation; and forasmuch as we are subject to
the infirmities of flesh and blood, He took also part of the same,
that through death He might destroy him that had the power of
death, and deliver them who, through fear of death, were all
their life-time subject to bondage.

Why then, my Hannah, should we fear? I did not know,
when I began, I should write so much on this subject; though it
is of all others the most important; and I will conclude it with
recommending to thy attentive perusal and frequent meditation
the fifth chapter of St. Paul's Epistle to the Romans, as containing a brief, yet comprehensive and full delineation of the benefits and privileges of the Gospel dispensation, fully justifying
our immediate appropriation of them, by their being described, not
as what the believers *were* to have, but what they *had*, and what
is intended *for us* to have. May it be our happy experience!
and then, though while we continue in these elementary bodies,
we shall be liable to the ebbings and flowings of our animal
spirits—to vicissitudes of light and shade, yet dark as sometimes
the gloom may be permitted to involve us, still we shall have an
hope which, as an anchor to the soul, both sure and stedfast, will
enter into that within the veil, and preserve us safely through
every storm.

I observe thy considering the depredation of the mouse as a
misfortune; but if he has only destroyed one of the many letters
I have written to thee, I think thy loss cannot be great; however,
as it seems desirable to thee, if thou can send me the date of it,
and it happens to be one of which I have a copy, I shall willingly
transcribe it for thee; indeed, I have lately thought of burning
many letters which I have written, and were then of some little
consequence, but will soon be of none; and yet I should not
like to have them fall into improper hands when mine can hold
them no longer. Of the letters I have received, I think it will be
right they should be returned to those of the writers of them

who shall be then living, and of those who shall have died before me, that they should be burned unopened; but I should like thy inspection of them and assistance in the meantime.

Please to give my love to our T. H., whose letter of the 8th I received yesterday, and hope to write to him soon, and to my grandson, from whom I have received another acceptable letter. I suppose my son Joe has consulted his brother Rathbone on his design of opening a bank at Wellington, in which I shall willingly assist him, though I think a little differently on the subject, to which he may be more competent.

P. Gurney and S. Allen are both with me at present, and unite in dear love to thee and all thine, with

Thy affectionate father,
RICHARD REYNOLDS.

Bristol, 12th of Fifth Month, 1808.

MY DEAR SON,

I shall attend to what thou says respecting the pre-emption of the Manor Mines and Iron Works being vested in my grandsons, Joseph and Michael Reynolds, for which thou assigns reasons that did not occur to me, not less to the credit of thy disinterestedness and integrity than to thy judgment in the case, whether they ever knew or not of their obligation to thee in this as well as in other instances. I am very desirous of putting it into thy power to consider Lincoln Hill with coppices—indeed all the land on that side of the Dale, from the New Pool to the end of Lincoln Hill, or at least the possession of it at thy option or absolutely, as will be most agreeable to thee, and therefore request thee to send me, before thou goes from home, a proper item or clause to insert in my will for that purpose. I am now employing an attorney to make it for me, and have peculiar reason to hasten the execution of it. I am, with dear love to the children, and thy sister Dearman,

Thy affectionate father,
RICHARD REYNOLDS.

Bristol, 8th of Twelfth Month, 1808.

MY DEAR SON,

I was comforted to find by thy letter of the 28th ultimo, that thou left thy brother Rathbone so much better than thou found him, and which was confirmed by a letter from T. Houlbrooke written early in the week after thou returned; but by one this instant received from thy sister Reynolds, I am again alarmed, though I have not heard from Green Bank since T. Houlbrooke's letter as above said. Thy cousin S. Allen, who is at present at Frenchay, has been expecting to hear from thee with directions for the pictures, which at present are at John Birtell's, carefully packed in cases, which should be as carefully opened. John Birtell has paid £48 4s. 7d. for the pictures, frames and cases, which should be repaid to him. I understood from S. A. it was thy wish to make thy sister a present of one of them, and in that case please to remit the amount to John Birtell; if she (S. A.) is mistaken, remit the money to J. B. nevertheless, and I will repay thee the half of it; but I insist upon one condition both from thee and thy sister: that as long as I live, the pictures be nowhere but in your bed-chambers. The first was begun without my knowledge, and indirect means used to accomplish it; at length I was candidly told it was determined to have it, and when I saw what was done, I thought it better to sit for the finishing than to have it a mere caricature; but I think it a very moderate performance at last. I was willing, too, to avail myself of the opportunity, if such a one must be presented, of exhibiting my belief of Christianity as exhibited in the 5th chapter of the Romans; and my estimation of certain authors, by affixing their names to the books delineated in the back ground. Thou dost not mention thy own, thy children's or thy sister's health. I hope you are well, as through mercy I am, excepting that I feel the increasing infirmities of old age; which though many instances convince us that the young may go, convince me that the old must go; and if both are prepared for their change, it is little consequence which goes first.

18

I hear nothing of the intended Iron Company at this place, only David Evans told me you were off your bargain with him. If thou wants the money mentioned in thy former letter, I believe thou may have it from me at the time mentioned, or sooner if more desirable; and on this subject I shall be pleased to hear from thee soon.

I am, with dear love to thy children, thy sister, and thyself,

Thy affectionate father,

RICHARD REYNOLDS.

In reference to this subject (his portrait) in a letter addressed to his son, about a twelvemonth after the above, he says, in a postscript—

I have received a letter from each of my dear grand-daughters, giving me a favoured account of their health, &c.

Hannah says, "I do wish thou would send me a little picture of thee—I should not like any thing so much: we all used to like to look at that in father's room."

This reminds me to mention what I intended to have mentioned before; that is, an alteration I propose to be made in the one here, and if this could be done in the others, I should like it; and which, I suppose, would be best effected by obliterating the books, and arranging them differently, according to the estimation in which their writings or character may be supposed to be held; with the addition of Kempis and Fenelon, not only for their intrinsic merit, but to show that our good opinion was not confined to our own countrymen. They would then stand thus :—

Fox and Penn.	Woolman and Clarkson.	Hanway and Howard.	Milton and Cowper.
Addison and Watts.	Barclay and Locke.	Sir W. Jones and Sir W. Blackstone.	Kempis and Fenelon.

⌐ I do not know whether I gave thee my reasons, as I did to thy sister, for the original selection. She may show thee my letter to her, and thou may communicate the above to her, with my dear love to all, repeated from

Thy affectionate father,

RICHARD REYNOLDS.

To R. G.

Bristol, 10th *of First Month,* 1809.

RESPECTED FRIEND,

Although I received thy letter of the 15th of last month in due course, I was not qualified to answer it before this day, when ——— commissioned me to give his love to thee, and with it £15, towards £30, for which I enclose two bills, as at foot.———I notice the three cases of distress mentioned in thy letter—alas, I could send thee many such, and more calamitous! I observe two of the three are the wives and children of soldiers. I would by no means discourage thee from relieving the wants of such, if no others want it worse; but, as I apprehend there is a difference made by the law for the families of our military men, especially the militia, so it may be proper to consider, whether a difference should not also be made between those who go voluntarily, and those who are compelled to go. If we had enough for all, no need to discriminate; but as we can relieve only a part, and that a small one, I have thought it right to consider who wanted it most, and who deserved it best. Though I willingly admit, thy knowledge of local circumstances must qualify thee to determine on the best mode of administering relief, and it is possible the payment of their rents may be the most eligible for the poor at Glasgow, I would just take the liberty to suggest, that in the little experience I have had, some fuel, additional clothing, or a blanket or two, has been more acceptable, more lastingly serviceable, and less liable to abuse or misapplication than money.

Thy respectful friend.

To the Rev. Theophilus Houlbrooke.

Bristol, 16th of Tenth Month, 1809.

My dear Friend,

I have been a few days from home since I received thy acceptable letter of the 18th instant. I thought it long in coming. Thy account of thy *tour* is pleasant as it was productive of pleasure to thee, and interesting as exhibiting some instances of very affecting as well as afflicting dispensations by the death of some young and amiable, with many others, whose numerous removals, since they were thy companions in thy studies and juvenile pursuits, has contracted the circle into very small dimensions. When I was with my cousin Sally Allen, at Oxford, in the year 1806, we met Archdeacon Corbet, with two of his daughters, in New College. She remembers them well, and says they were uncommonly elegant girls, in the prime of youth and beauty. We suppose it is one of them whom the other mourns, but from thy account of her, it appears most likely it will be but for a short time. It forcibly brought to my recollection a passage in Catherine Talbot's Ode, which begins—" What art thou, memory of former day," &c.; viz.

> " For stormy clouds too often intervene,
> And throw dark shadows o'er this mortal scene ;
> Blast the fair buds of Hope, or snatch from sight
> The dear companions of our social way,
> Absorb'd at once in Death's impervious night.
> Lost for a while—but when eternal day
> Shall gladsome dawn, at once its glorious ray
> Shows the fair scene of happiness complete ;
> Then friends, companions, lovers, joyful meet,
> Thence never more to part; and fully blown
> The buds of Hope their lasting bloom display."

This, I doubt not, will occasion thee to remember our mutual dear friend F. T. I am glad to find her last letter gave a better account of her health than the preceding—still I fear it is precarious. I had a kind letter from her the 6th instant. She speaks of going from home; if I knew where to write to her, I could only tell her I love her dearly, and rejoice in the happy state of her mind, and this thou can say for me, with something from thyself the next time thou writes to her.

I have been the more disposed to write in this manner, by my having this day attended the funeral of one of the most, if not the most valuable member of civil society with whom I was acquainted in this city, and who will be more sincerely lamented, as he was more deservedly beloved than any other who has died since my returning to this place.

John Birtill,* though not thereunto ordained, was sometimes an exhorter in the Moravian Society, and at all times in life and conversation, a preacher of righteousness to them and all men; cheerful, humble, pious, and learned, though not elaborately educated; an admirer of antiquity and the fine arts, though not in circumstances to be an expensive purchaser of them; and if he had been, I believe he would have preferred relieving the wants of the living to the possession of the productions of the dead, whether by the pencil or the chisel. With all this he was my particular friend and most intimate associate in anything I was capable of undertaking for the good of others, or my own; in short, he was *that* to me in this city, to which thou wast to me in the country; need I then say, I loved him living, and lament him dead? nor need I desire more for thee or for myself than that we may, as he did, die the death of the righteous, and our last end be like his, in the full assurance of hope, through faith in Jesus our Saviour. This event enforces the monitory warning, *prepare to meet thy God*, so justly repeated by thee when, counting with thy friend Edward Harries, you found but five remaining of his class or thine: thou says, "How soon may those five

---

* Mr. Birtill had placed in a private chapel, attached to his house, a marble tablet bearing this inscription :—

| "JOHN HOWARD. | JOHN FOTHERGILL, M.D. |
| JONAS HANWAY. | RICHARD REYNOLDS." |

be, with us, removed?" How awful then to me the important admonition, who am ten years older than either of you? May it have a proper—a permanent effect upon me! I was glad to hear he continues so capable of enjoying and contributing to the enjoyment of his friends; so long as that is mutually the case with you, your interviews will be increasingly interesting, as the contraction of the circle of friendship brings your minds into greater intimacy, (if I may use the expression,) into closer contact, and your communications will be more of intellectual than material subjects—more of the concerns of the next life than of the present.

The 9th instant I received a letter from my daughter, with a good account of their health at Green Bank. She says but little of the concerns of her sons William and Richard; but if the trials and vexations her dear boys meet with may but have the right effect upon their minds, she desires nothing more. I am obliged by thy kind solicitude for my sister. I went to see her in the last month, when she was very poorly, but she was finely recovered before I left her. I had a letter last night from her son Gawen, who, with his brother Joseph from London, is at present at Bridgewater, but I expect them here the latter end of the week. My sister had been again very poorly, but was better; her health is very precarious, and frequently reminds her that here she has no continuing city, which her age alone might sufficiently do, she being nearly seventy-three, but little more than one year younger than I am, who ought therefore to be proportionably mindful of the little time I have to continue a probationer for a better inheritance in a better world. Remember me affectionately and respectfully to Isabella and the family of the Douglass', when thou writes to her. My friend, P. Gurney, is at Bath; when I write to her, I will desire her to inquire after Todd Jones. My cousin S. Allen and I are pretty well; she desires to be remembered to thee, with

Thy affectionate friend,
RICHARD REYNOLDS.

To his Daughter.

1st of Tenth Month, 1810.

—— The listlessness, amounting almost to lukewarmness, of which thou complains, is felt I believe at times, by every professor of faith in Christ, however sincerely desirous to be his disciple; at least I am sure it is as well as by thee; and like as by by thee, lamented by thy father; but may we not hope we shall in the Lord's time experience deliverance from it, and does not the sorrow it occasions excite our prayers at the same time that it proves we are not left in a state of torpid insensibility? How often have we desired to suffer pain rather than to become insensible? "While there is life there is hope;" and however sincerely as justly we may disclaim the least shadow of merit, are we not conscious that ours is not the hope of the hypocrite, and may we not confide in His promise who has said, "I will never leave thee nor forsake thee?" I was glad to find it was thy practice to begin the day with religious retirement, and reading a portion of the Holy Scriptures. The regular and frequent recurrence of any practice is too liable to reduce it to a form; but though less lively at some times, at others we experience a revival, and to consider the promises and exhortations which we read in the Scriptures, the New Testament especially, as addressed to us immediately and individually, will increase their interest, by authorising us to appropriate the abundant fund of consolation and encouragement contained in the gospels and epistles. And if we read the experience of those whom we have reason to believe have been among the excellent of the earth, and without partiality I think I may refer to some of our own Society; from these it will appear that a great advancement in religious experience does not exempt from mental conflict and apprehended desertion. May I without blame, as it is with awe and reverence I presume to refer to the unparalleled and tremendous agony of our Saviour's expiring conflict, and—may it never be named without devotion, humility and thankfulness—it was, my Hannah, for us He endured it. And can we doubt our safety, seeing, as the apostle expresses it in my favourite chapter, we have now received the atonement, and, knowing that under every future temptation his grace is sufficient for our preservation, and that our prayers will be heard by God, who giveth liberally to all that ask Him and upbraideth not.   Let us then, my daughter, duly prize the sacred pages, considering them as written for our learning, "that we through patience and comfort of the Scriptures may have hope," inasmuch as they are "able to make us wise unto salvation, *through faith which is in Christ Jesus.*",

To THE REV. THEOPHILUS HOULBROOKE.

Bristol, 21st of Second Month, 1811.

—— A friend in Edinburgh writes to me thus :—"I was much gratified by an instance of usefulness which I met with a day or two since in this place.   Two religious young men, of the name of ——— who are banker's clerks, have established a school for the instruction of negroes, in reading, writing and accounts ; as also with a view to their religious information and improvement.   The school is open every evening, except on Seventh-day, and the brothers attend alternately.   The meeting on First-day evening, which was that which I attended, seems to be almost exclusively appropriated to religious instruction.   The negroes read the scriptures, a verse each in rotation ; then the young men read a portion, and catechised them on the subject of their last lecture, which they appeared to remember well, and mostly gave sensible and pertinent answers.   They each repeated the text they had heard at their respective places of worship, and the meeting concluded with prayer.   An inquiry was made after their temporal necessities, but none were in want.   Between twenty and thirty attended ; but being mostly servants they cannot often all attend together.   The young men raise the necessary funds among their acquaintance.   The blacks appear fond of being brought together, and are very assiduous."

It occurred to me, when I read this, how many more negroes there were at Liverpool than in Edinburgh; and how much more extensive the good effect of such an establishment would be at Liverpool; and that, as no undertaking of this sort can be carried into effect without incurring some expense, I shall be willing to contribute —— towards it, in such proportion as thou shall recommend. * * *

Bristol, 9th of Third Month, 1811.

—— For though the times may not mend, nor the prospects as referring to public affairs brighten, I trust, that if we are favoured with health, our philosophy, or, I would rather say, our religion—will inspire us with fortitude to bear the worst that will be permitted in this world; and with confidence, in expecting happiness without abatement and without end, in the next. Nearer eighty than seventy years of age, I have the consolation, under my conflicts of mind or body, that they cannot continue long; and convinced that a total exemption is not to be expected on this side of the grave, I consider the short time that remains to me, as calling for all the exertion of which I am capable, to bear them with patience and cheerful submission to the divine will, as the dispensations of a providence merciful as wise—while faith in Christ, as a propitiatory sacrifice for the sins of the world and for mine, dissipates the fears that my consciousness of my own demerits would otherwise inspire, and introduces the hope, which as an anchor to the soul, will keep it safely through the awful transition from time to eternity.

It appears from the statement in the letter from New York, of the number of failures in that city, and from the number of bills returned to the West Indies protested, that the commerce of America is nearly ruined, and ours, as thou says, is hastening to its crisis. I am much less affected by the concerns of the rest of the world, than I am by my own impending state in futurity —the thought of this is almost always present with me. The former seems as that in which I once was, but am not now interested, so that I sometimes think myself too selfish.

I am thankful, however, that I am not altogether without sympathy with my fellow men and compassion for the sufferings to which the want of employment subjects the poor manufacturers; and the failure of trade and of payments, equally, or perhaps to sufferings still more severe—some of their former employers. Thou mentions Rochdale, Bolton, Leeds and Halifax. Will thou apply the inclosed toward the relief of some of them, at thy discretion; those who want it most and deserve it best should have the preference—the aged, honest, sober and industrious. I am sensible how limited the benefit from such a sum in so populous a district, and of the difficulty of personal investigation before distribution. If it could be made subservient to the procuring an extensive contribution it would be of more important service. If it cannot, I think it would be best to commit it to some judicious person or persons in each place, to distribute with the utmost privacy, and (that) for their own sakes, were it only to avoid applications from more than they could supply, and yet the refusal would subject them to abuse. But in whatever manner thou shalt dispose of it, I send it upon the express condition, that nobody living ever knows thou hast it from me; this is matter of conscience with me. In places where we are known, and on public occasions, when one's example would have an influence, it may be as much a duty to give up one's name as one's money; but otherwise, I think we cannot too strictly follow the injunction :—"Take heed that ye do not your alms before men to be seen of them, otherwise ye have no reward of your Father which is in heaven."

When thou acknowledges the receipt of the inclosed, do not mention the sum; it will be sufficient to say, my letter of this date, with its contents, came safely to thy hands.————

8

Bristol, 10th of Fourth Month, 1811.

RESPECTED FRIEND,

When I took the liberty of soliciting thy contribution toward augmenting the income of the almshouses in this city, thou wast pleased to say thou would consider of it. Permit me to submit to thee that there are 23 almshouses or endowments for the reception and support of 239 poor persons of both sexes—mostly aged, many as old, and several older, than we are—that 85 of them have but 2s. 6d. a-week; 47 but 3s.; 38 from 3s. 3d. to 3s. 6d.; 46 have 4s.; 5 have 4s. 8d.; and 5 have 4s. 6d. a-week. Two of the almshouses have been built and endowed more than 500 years; five more than 300 years, and most of the rest more than 150 years. From the reduction of the value of money, and the increased dearness of all the necessaries of life within the shortest of those periods, that which might, at the commencement of it, afford to the poor creatures a subsistence, will not now keep them from starving; and had not extraneous assistance been from time to time administered to them, many must have been famished. I believe many have suffered severely, and their lives been embittered as well as abridged by the want of food, of clothes, and of fire—the consideration whereof has induced the attempt to raise a fund for the purpose of increasing to five shillings a-week the allowance to these our poor fellow-creatures and fellow-Christians, many of whom, in early life, had as little reason as ourselves to expect so calamitous an old age.

This very moderate addition would be deemed an important improvement of their present condition, though not such as to preclude the necessity of further aid from the benevolence of our successors. But to effect even thus much will require such a sum as leaves me only the hope that what may be at present procured, will be the commencement of a contribution which subsequent additions will at some future day render sufficient to accomplish the purpose intended.

The liberality of the few to whom I have applied, warrants,

I think, my indulging the hope. Among them I am thankful
to name thy son Richard's donation of two hundred pounds. I
am unknown to thy son James, and have not the pleasure of
knowing him; but from his general character, I might have made
bold to apply to him when I was at Wraxall, had he been at
home. I may yet be emboldened, if I have to exhibit the example of his father, as well as of his brother, with due advertence to the respective abilities of each, remembering "that if
there be first a willing mind, it is accepted according to that a
man hath, and not according to that he hath not."

May I without offence refer to the infirmities attendant on old
age, and our experience of them—how distressing, with every
alleviation that money can purchase or friends administer. To
the same, or to a greater degree of suffering are so many of our
fellow-creatures, older and more infirm than ourselves, subjected
—wretchedly lodged, scantily as well as meanly fed, without a
friend to pity or assist them; in want of clothes, food, and fire,
without the means to keep their apparel clean, if they had it,
with less than sixpence a day to supply all their wants. Though
so unequal the dispensations of the present life, these are, equally
with us, the objects of redeeming love, equally interested in the
benefits of the sufferings, the death and the mediation of Jesus
Christ, our common Saviour.

Should we not consider who made us to differ from them, and
what have we that we did not receive? Is not that which we
have received and do not want, the property of those who do want
and have it not? Is it not committed to us as stewards for the
poor, who often are incapable of managing for themselves. For
these and other talents entrusted to us for improvement, we must
very soon give an account—the time is so near that I trust my
freedom will not offend. It is not likely we shall ever meet again
in this world, it is certain we shall soon be in another—may we
meet in a better!

Our time of life justifies our considering what we now offer as
an *evening* sacrifice, which will not be the less acceptable because
intended for those who cannot thank us, and to continue to their

successors when we and all ours shall be extinct. For the little time we can have the means and the power, may we "be ready to distribute, willing to communicate, for with such sacrifices God is well pleased."

I have written more than I intended to write, or than, I fear, will be easy to thee to read; but I hope I shall obtain thy excuse, and thou enjoy the peace of God and the blessings of the poor for that which thou shalt be pleased to add to the contributions annexed, and which will be thankfully received and faithfully applied by

Thy very respectful friend,

RICHARD REYNOLDS.

To one of his Grand-daughters.

Bristol, 5th of Fourth Month, 1813.

MY DEAR GRAND-DAUGHTER,

I duly received thy acceptable letter of the 5th of last month; I have since had the pleasure of a visit from thy father and brother Thomas   *   *   *   I am pleased to hear the gentlemen at Leicester have entered into a large subscription for the relief of the poor. I approve of the spirit of independency in the two poor men thou mentions, but not equally the manner in which they exhibited it. He that told the gentleman who visited him from benevolent motives, that he had maintained his family hitherto, and though the times were hard, yet he would not be dependent on any body, and did not want them in his house, for he had never asked them, should have acknowledged their kindness in more grateful expressions : the other, who said he had brought up twelve children and was very poor, but refused all assistance, because he thought there were many others who were still poorer than him,—this man I admire as well as approve, and if he is not quite comfortable, would willingly contribute towards making him so, as I hope thou and thy sisters will do, according to your abilities, if there is occasion. I am pleased to find the oranges were received, and hope they were

19

good ones. Please to tell thy sister Rebecca, that with my love to your brother John, when she writes to him, I would have her tell him, that I shall be much pleased to receive a letter from him, being his as I am

Thy very affectionate grandfather,

RICHARD REYNOLDS.

To G. H.

Bristol, 9th of Tenth Month, 1813.

—— Thou tells me, and I admit it, that thou art now entitled to know my mind on this most interesting subject.* I wish I was competent to pronounce upon it; but, conscious with due deference to the judgment of the better learned—of the contrary, I shall only venture to suggest my *opinion,* admitting, without hesitation, that every child should be taught to read the scriptures.

Much as it may be desired that we might have a correct translation of the scriptures, I cannot think it indispensably necessary as a preparatory step, or that the British and Foreign Bible Society should not have distributed the scriptures till such a translation should be obtained; because the diversity of opinions among the learned and the zealous, would, I conceive, delay the completion of such a translation so long, that the probability is, that the good that has already been done, and is increasingly doing, would never have been done: and with increased light and liberty, it may be hoped corrections and improvements will gradually be made, by translations more faithful to the original.

I have frequently urged the propriety of distributing the New Testament in preference, inasmuch as our object is not to convert heathens or Mahomedans to Judaism, but to Christianity: and as life and immortality were brought to light by the gospel, *that* is what we should most zealously promulgate. I am of the same opinion as to the poor and illiterate objects of our bounty on our

* Referring to a proposed new translation of the Scriptures.

own island, and in Ireland; and have confined the little I have done for the latter to the giving of New Testaments only. On this subject I had some conversation with ——, and though I continue to be of the same mind I was before, I am convinced that selecting certain parts of the history, the Psalms, and the Prophets, from the Old Testament, which I had thought might accompany the New Testament, for the use of the continents of Asia and Africa, would be attended with greater difficulty than I had apprehended.

I think —— must be convinced by the perusal of thy remarks, of the expediency, if I do not say the *necessity* of a prior civilization, by means of the increase of the comforts and arts of social life, in order to the extensive adoption of Christianity from the dispersion of the scriptures, or the labours of missionaries, such as have hitherto been sent abroad for that purpose. And I am of opinion, that but for the present shocking war, injudicious and injurious to both countries, the comparative success of the endeavours of Friends in America among their Indian neighbours, would have evinced the superiority of their mode, and proved the justness of thy opinion. I admit the purity of the motives, and admire the zeal of the missionaries in the East Indies, and other parts of the globe: nor will it, I trust, be considered as an impeachment of either, if, upon comparing the time and the expense, the labour and the encouragement given, with the result—I have been ready to exclaim, "Who hath believed our report," &c.

The argument respecting Atheism, quoted from the *Commonplace Book*, is more compendious, and perhaps equally conclusive with Paley's masterly refutation of it on the ground of contrivance and contriver; which yet is not new, though he might not have seen it advanced, as I did, when I was a youth, in the third volume of *Spectacle de la Nature*, in an appendix, entitled, "Useful Reflections on the whole." * * *

Bristol, 19th *of Tenth Month,* 1813.

MY DEAR GRANDSON,

It is not because I have not frequently remembered an expression in the letter I some time since received from thee, that I have not sooner cultivated the correspondence with thee; but besides the increasing inaptitude for writing, the effect of advancing, or rather advanced, old age, my frequent letters to my daughter and others at Green Bank, left me nothing to say of my health and general concernments. I had also, by the means of their letters to me, the pleasing information of thy being as comfortable as their kindness could make thee, with, perhaps, the abatement on thy part, which the want of sufficient employment in service to them would make in a grateful heart.

But my solicitude, my dear John, has been lately excited by my hearing from thy father of thy being very ill; and though I am measurably relieved by a letter from thy sister Rebecca, giving an account of the hope entertained of thy gradually, though slowly recovering, I do not refrain from bearing thee often in remembrance, accompanied with an earnest and affectionate desire that this visitation may be sanctified to thee, and the means of inducing an increasing consideration of what might have been the issue of it—the instant recollection of thy cousin William, who, about six years ago, at very nearly the same age, and with very little, if any, more warning, was called away from works to rewards, loudly proclaims the more than propriety of our being also ready; for to us also, in an hour when we think not of it, the summons may be sent. But come soon as it now may, I trust it will not come unexpected. Thy recent reminding of the uncertainty of health may keep it in thy frequent recollection; and my constant adventure to it ought to be ensured by the lapse of so many years beyond the longest admitted estimate of human life—how soon must the scenes of eternity be opened to me—how soon may they open to thee? O! that the consideration may have an effect on us in some proportion to its awful importance—to the full it cannot.

All that can occur to us, that can yield us pleasure, or give us pain in this world, will make little difference, but as it shall affect our condition in the next; and often, I believe, future happiness has been promoted, perhaps insured, by the merciful allotment of painful, though mysterious, dispensations—of blessings in disguise. May it be thy experience in the present and every future affliction, whether of body or of mind—for to both, however before exempted or insensible, thou wilt be liable, or rather art by thy fallen nature subjected—and miserable should we be had not the mercy of God in Christ Jesus provided the means for our redemption.

I am not disposed at present, nor perhaps would it be suitable —I trust it is not necessary—to enlarge upon this mysterious subject, to convince thee of its reality; the effect of which no individual's experience will invalidate. May we as experimentally witness the necessary change produced in us by the operation of the grace of our Lord Jesus Christ—in him we may trust for the remission of sins that are past, and hope for preservation in future.

But it is probable thou will think I have written enough for once; and so do I—though I have as little prospect of writing again as I had when I began of writing so much; and therefore thou will take it, concise, or rather crude, as are the thoughts, and mean the expression of them, as proceeding from a desire for thy welfare in every respect, but especially in the most important, with all sincerity and tenderness in the heart of

Thy affectionate grandfather,

RICHARD REYNOLDS.

—— As I understand it, a settlement is intended to except the property so settled on the wife from the legal claims of her husband's creditors, though they may have become such in consequence of the credit acquired by his having such addition to his property as his wife's fortune gave him—that, though it is intended the wife shall be benefited by his successful occupation of his own and her fortune—yet, if he proves unfortunate, though by inevitable losses or the immediate dispensations of Providence, his wife shall retain all she brought, and perhaps more, and his lawful creditors be unpaid, though their families shall be thereby reduced to the want of bread.

From the possibility of a man's becoming so wicked as to dispose of his property to somebody else, to the injury of his wife and children, perhaps it may be allowable to prevent it by a previous settlement; but I submit, whether *that* should be done to the exclusion of the payment of his just debts, and whether every settlement or deed intended to operate as such, should not be subject to the proviso, that such debts be first paid, as every honest man in making his will, bequeaths, after the payment of his just debts and funeral expenses.

These considerations appear to me to apply, confining them to doing justly, to mere morality. But if we consider the case in a religious point of view, as including a dependence upon the all-sufficient Providence of the Almighty, and the wisdom and goodness of all his dispensations, the extent of his care of the animate part of his creation, I think we may rely on him for ourselves and our children, and that, if we walk uprightly, no good thing will be withheld from us or our children, and He knows best what is, or will be, best for them and us.

That riches are not always best for all that have them, we have abundant proof. They are always trials, and may be blessings, if the possessors make them such to others; but how few are fully faithful in the discharge of their stewardship! how awful the responsibility attached to great wealth! Though my charge is less than many, it is more than some; and I greatly fear for myself.

The prayer of Agur is wise—"Give me neither poverty nor riches." But why should poverty be so much dreaded or deprecated? "Hath not God chosen the poor of this world rich in faith and heirs of the kingdom which he hath promised to them that love him; and hath he not said, Leave thy fatherless children, I will preserve them alive; and let thy widows trust in me?" What, then, have we to fear for ourselves or our children, that we should endeavour to prevent, by means scarcely, if at all, consistent with justice and equity?

I hope the young couple are influenced by the love of God and a desire to live in his fear, to rely on his providence, and by seeking first his kingdom and his righteousness, to ensure the addition of all that shall be necessary for them.

I fear I shall be too late for the post, or I might scribble more (perhaps I have written more than enough already); but thou will excuse the *manner*—haste must be my apology for *that*, and my sincere good will and desire to comply with thy wish, for everything else. Give my dear love to thy Eliza and all yours, and accept it from

Thy affectionate uncle,
RICHARD REYNOLDS.

Bridgewater, 11th of Sixth Month, 1814.

Dear ——

The sentiments to which thy brother alludes, though I know not that I expressed it to him, was in consequence of a reference to some *post mortuary* charities, if thou wilt allow of the expression, when adverting to the saying of the apostle, that we are to receive hereafter according to the things done *in the body*, I contended that *these* were not deeds done in the body; and I do not think the assertion need be qualified by the alteration thou suggestest, of being *best* done while we are in the body; for, in the case under consideration, we keep what we have as long as we are in the body, and would keep it longer if we could. All that we do is to prevent our heirs doing as we have done, by obliging them to do that which we should have done; and the deed is not done either by them or by us while *we* are in the body. If we should admit there is any merit in the deed, it certainly cannot belong to us, who do it not; and that which we do, by enjoining what others shall do, is lessening as much as we can every thing like merit in them, by depriving them of free agency, especially if they are not the persons to whom the money would have gone if we had died intestate: these, if any, have a right to take credit on account of the act. Perhaps those, if any such there be, who prevent others from having that which the law would give them, would do well to consider whether the account is properly adjusted by their obliging those who do give it to apply it to charitable purposes, which can do them no credit. The testator certainly can claim none as for a deed done in the body, which, as I said before, neither was then done, nor would have been done, had he continued in the body. I am pleased to find the reflection warmed thy heart—I hope it will move thy hands also upon an occasion of which the same post that brought me thy letters brought me an account, styled *a case of distress,* relating that —— of —— was drowned near ——, leaving a wife and nine children, without any provision for their support; that contributions would be received at the banks there till the 5th instant, after which time the inhabitants would be applied to personally. I suppose thou art not a stranger to the case— most likely not to the individuals, and as a neighbour—still more as a parent of a numerous offspring, I conclude thy assistance will be proportionably liberal, nor the less for it being a deed done in the body. I know not who sent me the case, which I did not receive till the time was expired for public contributions. Nevertheless, if thou wilt inform me what thou and others have done, and you have left room for more, though a stranger to the persons and remote from the place, my mite shall not be withheld by

Thy affectionate friend,

RICHARD REYNOLDS.

Bristol, 4th of Eleventh Month, 1814.

——I think the doctrine of perfection, as contended for by our primitive Friends, is consistent with the tenor of the New Testament generally, as well as with particular exhortations and injunctions therein contained ; and I presume thou will admit that infirmities, the unavoidable consequences of the elementary composition of our frail tabernacles, and the intimate connection between them and our minds, with the consequent reciprocal influence on each other, will account for certain aberrations from the standard of abstract perfection, without invalidating the doctrine as held by our ancient Friends.

Consistently with such an opinion, I rejoice in considering thee, among some others—too few, I acknowledge—who I believe have, by a proper use of the means afforded them for that purpose, attained to that degree of perfection intended by the apostle, when he exhorted those who were perfect, to walk by the same rule, and to mind the same things whereby they had so far attained, without considering themselves as having arrived at the utmost degree of attainment, or were so perfect, that there was no further advancement to be made by them, from whence I conclude that there is no impropriety in considering that degree of attainment, which is the result of a faithful occupation of the talents committed to us, whether many or few, equally that state of perfection to which the apostle refers, and for which our friends so earnestly contended.

I cannot account for my thus writing on this subject to thee, but by attributing it to the freedom which friendship inspires, and induced by thy observation, without expecting to say so much, unnecessary if not impertinent, to one of thy superior judgment ; but thou wilt excuse me, and I will conclude with sincerely desiring that, even according to my own limited idea of perfection, we may not be found wanting in the great and swiftly-approaching day of account ; that I shall not, my dependence truly is not upon any works of righteousness that I have done, or can do, but upon his mercy, who saveth us by the washing of regeneration and renewing of the Holy Ghost, through Jesus Christ our Saviour; that being justified by his grace, I shall be made an heir according to the hope of eternal life. Though, through mercy, I am enabled at times to confide that such will ultimately be my happy experience, frequent fears assault me; the absence of all sense of good, or the comfortable influence of divine favour, suggests with fearful apprehension the possibility of my taking up a rest short of the rest which remains for the children of God; but whatever sufferings it may be necessary I should endure or deprivations sustain, to prevent so fatal a delusion, may I be preserved from it; and however inferior my talents, or imperfect my obedience, may I through the mercy of God in Christ Jesus, have hope in my death—till then remember in thy prayers, when so permitted,

Thy poor but affectionate friend.

To GAWEN BALL.

Bristol, 10th of Eleventh Month, 1814.

—— I began this letter according to the date, but have not had leisure to resume my pen till this the 12th instant, and on this day I commence the eightieth year of my age—a circumstance so awful, that it indisposes for every other employment, but the consideration of the probable speedy termination of a life already protracted so much beyond the admitted natural term of human existence, and that term not attained by the hundredth part of those born into the world. I cannot describe the effect of the retrospect of the time that is past, the events that have occurred in the course of a long life: how important many of them were thought while in expectation, how much reduced when attained; and now, of so little consequence, that the wonder is they should ever have been thought of so much. Where are now the companions of my youth?—my associates in the animating endeavours to acquire knowledge?—those whose friendship I cultivated with pleasure and advantage?—those with whom

I entered the busy scenes of trade, some in concert with me, some in competition? Not one of them remaining! not a relation, not a friend, scarcely an acquaintance, but who is my junior. Most reasonably, therefore, may I expect soon to follow those who are gone from this state of probation and intended refinement—from works to rewards: and earnest are my desires, nor always faint my hopes, that through the mercy of God in Christ Jesus, it will be to be again united in heaven with those whom I have loved best on earth. Not as though I had already attained a sufficient degree of refinement, or were already perfect; alas, much remains to be removed, much to be acquired, and in how short a time! If it depended on my own unassisted efforts, or my expectation rested upon works of righteousness which I have done, or can do, my hope would perish and my confidence fail; but I trust I may, in all humility, though in a very limited degree, adopt the language of the apostle, and say, " I know in whom I have believed," and commit my soul to Him, as unto a faithful Creator, and all-sufficient Redeemer.

Farewell, my dear nephew; unite thy prayers with me and for me; and if we never meet again in this world, may we in that into which our nearest relations and dearest connections have already entered; there to unite with them in praises to Him who sitteth upon the throne, and to the Lamb, who is worthy for ever, amen!

So prayeth for thee, as for himself,

Thy affectionate uncle,

R. R.

Bristol, 20th of First Month, 1815.

MY DEAR GRAND-DAUGHTER,

If thou remembers how we were circumstanced when thou left us, and knows the addition we have since had to our engagements by the succession of company and increase of occupation

in consequence of the year's end—that I have not sooner acknowledged the receipt of thy acceptable letter of the 21st ultimo, will not surprise thee. I have more than once taken up
my pen, but have as often been interrupted and prevented from
proceeding. But I will now begin by expressing my pleasure
to find your safe return to Ketley was also so pleasant. Thy
description of the inundated country between Gloucester and
Worcester, enlivened by the reflection of the bright moonlight,
and of the stars, and of the winter scene at Hagley, is animated
and just. It made me recollect some passages in Thomson's
Seasons, and especially Addison's beautiful hymn, in the 465th
Spectator, which I never remember without pleasure.

The meeting of the Prudent Man's Friend Society, which thou
would willingly have attended, and at which our S. A. would
have been pleased with thy company, was small, but satisfactory, though the mayor, who was to have taken the chair, was
prevented from coming, and Dr. Randolph, who took it on the
spur of the occasion, was under an engagement to be soon at
another place, and thereby obliged to be more brief in his com-
mendatory remarks on the utility of the institution, and the conduct of the committee in the conducting of it, than I suppose he
otherwise would have been. However, upon the whole, it
concluded agreeably; and the report which he read was much
approved, and did great credit to S. M., the secretary, who wrote
it. I do not know whether our friend, Theo. Houlbrooke, and
his wife, went by Ketley in their way to Liverpool: they were
undetermined when they left us; they came on the 10th instant,
and left us the 13th: they appeared to be much pleased with
each other, and I hope will so continue as long as they live. I was
very poorly when they came, not being recovered from an illness
which commenced the preceding week: and though I am now
pretty well again, it has not so entirely left me, but that frequent
relapses repeatedly remind me that here I have no continuing
habitation: may I successfully seek one that has foundations
eternal in the heavens!—The unusually long time that I have
occupied a crazy tenement in this world, should make me con-

stantly expect to be summoned at a short notice, or ejected without any. But so precarious is human existence at all times, that even my grand-daughter may properly remember the exhortatory injunction, "Be ye also ready." Forasmuch as she no more knoweth than I do, at what hour she may be called from works to rewards—from the uncertainty of time to an unchangeable eternity. May it also be happy to us both!

Thy brother is very well. Give my dear love to thy father, from whom I have not heard, as he gave me to expect—to thy brothers and sisters and aunt, and accept it thyself, from

Thy affectionate grandfather,

RICHARD REYNOLDS

To GAWEN BALL.

Bristol, 28th of First Month, 1815.

—— A letter which I received last evening informs me of the favourable termination of an affair that has occupied much of my time of late, and which I think will appear of sufficient interest to warrant my relating the circumstance to thee, as follows. About six weeks ago a negro lad was brought by his master from Jamaica. He had been kidnapped in Africa, being then, it is conjectured, about eight years of age. He was purchased as a slave for his master, who being about to bring him to England, and aware that he could not retain him there as a slave, had him baptized and bound to him as an apprentice. The lad being apprehensive that as his master intended to send him back to Jamaica, he should be sold as a slave, ran away from his master, who pursued and attempted to bring him back. The boy resisted, and the contest excited the notice of the neighbours, some of whom rescued the lad and put him under the protection of a constable, who brought him to me for my advice and assistance. I applied to counsellor Smith and to the mayor, who had resided in the West Indies, and has at present planta-

20

tions and many slaves in St. Vincents, but was favourable to the
boy's emancipation.

After some ineffectual attempts on his part, and mild remon-
strances on mine, the master consented to relinquish his claim
and let his slave go free. This he did with so good a grace at
last, that I offered to pay a servant's wages to attend him while
he continued with us; this he refused. Considering the incon-
venience he sustained by being deprived of the boy's services, I
proposed in as delicate a manner as I could to avoid offending
him, to make him a present of twenty guineas. This he also
declined accepting, with acknowledgments of the kindness of the
offer, and we parted very good friends. He is a young man, a
mulatto, with wool on his head, and a complexion almost as dark
as his slave, who is a complete negro.

I placed the boy at our British and Foreign School, and had
the satisfaction to find him uncommonly quick at learning, and
of a capacity equal to most, if not to any one of his schoolfellows
of the same age.

The probability of his being qualified in due time to go out
as a teacher in the school established at Sierra Leone, induced
me to apply to the board of directors of the African Institution,
through Thomas Harrison, their secretary; and last evening I
heard from him that the Institution would send him to the Bor-
ough-road School for a year, in the hope that he would by that
time be qualified for the situation I had in view for him. The
certain benefit to the youth,* as rescued from slavery and ignorance, and the possible, not to say probable, extent of the benefit
of his services to his countrymen, and the promotion of the civilization of Africa, is so satisfactory, that, under the immediate influence of it, I have written perhaps more than may be agreeable
to thee, but thou wilt excuse it.

* The boy's name was William Symonds—he went to Sierra Leone, thence
to Hayti, and was afterwards tutor in Toussaint's family.—ED.

Bristol, 30th of Third Month, 1815.

—— Thou says —— has made a good thing for himself of that which proved ruinous to others. I am surprised thou should be far from thinking he has been guilty of any thing which would be deemed dishonourable among *tradesmen.* I think a tradesman ought to have, and I trust some tradesmen have, as high a sense of honour as any other men—I think too, that liberality, equity, justice, and the golden rule are incumbent upon tradesmen, and a conduct in opposition to them disgraceful to them; but I cannot think any modification can make that admissible in one rank or description of men, which would be reproachful in another. The money spent or lost at Sierra Leone has been enormous, the benefit in proportion to it we must confess very little, and I fear the public will not be very forward in contributing toward the expense, incurred by petitioning; however, I am willing to contribute liberally when I know of its being commenced, and the scale upon which it is undertaken.

The following extract of a letter from a friend in New York, dated the 9th of Fifth Month, 1815, having been found copied by my grandfather, it has been considered desirable to insert it here.

One of the Friends who has resided a number of years with one of the Indian tribes to promote their civilization, told me that a missionary came there lately from this place, who having called the council together, told them he had come, sent by such and such, out of love and pity for them, poor, ignorant, and benighted people, to teach them the way to happiness, and to bring them that holy book, the Bible, without the knowledge of which, and their observing the doctrines which he had come to teach them, they must be forever miserable, or words to the same import.

Red Jacket, the Indian Chief, replied, " that he did not know wherefore the Missionary and his friends that sent him should call them a poor, ignorant, benighted people; they were not without religion, but possessed the same that their forefathers had handed down unto them—that is, the good Spirit taught them to be kind, hospitable, sober, patient, to love all men, forgive injuries, and to persecute no man for differing from them in religious sentiments; but, said he, we hear that you who have that good book, quarrel and fight together, and that you do not agree about the contents of that book—therefore go first and agree together, then we will consider the matter."

To Priscilla H. Gurney.

28th of Fifth Month, 1816.

The receipt of thy letter of the 15th was a consolation to me when poorly in the evening, and the re-perusal of it comforts me now. It is true that in this variable state of things, and especially as we advance towards the termination of the probationary scene, the bitters may at times appear to exceed the sweets; yet it is with thankfulness I acknowledge that ever since we parted I have experienced a degree of support sufficient to prevent my sinking below hope in seasons of apprehended desertion, depression and weakness, which have sometimes been such as to deprive me of the power of praying for the help I so much needed; yet in hearing the Scriptures read I have even at such times been enabled to apply (I hope I was not presumptuous if I thought I was permitted to appropriate) the gracious invitations and promises of our blessed Saviour, more to my encouragement and confirmation, than at some opportunities in times of greater bodily strength and mental energy.

To Gawen Ball.

Liverpool, 12th of Seventh Month, 1816.

—— I set out on the 24th of last month for Coalbrook Dale, where we arrived the evening of the next day: and whether the exercise of the preceding days, or of those spent at the Dale, was too much, I know not, but I was so much worse and weaker than I was when I set out, or expected to have been, that I feared I should not be able to accomplish my purpose. However, we proceeded to Ketley on the 28th, to my son Joseph's, and kept the house the next day, went to the New Dale Meeting on the 30th, and came to my daughter's at Green Bank the 3rd instant, finding her and her children at this place in good health, (for which I desire to be thankful,) and confirmed in the persuasion I have for some months past admitted, that my continuance in this world will not be long. I have no specific complaint, unless a troublesome cough, especially at night, can be considered one: but with every assistance that diet, exercise, and change of air can afford, I continue as weak or weaker than before. My appetite fails me, especially for animal food, and I, like Barzillai at my time of life, incapable of enjoyment from all animal gratifications, and indifferent to all this world can threaten or indulge, and desirous as he was, when, in answer to David's invitation to him to accompany the king to Jerusalem, he desired to be permitted to return home that he might die in his own city, and be buried by the grave of his father and his mother; which I hope to accomplish so far as to return home on the 19th, and wait with patience my appointed time. My mental faculties, as well as my bodily strength, fail me much, especially my memory: but though indifferent to everything else, I hope to be preserved alive to my eternal interests, and that I may rather be in a state of present suffering than of insensible indifferency. I have not been hitherto without hope, and through the mercy of God in Christ Jesus, I desire to be enabled to trust therein to the end.

To Gawen Ball.

Bristol, 30th of Seventh Month, **1816.**

—— I know not how to acknowledge as it deserves thy most affectionate and affecting letter of the 26th instant. I can write but little, and, had I more strength, I could not express my thankfulness for the favour, which I receive as the medium of a manifestation of continued Divine regard, most seasonably vouchsafed at a time of deep depression, under a long continued sense of the withdrawing of the light of His countenance, whose loving kindness is better than life.

That I have been a participator with thee in a degree of spiritual union, so far exceeding my conscious deservings, humbles me as it ought: that it has been to thy comfort and advantage is cause of thankfulness to me, while it excites the fervent prayer, that during my short continuance in this world our spiritual fellowship may increase, and that we may, with the deepest humility and self-abasement, be permitted to adopt the language of the beloved disciple, and say, "Truly our fellowship is with the Father, and with his Son Jesus Christ."

I do not find myself stronger since my return; the pain in my side is less. When medical men are called in they must do something, and the patient goes through a certain routine of medicine and treatment: but as it is appointed for all men once to die, so I have been, since the commencement of my present illness, of opinion, that the time of my departure was approaching, and nothing has occurred to alter my opinion; and thankful I am, that the process, sometimes more rapid, sometimes more tardy, is attended with no very severe bodily suffering. I hope I shall with patience wait the appointed time when my change shall come.

I shall be very glad to hear thy plan of proceeding will admit of thy coming to Bristol while I am living; for to see thee once more in this scene of mutability and conflict would be very pleasant to

　　　　　Thy very affectionate,

　　　　　　　　　　R. R.

To George Harrison.

Bristol, 2nd of Eighth Month, 1816.

I have had, for some weeks past, a constant, though not always equally severe pain in my side, loss of appetite, with an aversion almost to the sight of animal food, and frequently, as at present, a degree of sickness that renders every exertion, even writing, difficult and a task; but it is so long since I received thy kind letter, that I would no longer refrain from acknowledging it. I will not conclude without mentioning that, through my illness, I have not been without hope, and which, with humility and thankfulness, is continued, and I trust will be to the end. But it is solely founded on the mercy of God in Christ Jesus, who died for us, in whom we have redemption through his blood, even the forgiveness of sins.

Farewell, my dear friend; it is not likely we shall meet again in this world; I hope we shall in a better. Excuse this scrawl, which is written with difficulty by

Thy truly affectionate friend,

R. R.

It is not to be expected that the following portion of the Correspondence of Richard Reynolds will possess much interest for the general reader; yet, as the various subjects, which it embraces, were to him important, and occupied much of his time and thoughts, such letters could not be altogether omitted, and a few of them have therefore been selected, as exhibiting the writer in a point of view of a less peculiar and private character than could be afforded by letters addressed to members of his own family, or his intimate friends.

TO THE CHANCELLOR OF THE EXCHEQUER.*

Ketley, near Shiffnall, Shropshire,
12th of Seventh Month, 1784.

As from my situation and connection in coal-works and iron-works, I was better apprised of the ill consequences to be dreaded from a tax upon coals than some others, I doubt not I shall obtain thy excuse for my endeavouring to prevent it, by communicating to Lord Gower, to whom I have the honour to be known as his tenant, as well as to Thomas Gilbert, Esq., and some other gentlemen, such an account of what would have been its operation, as was sure to obtain from thy candour and true patriotism the relinquishment of so obnoxious a tax. I have communicated to Sir Richard Hill, whom I have requested to be the bearer of this, such hints as have occurred to me on the subject of a substitute in lieu of the coal tax, as well as some remarks on the brick and tile tax. And I shall think myself fortunate if this is accepted by thee, though it were only as proceeding from a wish inspired by gratitude and respect to endeavour to lighten the task which thy office imposes, and which I am convinced thou would exercise in the manner most favourable to every individual.

I shall now mention another tax, which, affecting a description of men whose power, and my connections with them, renders it necessary that I should have an absolutely safe reliance upon thy secrecy, whether anything be done in consequence of it or not.

The tax upon bills of exchange is a shilling on all above £50. I would propose, that sixpence be paid for every additional £50 above £100. At present, little tradesmen, whose returns do not exceed £1000 per annum, may be supposed to pay as much as many whose returns are fifty times that sum; and, as there are more competitors where the capital employed is small, and the profits thereby reduced, it seems more tolerable, as well as more

* The Right Hon. William Pitt.

consistent with equity, that the larger the sum the higher should be the tax in proportion; but if it is only after the same rate, there can be no reasonable objection. And it would obviate a difficulty there might be in procuring a very high stamp on particular occasions, by making use of divers lower stamps to the same amount.

I do not write this because I should not be affected by the alteration. For the use of the works under my immediate inspection, I have taken, for some time past, £2500 monthly, in cash, to pay the workmen. It may be supposed that I give, as often as I can, such bills as I receive; but I sometimes draw on our bankers for the whole sum, in one bill, for one shilling.

If every one's will to do good was in proportion to their power, I should have no occasion to engage thy honour for thy secrecy on the present occasion; but, as the disposition to resent is more natural, thou wilt excuse my repeating it, and requesting that thou will be pleased to return this letter to me. I have too just an opinion of thy good sense to apologize for the simplicity of the language, which, consistently with my religious profession, I have made use of in it, and of the value of thy time, than to intrude on it longer than to desire to be considered as

Thy very respectful friend,

RICHARD REYNOLDS.

To GEORGE ROSE, ESQ.

Ketley, 7th of Second Month, 1785.

RESPECTED FRIEND,

I replied to thy favour of the 3rd instant yesterday, and afterward received that of the 4th. Though I continue of the opinion that my journey will rather prove my will than my power to render the Committee any important service; yet having, on the receipt of thy first letter, sent a person to overtake the post, with one from me to William Gibbons of Bristol, request-

ing him to attend in London without delay, and promising to
meet him there; and there not being time to prevent his setting
out, I fear he would have reason to think himself ill-used if I
now declined it. I therefore continue my intention of setting
out to-morrow, and hope to be in town the evening of the 9th
instant, and yet see, in my way through Birmingham, some intelligent and extensive manufacturers of iron in that place. I
might therefore, perhaps, more properly defer attempting any
reply to the query in thy last favour till I have the pleasure to
see thee; but as thou desirest an immediate statement of it, I
will just recite it, with a short remark or two.

Thou art pleased to ask my opinion " whether, if the manufacturers of iron of Great Britain and Ireland, were made subject to the same duties upon *importation* into each country respectively, the manufacturers of Great Britain would have any
reason to fear a competition ?"

As there is very little, if any, iron made in Ireland, I presume by iron of Great Britain and Ireland is meant bar-iron,
whether foreign or made in the country; and taking it for granted
that if the duties *are equal*, it will not be regarded how low they
are, I will venture to give it as my opinion that we should have
nothing to fear, provided the duties on the *importation* of the
iron manufactures of each country respectively are sufficiently
low; or rather, that it would be still better there should be none
on either side: because duties upon importation go in aid of the
revenue of that country which lays the duty, and against the export trade of the manufacturing country, by enhancing the price
to the consumer, which operates, in proportion to the amount of
it, to prevent the consumption.

If the duty is high, it also induces smuggling. In the present
case, if Ireland pays an equal duty with England upon all foreign
iron imported—and which is most desirable, or rather, absolutely
necessary—we need not fear them as rivals in manufacturing of
it, so long as our fuel is untaxed, and our national spirit of industry and exertion continues.

Thou art pleased to add, " There are many questions of fact

to which it would be very desirable to have answers, if you had been present." I should be very glad to have those questions in writing, directed to me, on the receipt of this letter, at Smith, Wright, and Gray's, 21 Lombard Street; because I might be thereby better prepared to answer them, and in less time, when I shall have the honour to attend thee, which thou will also be pleased to mention for my government and punctuality.

I am very respectfully,

Thy assured friend,

RICHARD REYNOLDS.

To EARL GOWER, LORD PRIVY SEAL, &c.

Ketley, 31st of Twelfth Month, 1785.

The bearer hereof is William Rotch, of the Island of Nantucket, who is deputed by its inhabitants to solicit assistance and relief from the British Government, under their present, and, so far at least as relates to their country, unmerited sufferings.

I was so unfortunate, by being from home when he was in Shropshire, as to miss the opportunity of profiting by a personal acquaintance with him; but I am emboldened by the concurrent testimony of divers persons, whose judgment I prefer to my own, and who have had the means of perfect information, in the warmest manner to recommend him as an individual respectable and intelligent, worthy of thy attention and favourable notice, as the representative of a very considerable body of useful and industrious people, appealing to thy humane feelings for a mitigation of their distress, and claiming thy patronage as affording the means of benefiting this country. And permit me to add my wish, that Britain may attribute the solid advantages of an extended trade, and an increased population, to thy influence on the determination of its councils on the present important occasion.

§ The island of Nantucket has been peculiarly unfortunate. The peaceable inhabitants (3,000 out of 4,500, at which number they are computed, being of the Society called Quakers), refusing to take any part in the American rebellion, when required so to do by the state of Massachusetts, to which they belonged; and considering themselves, and supposing they would be considered by this government, as in the king's peace, had, notwithstanding, taken from them by the English, during the war, about two hundred sail of vessels, with other effects, to nearly the value of £200,000; by which and other events of the war, the bearer and his father lost nearly £30,000.

Nor did the return of peace restore to them the power of retrieving their losses; for being, by our revenue laws, subjected as aliens to the payment of a duty amounting to a prohibition on the oil they brought to London, which was almost their only market, as the whale-fishery—especially of the spermaceti kind—was almost their only employment: they are disabled from following it at that island; and now solicit the assistance of that government which they would not oppose, and under which they have suffered, to enable them to settle in the British dominions, and prosecute a branch of business important to every nation as a nursery of seamen, and profitable, as producing wealth by the acquisition of an article useful as light, and necessary in many of our manufactures, by their superior skill in taking the fish; for which we may be otherwise obliged to pay foreigners, besides transferring to them the collateral, but not inferior, advantages of population and revenue; which latter, in consequence of Lord Sheffield's being called upon to account for what he had adopted from the letter, I took the liberty of addressing to thee on the trade of making iron in this kingdom, I have had occasion to reconsider, and am fully convinced it amounts, as I then supposed, to more than six pounds a year for each man employed in it.

The patronage and assistance offered by Ireland to the oppressed Genovians did no less credit to the good policy, than to the humanity of our sister kingdom; and without, at this time, urging it as only a compensation to the people of Nantucket for their sufferings, for their fidelity during the late troubles. As an Englishman, I had rather this island than Ireland, or any other country, should be benefited by an acquisition of sailors and fisher-men, still more valuable than watch-makers from Genoa; and that both parties, experiencing the accumulation of national riches and strength, thereby may have to remember with gratitude the interference of Lord Gower in their favour, rather than any other person in England; for I am, with great truth as well as with deference and respect,

Thy faithful and much obliged friend,

RICHARD REYNOLDS.

To LORD SHEFFIELD.

Ketley, 19th of Tenth Month, 1786.

—— The clause respecting linens appears to me likely to in-crease the revenues of both kingdoms, and the satisfaction result-ing from the consideration of the whole is heightened by the hope it inspires, that the mutual advantages received will be the means of preventing war between the two nations, perhaps of ensuring the peace of Europe, and at last of the world.

Thy obliged friend,

RICHARD REYNOLDS.

To LORD SHEFFIELD.

Ketley, 10th of Twelfth Month, 1787.

Thy observations on my hoping the present treaty will be the means of preventing wars between the two nations, makes me almost wish I had let the following passage stand in my last let-ter, but which, from a consideration more easily assigned than justified, I suppressed; for I believe thou would not think the worse of a man, as a member of civil society, for a reflection

21

escaping him which might be coloured by his particular or peculiar religious sentiments.

I had remarked that the interests of humanity appeared to be better understood by modern, than by ancient patriots, and that the attention many of the European governments are paying to the improvement of their internal and the extension of their foreign commerce, furnished some reason to hope that former rivals in arms will become mutual helps to each other in the free intercourse of trade; and that a reciprocation of the benefits and blessings of peace may lengthen the continuance of it. I had added—but as avarice is as opposite to virtue as ambition, and commercial advantages as desirable to one as dominion to the other, so nothing short of the divine philanthropy enjoined by the gospel, and only acquired by the influence and operation of the Holy Spirit, will prevent the return of wars and the destruction of their fellow men by those who should " love as brethren."

And though this continues to be my persuasion, I flatter myself thou wilt, notwithstanding, permit me to subscribe myself, with much respect and esteem,

Thy obliged and faithful friend,

RICHARD REYNOLDS.

To THOMAS GILBERT, ESQ.

Ketley, 25th of Sixth Month, 1786.

RESPECTED FRIEND,

I certainly ought earlier to have acknowledged the receipt of thy plan for the better regulation of the poor, if I had been capable of suggesting any improvement; but I thought that without it, a profession of the just sense I, with very many others, have of our own, and indeed of the nation's obligations to thee for thy continued endeavours to serve it so essentially, would be an intrusion on thy time, so importantly engaged : nor should I now be thus troublesome to thee, but on an occasion interesting to one part of the poor, and to the community at large. The great success and advantages of those called Sunday-Schools in other places, and a consideration of the very great want of such means of improvement and civilization among the numerous poor children of the Marquis of Stafford's cottages, whose parents are employed in the works we rent of his lordship, hath induced me to determine to attempt something of the kind in this neighbourhood, and no place appears so proper on which to erect a suitable building for the purpose, as the unenclosed land near this house, which is part of the farm rented by Robert Clayton. I have spoken to him, and have his consent, but I thought it proper to obtain his lordship's also; and I therefore make bold to request thy good offices on the occasion. Without going out of the township of Ketley, there are at least three hundred proper objects; and I think a building about eighty feet long, fourteen feet wide, and seven or eight feet high, without a ceiling, divided into four parts, will answer the purpose, and, so situated, bring the conduct of the children and the teachers under my own occasional inspection, or my sons, or other suitable persons, if such can be found.

There is not another person among the Marquis of Stafford's tenants in this township to whom I can apply for assistance in the building—a few may be asked to subscribe toward the annual expense of teachers, books, &c.; and if I obtain his lordship's permission *only*, I will proceed to erect the building; but if I might without offence, I would suggest how acceptable his lordship's contributing to it would be, not only as giving a sanction to the undertaking, and placing his lordship in the most amiable point of view, as the father of the helpless part of his tenantry, but exhibiting an example more likely to be followed by the neighbouring gentlemen, than anything that could be done by so insignificant an individual as

Thy very respectful and obliged friend,

RICHARD REYNOLDS.

To LORD SHEFFIELD.

Ketley, 22nd of Twelfth Month, 1785.

Thy favour of the 11th instant was longer in coming to my hands than might have been expected, owing, I apprehend, to the irregularity of the cross posts since the introduction of coaches for the carriage of the London mails, which I mention to account for the appearance of delay in my acknowledgment and reply to it.

I shall be sorry, if what I advanced as a matter of *opinion*, has been the occasion of thy being called upon for proofs in consequence of thy advancing it as a matter of *fact;* but if the only place in which thou speaks of the workmen employed in the making of iron as. paying six pounds a year or upwards to the revenue, be, as I conceive, in page 211 of thy *Observations on the Manufactures, &c., of Ireland,* it is *there* advanced only as a supposition, or matter of *opinion.* In the letter I took the liberty of addressing to Lord Gower, to which I presume the reference in thy letter is made, I expressed myself to this effect:—"The value of each individual to the revenue will not be ascertained by a reference to the country excise office, because that includes only the exciseable articles they consume, the duty for which is paid in the district wherein they reside; and not those they have from *other parts of the nation,* or *from abroad,* the *whole* of which has been computed, *I believe,* to be equal to six pounds a year; but I am persuaded that in this country it is more."

Now, though I might be mistaken in supposing that it was *generally computed* at so much, as I confess myself much a stranger to political calculations, as well as but little skilled in political disquisitions, and consequently, not qualified to form an opinion that may be safely relied on—yet as I was not intentionally wrong, however hasty in my conclusion, so I do not at this time see any reason to alter my *opinion:* for when I consider that six pounds a year is not quite four-pence a day, and how many are the articles of consumption, in food and clothing,

that are taxed, and how highly some of them, as spirits, ale, to-
bacco, candles, soap, leather, &c.—I must still conclude it would
not, nor has one with whom I have since had an opportunity of
conferring, supposed it would, be so little as six pounds a year
to each.

I might urge, that as in the beforementioned letter I was considering the importance of the trade of making iron in England
as in competition with the importation of foreign bar iron, so I
was thinking of and intended workmen engaged in the making
of iron, particularly furnace-men and forge-men, whose employment is supposed to render necessary, as their wages enables
them to provide, better or more expensive food and liquor than
common labourers or husbandmen; but, and this I suppose will
be readily admitted—if by so much as any article is advanced in
price to the consumer in consequence of taxes imposed by Government, by so much is that Government advantaged by such
consumer—then I think it will be evident that six pounds a
year is less than *every workman* pays, without confining it to
furnace-men and forge-men ; for as through every stage of every
article of food and clothing, from the corn in the furrow and
the flax in the field—from the ox and the sheep in their pastures
to their hides and their fleece, passing through various hands and
various processes into clothing, and their flesh salted before or
after it is on the table as food, or furnishing them with light,
and contributing to their comfort and health, by conducing to
cleanliness when converted into candles and soap—as all these
are regularly increased in price, by the addition the farmer and
every one after him must make, in consequence of the taxes to
which each is liable, as well as the particular duties or excise on
many articles used in the varied process, so the price the consumer pays for all he eats, or drinks, or wears, will be found to consist of an accumulation of duties and excise, advanced indeed by
others as the articles pass through their hands in their several
stages to perfection, but paid by him at last, with an addition
for rent, interest of capital, and their labour respectively, which
in divers instances constitutes the least part of the price.

21*

Nor is this reasoning confined to the produce of our own land. It is equally conclusive when applied to that of our colonies, and to foreign commerce; for if in the first instance a farmer renting an estate of £100 a year, pays in taxes of all kinds £20 a year, and I *know* in some places it is much more; to make his rent he must sell his produce to the manufacturers for £20 more than if he paid no taxes. The manufacturer must be paid for his labour 20 per cent. more than he otherwise would, and the articles made by him for the export trade, whether sent to the Indies or to America, up the Mediterranean or the Baltic, must be sold at a rate proportioned to such advanced price, which must be repaid in the price of the raw material or manufactures taken in return, and this perhaps is the best reason to be given, as it heretofore has been, for the higher price paid by the consumers of West India produce from the English than from the French Islands.

From the preceding it appears to me not only that my former opinion was well founded, but also that, however speculative politicians may estimate any class of men, it is merely, and only in proportion as they are *consumers* of the produce of the soil, the manufactures of the country and the imports of its merchants, that they contribute to its revenue: and this shows the importance of population to a nation, and of trade as furnishing employment for the people. Indeed, like action and reaction they in great measure produce each other, and, eventually, they will stand or fall together; which should induce the consideration, whether raising the supplies by taxes upon raw materials and implements of manufacture, or others that ultimately affect trade in general, as has been so much the practice of late, is good policy.

So long as the consumption of our manufactures and imports at home or abroad continues, so long the burden may be borne, but the higher the impositions the higher the price of them must be, and the sooner we shall be undersold in foreign markets. The want of a *foreign trade* would deprive many of our manu facturers of employment, and by obliging them to emigrate, lessen our *home consumption*, and defeat the revenue of the duties upon *both*; but I expect this will be sooner felt than seen, by those who should know that in all cases it is better to prevent than to cure; and that in some, that which might have been prevented cannot be cured.

I have now written a longer letter than I at first expected to write, and have only to apologise for it by saying, that long as it is, I have restrained the wanderings of my pen: for the subject (of trade) is so various, so complicated, and so beneficial to society, that one is almost unavoidably led into reflections more diffuse than comports with the bounds of a letter—and yet I will add to this, by wishing thy most valuable observations on the commerce of America and Ireland had been seen by some modern writers. It might have prevented some reflections of theirs, as absurd as they are illiberal. I am going to spend two or three weeks at Bristol. If I can render thee any service there, I shall be glad to receive thy commands, at Mary Cowles', in Castle Green; and I trust it will not be attributed to an affectation of humility, if I request it may be without an addition to my name—which, considering its military origin, is ill applied, and would be worse assumed by one of my peaceable principles—which, however common, but few are entitled to—and which, whatever Johnson or Boswell may have thought to the contrary, is not necessary to elevate the real rank in society, of *a tradesman*—or, as they as elegantly as justly express it, of "a fellow sitting all day at a desk,"—or even of such an one as is bold to subscribe himself, without a fear of offending thee,

Thy very respectful and obliged friend,

RICHARD REYNOLDS.

To John Smitheman, Esq.

Coalbrook Dale, 14th of Seventh Month, 1795

RESPECTED FRIEND,

It is likely thou will have heard that there was a numerous meeting of gentlemen, farmers, millers, and tradesmen, held at the Tontine Inn, the 9th inst., on the alarming occasion of the present scarcity of corn and dearness of all other provisions, at which a committee was appointed of certain persons especially, and generally of all subscribers, for the immediate collection of contributions and the purchase of such grain as can be procured to be distributed to the necessitous, at the reduced price of one-fourth, or nine shillings for twelve.

It was cause of regret that the meeting had not the advantage of thy company and advice, for of thy contributing with them they doubt not; and I am directed by the committee, on behalf of the meeting, to apply to thee on the occasion, the urgency of which admits not of delay. The wants of the poor are far beyond what has been at any former time experienced, and from the best account that could be collected, the quantity of grain of all sorts in the country is three thousand bushels short of the consumption before harvest. There are many families now in want of bread, and the present supply is very scanty in proportion to the increasing demands. The colliers, &c. have hitherto been prevented from rising by assurances that the gentlemen of property were disposed to contribute liberally to their relief, as well as to adopt measures for obtaining from distant parts such aids as can be procured; and I have by their direction sent to Liverpool for one or two thousand bushels of Indian corn; but such are the increasing wants, and such the consequent murmurs of the poor, that it is impossible to say what will yet be the consequences, and I should not be surprised if they applied in a body at those houses where they expected to find provisions, or from which they thought they ought to be relieved. They already begin to make distinctions between those whom they consider as their benefactors and those who (as George Forester expresses it in the annexed letter) are at war with their landlords; and I fear those whom they would consider as deserting them in their distress would not only incur their disapprobation, but might be the next to suffer from their resentment. I therefore the more readily attempt to fulfil my appointment by recommending thee in the most earnest manner to send by the return of the post to Richard Dearman at this place, who is appointed treasurer on the present occasion, a bill for such a sum as thou shall think proper to contribute, and at the same time to write to thy servant at the West Coppice to give notice to thy tenants, (as G. Forester has to his), and especially to William Parton of Little Wenlock, that it is thy desire that he and they should conform to the general practice and deliver immediately all his wheat to the committee, at twelve shillings per bushel, for the use of the poor. And if there is any wheat, barley, beans, or peas, at the West Coppice, or elsewhere in thy possession or power, I recommend thee to order it to be sent without delay to the Committee; and then if the colliers, &c., should go in a body, or send, as I think more likely, a deputation to thy house, thy having so done, and thy servant showing them thy order for so doing, as well as thy contributing liberally as above proposed, will be the most likely means to prevent the commencement of mischief, the end of which, if once begun, it is impossible to ascertain.

Annexed is a copy of the letter from George Forester, before alluded to, and the enclosed advertisement will show thee the parishes included in the present Association for their relief, and the amount of the sums immediately subscribed, among which are the following, viz.—George Forester, £105, Cecil Forester, £105, J. H. Browne, £105, the Coalbrook Dale Company, £105, Richard Reynolds, £105. Thy neighbour, John Wilkinson, is among the subscribers, and has also engaged to deliver a quantity of wheat under the market price to the amount of £50,—and as some money was immediately wanted to purchase corn, &c., George Forester, J. H. Browne, and myself consented to advance £700, each, to be repaid from the produce of the corn which is to be sold at the reduced price.

The donations are to pay the expense of grinding, &c., as well as the loss of three shillings out of twelve shillings, and thou will easily calculate how much it will require to do that on 9000 bushels, which, at the most moderate computation, will be wanted to support the country for six weeks to come; and the Committee assure themselves thy liberality will be in proportion to the occasion, of which, such is the urgency of the temper of the people, that there is not a day to lose if we are desirous to preserve the poor from outrage, and most likely the country from plunder, if not from blood.

Though general calamity doth not require particular or local inducements to obtain relief from the affluent and humane, permit me to suggest that the inhabitants of this parish, and particularly the colliers and miners, are disposed to look up to thee in an especial manner as their former master and their present friend; nor are their or our hopes the less, or the less founded, by thy income being increased by passing thy mines or the produce of them into a different kind of property, or to the purchase of land in a less populous part of the country.

I make no apology for the freedom of the proceeding, conscious that it is what I should have used under similar circumstances to my father, had he been living, and the strongest proof I can give thee of my being as truly as I am respectfully

Thy faithful friend,
RICHARD REYNOLDS.

To SIR RICHARD HILL, BART.

Coalbrook Dale. 5th of Third Month, 1796.

RESPECTED FRIEND,

I was obliged, by thy favour of the 19th past, giving me the agreeable information of the success of the motion by W. Wilberforce, for the abolition of the slave-trade. I hope the Bill for that purpose will be equally prosperous in passing both Houses, and obtaining the royal assent.

Understanding from the public prints that a tax is intended to be laid upon dogs, I have taken the liberty to mention it in my acknowledgment of a letter from thy worthy colleague, as introductory to a subject to which I also beg leave to engage thy attention, and that is, my hope that the tax upon dogs, in which, I trust, the sum imposed on bull-dogs will amount as near as possible to a prohibition, may be made subservient to the suppression of the infamous practice of bull-baiting, the ill effects whereof upon the tempers and manners of the frequent use of them I need not describe, to justify the introduction of such a clause, if it be possible. If that cannot be done, I really think, as I presume no law at present in force will apply to the prevention of the evil, it is of sufficient importance to warrant the bringing in a bill for the especial purpose; and I cannot but wish the representatives for the county of Salop may have the honour of abolishing a practice which is a disgrace to the nation, inconsistent with religion, and degrading to human nature; and if the practice of cock-fighting, but little less objectionable, could be included, it would lessen the number of existing evils, and add much to my satisfaction. Perhaps thou wilt confer with John Kynaston upon the occasion. Sensible of thy many engagements, I will not intrude upon thy time, by apologizing for the liberty I have taken, or by adding more than that I am, with much respect and esteem,

Thy obliged friend,
RICHARD REYNOLDS.

To John Kynaston, Esq.

Coalbrook Dale, 5th of Third Month, 1796.

Respected Friend,

I accept very cordially thy congratulations on the success of William Wilberforce's motion for the abolition of the slave trade, and received very gratefully the printed bill intended to effect it, assuring myself of its having thy support as well as that of thy worthy colleague, whose attention I shall solicit as I do thine on the following occasion. I understand from the public prints, it is intended to lay a tax upon dogs. If more consistently with my wish than my expectation, it should be done, and a difference made in the species, I hope bull-dogs will be highest taxed, so high if possible as to amount to a prohibition, but I wish still more earnestly that the occasion may be made introductory to the abolition of the cruel practice of bull-baiting, disgraceful as it is to the nation, inspiring with a degree of ferocity the human brutes, who with their dogs are immediately concerned in it, as well as inducing idleness, dissipation and intemperance among the mob, who assemble to partake of this worse than savage diversion.

I hope thou wilt find an opportunity to confer with Sir Richard Hill on the subject, and am very respectfully,

Thy obliged friend,

RICHARD REYNOLDS.

To Sir Henry Bridgman, Bart.

Coalbrook Dale, 2nd of Fifth Month, 1789.

Respected Friend,

I was not at home when thy favour of the 24th past was brought to this place. I returned last night, and take the earliest opportunity to acknowledge so condescending a mark of thy attention.

It is not, I trust, necessary for me to employ any arguments to justify thy very obliging compliance with my request in favour of the abolition of the slave trade, but whether it should be effected by an immediate total prohibition of it, or be extinguished in a very few years by the gradual operation of provisions to be enacted by parliament for that purpose, I shall most cheerfully submit to thy better judgment. Still thou wilt give me leave to hope it will be one or the other, as well as permit me to object to the proposal of an act to *regulate* the slave trade, and render it *less shocking* to humanity; because no modification of that which is evil in itself can convert it into right, and especially because by making it less shocking it would probably be rendered more lasting—and the violation of their rights as men and of our duties as Christians be entailed upon thousands yet unborn, by the specious provision for their more lenient treatment as slaves who should always have been free men. Thou will excuse this further freedom, and believe me with much respect and deference,

Thy obliged friend,

RICHARD REYNOLDS.

TO LORD SHEFFIELD.

Coalbrook Dale, 21st of *Sixth Month*, 1790.

Before I received thy favour of the 17th instant, I had replied to my friend on the subject of it. I apprehend thy election will not be opposed. I trust it will be allowed as the strongest proof the nature of the case admits, of my thorough conviction of the total repugnance of the slave trade to our duty as Christians, and to all that ought to distinguish us as men, that a diversity of sentiment and conduct on that subject would prevent my giving a vote for the person, who, of all others, I should otherwise think best qualified and most eligible to represent the commercial city of Bristol, and whom I had considered as such, with an hope thou would be its choice, before the business of the slave-trade was agitated in this nation, and long before the dissolution of the late parliament was expected.

I think too it will be made to appear that the slave-trade is no more *necessary* to the existence of our West India trade, than it is inconsistent with equity, humanity, or the golden rule—but this is not the time, were I qualified, as I am not, to discuss a subject of such magnitude as well as importance. Let it, however, suffice to assure thee of the continuance of that respect and esteem, with which I have hitherto subscribed myself,

Thy obliged and assured friend,

RICHARD REYNOLDS.

TO THE CHANCELLOR OF THE EXCHEQUER.

Coalbrook Dale, 12th of Tenth Month, 1799.

I will not take up thy time by apologising. Always a friend to government, and desirous to promote the public weal, thy candour will excuse without it, my submitting to thy consideration the expediency of discontinuing the use of hair powder in the army. The lateness of the harvest, and continued wet weather, not only injurious to the present crops, but, by preventing the sowing, entailing a scarcity on next year, justly excites the public fear, the effect whereof is not lessened by the present disastrous conjuncture. The attention of government will be very opportunely displayed in suppressing at all times an unnecessary, and at this time an injurious, profusion by the misapplication of so much of the most essential support of human life, at present with difficulty procured by many poor families, and eaten by more with too *justly* founded apprehensions of speedy want, if not timely prevented, and towards which this measure would contribute a quantity more easily calculated by thee than by me.

I am of opinion, that upon a very moderate allowance per man to all the military in this kingdom, it would be found to be, if not the whole, a very large proportion of that which will be necessary for the foreign troops expected to be wintered (and a long winter it may be) in England. Even if they come not, the failure of the crops in other countries, as well as so generally in this land, will render every exertion little enough to secure a very moderate supply for this kingdom and its dependencies; and how conducive to public dissatisfaction and tumult is the want of bread I presume thou art sufficiently sensible, to promote a measure so expressive of the king's desire to alleviate the sufferings of the lowest rank of his subjects, whose loyalty and submission to the laws entitles them to encouragement and assistance from every branch of the legislature. I presume this might have been addressed with more official propriety to the Secretary at War, or the highest military officer; but having before now expressed my sentiments to thee, on a different occasion, and sensible of thy power to give weight to a representation from an insignificant individual, I am desirous the exertion of thy influence may convince the many who will be benefited by the measure, that it is as consistent with thy disposition to serve them, as that disposition is confided in by

Thy respectful friend,

RICHARD REYNOLDS.

To SIR RICHARD HILL, BART

Coalbrook Dale, 5th of Twelfth Month, 1799

RESPECTED FRIEND,

If the trouble thou has taken to bring under the notice of the Chancellor of the Exchequer the measure suggested in the letter I took the liberty of addressing to thee, produces, by his adopting it, the salutary effect intended, thou will have a more adequate recompense in the relief it will afford to the poor, than from my acknowledgment of thy condescension, which yet be pleased to accept, as it is tendered with gratitude and respect.

Conscious how inapplicable are the terms in which thou hast spoken of me, I must attribute to thy desire to give some weight to the proposition, thy representing the proposer of so much more importance and influence in his neighbourhood than attaches to him. Formerly, my concerns in trade gave me a little consequence among the occupiers of mines and makers of iron; these I have some years since relinquished to my sons, who, with abundantly more science, as well as experience, have made improvements in the quality of iron proportionably important to the nation, though I cannot say with equal emolument to themselves; so that whatever of weight or distinction in the commercial part of the community I once possessed—and I never possessed any other—I am now, not more compatibly with my time of life than consistently with my inclination, in that state of retirement, and I hope of safety, which was the privilege of those of whom the poet says—

> "Exempt from danger as remote from fame,
> Their life's calm current flow'd without a name."

Yet, though detached from actual participation in the losses or gains of iron works and mines, I partake with my betters in the feelings of humanity in these times of complicated distress, from war and want of bread, and I think myself honoured in being permitted to unite my feeble endeavours with thine, to mitigate the latter; as to the former, it is altogether out of my province. I would it were as much in thy power as I am confident it would be thy wish, to induce the rulers of the nations to become more, than in a profession flagrantly false, the followers of the Prince of Peace; but on this subject it was not my intention to have touched, and I hope thou will excuse me.   *   *   *

Thy respectful friend,

RICHARD REYNOLDS.

To Earl Gower, President of the Council, &c.

Seventh Month, 1784.

Unacquainted as I am with the customary mode of addressing a person so much my superior, the experience I have already had of thy condescension on other occasions would, embolden me to reply to thee on the present important one in our usual plain manner without a fear of incurring thy displeasure, or of failing to procure that attention which the magnitude of the object I desire to submit to thy consideration will be found to deserve.

I understand by the papers, as well as by a letter from Isaac Hawkins Browne, Esq., that the Chancellor of the Exchequer has proposed a tax upon coals of two shillings per ton, which, if enacted, will be of the most fatal consequences, I apprehend, to many branches of manufacture and commerce, and particularly destructive of those which are the support and employment of thousands in this and the adjoining counties; nor do I believe the produce of the land of at least one parish in this neighbourhood would in that case support the poor of it, neither is it to be computed the ill consequences it must have on the landed estates in general; but the difference to those who have mines of coal and ironstone, may be estimated by the consumption of both in the very extensive works in this and the adjoining counties. The advancement of the iron trade within these few years has been prodigious; it was thought, and justly, that the making of pig iron with pit coal, was a great acquisition to the nation by saving the woods, and supplying a material to manufactories, the make of which, by the consumption of all the wood the country produced, was unequal to the demand, and the nail trade, perhaps the most considerable of any one article of manufactured iron, would have been lost to this country, had it not been found practicable to make nails of iron made with pit coal. We have now another process to attempt, and that is to make *bar iron* with pit coal; and it is for that purpose we have made,

22 *

or rather are making, the alterations at Donnington Wood, Ketley, &c., which we expect to complete in the present year, but not at a less expense than twenty thousand pounds, which will be lost to us, and gained by nobody, if this tax is laid on our coals. The only chance we have of making iron as cheap as it can be imported from Russia, is the low price of our fuel, and unless we can do that, there will not be consumption equal to half the quantity that can be made, and when we consider how many people are employed in making a ton of iron, and the several trades dependent thereupon, we shall be convinced the revenue is much more benefited even by their consumption of exciseable articles, &c., than by the duty on a ton of foreign iron, nor will it I believe escape thy observation, that the iron trade, so fatally affected by this absurd tax, is only of the second, if indeed on some accounts it is not of the first, importance to the nation. The preference is given, and I believe justly as to the number of hands employed, to the woollen manufactory, but when it is remembered that all that is produced by making of iron with pit coal, is absolutely so much gained to the nation, and which without its being so applied would be perfectly useless, it will evince its superior importance, for the land grazed by sheep might be converted with whatever loss to other purposes of agriculture or pasturages; but coal and iron stone have no value in their natural state, produce nothing till they are consumed or manufactured; and a tax upon coal, which, as I said, is the only article that in any degree compensates for our high price of labour, &c., or can be substituted in the stead of water for our wheels and bellows, would entirely ruin this very populous county, and throw its numerous labouring poor upon the parishes, till the emigration of those of them who are able to work shall strengthen our opponents, and leave the desolated wastes, at present occupied by their cottages, to the lords of the soil.

I flatter myself what I have urged, though abundance more might be said did time permit, will obtain that opposition to so ruinous a tax, which thy abilities and thy station enable thee to give, and for which, as a lover of thy country at large, as the protector of thy tenants, and as the hereditary patron of the manufactories in this and the adjoining county, so many look up to thee with confidence, proportionate to their apprehensions of danger, and of thy disposition to save them from it. As to the tax on bricks and tiles, if it is not confined to those used in building dwelling-houses, it will be very heavy on those concerned in collieries, &c., and at any rate be very partial; few bricks, if any, being used in divers counties in England.

Let the importance of the occasion excuse any warmth of expression, if such has escaped me. May my religious profession, the simplicity of my manners, and the sincerity of my respect, obtain thy permission to subscribe myself with due deference, though in much haste,

Thy obliged faithful friend,

RICHARD REYNOLDS.

To EARL GOWER.

Bath, 28th of Third Month, 1785.

Observing that the consideration in the House of Commons of the Commercial Treaty with Ireland, is adjourned to the 31st instant, and not expecting to be in Shropshire before this day week, I take the liberty of addressing a few lines on that subject to thee from this place.

Nothing would induce me to be thus troublesome, but a thorough conviction of the fatal tendency of the resolutions proposed to be adopted from the Irish House of Commons, to the trade and manufactures of this kingdom in general, as well as their prejudice to the landed estates of many noblemen and gentlemen, and to the property of those who have adventured their fortunes, and the provision for whose families, as well as the payment of their rents, depends on the success of their engagements in the ironworks and mines which they rent or occupy.

There was a petition sent from Shropshire by the makers of pig and bar iron, the proprietors of mines, and others interested therein, which was to be presented to the House of Commons the 21st instant, and which I doubt not will obtain thy attention. As a family very materially affected, and who have been emboldened to look up to thee for protection as thy tenants, as well as having experienced thy assistance in their undertakings, permit me in the name as well of my relations at the Dale, as of my children and in my own, to solicit thy effectual interposition against a measure so injurious to us, and to the many hundreds of poor people employed by us in working and carrying on mines, &c., for the supply of a large sale of coals by land and water, and of coals and mine for sixteen fire engines, eight blast furnaces and nine forges, besides the air furnaces, mills, &c., at the foundry at Coalbrook Dale, and which, with the levels, roads, and more than twenty miles of iron railways, &c., still employs a capital of upwards of one hundred thousand pounds, though the declension of our trade has, as stated in a former letter, obliged us to stop two blast furnaces, which are not included in the number before-mentioned. Nor have we ever considered ourselves as the first of many others, concerned in iron works or coal works in this kingdom.

However we may have thought we had reason to complain of being sent for by the Chancellor of the Exchequer, to give information on subjects at that very time brought forward and determined in the Irish House of Commons, if not also intended to be adopted without any qualification or alteration in that of England, we are only influenced by a regard to the real interest, and the just and fair regulation of the commerce of the two countries, equally free from party influence, and the least intention to embarrass or obstruct the business of the nation.

So much has been said of the equalizing of the duties between the two countries, that, confining myself to that trade of which it may be supposed I have some knowledge, (the importance of which to the nation at large, and to the counties of Salop and Stafford in particular, I have already taken the liberty to remark to thee,) I trust I shall be excused, if, conformably to what is stated in our aforesaid petition, as well as our examination before the Committee of the Privy Council, I advance, that while there is so great a difference between the *import duties on foreign iron*, the notion of an equal duty on iron wares *exported from each country* is an illusion, and the trade of this country must be lost. At the same time, a reduction of the duty on the importation of foreign iron into England, to the same rate that is paid in Ireland, would not only immediately and greatly decrease our revenue, but still more extensively, as well as more importantly, injure it and the country also, by ruining the iron works of this kingdom; and, therefore, the Irish paying an equal duty to ours on all foreign iron imported, as it is the shortest, so it is the truest, though not the only way, of putting the iron trade of the two kingdoms on an equal footing; for the same end would be in great measure obtained by the Irish imposing a duty on all manufactured iron exported, equal to the difference of the duty on the bar-iron wrought into the iron wares so exported; but that would not be so easily or so exactly ascertained; yet it might be done sufficiently near, for we are not disposed to contend about trifles.

Conceiving the impending conclusions of our Parliament likely to affect not only myself and the present generation, I hope I shall obtain thy excuse for what I have written, as I could not think I had discharged my duty to my children, to my country, and to posterity, if I had not solicited the interposition of a nobleman most capable of knowing the truth of my assertion, and best qualified as well as disposed to prevent the ruin of his country. And in hopes that, under such influence, a commercial arrangement will take place between the two countries upon the permanent foundation of a liberal, equal, and fair regulation of duties on importation and exportation, permit me to subscribe myself, with due deference.

Thy obliged faithful friend,
RICHARD REYNOLDS.

To WILLIAM PITT, ESQ.

Coalbrook Dale, 27th of Tenth Month, 1802.

RESPECTED FRIEND,

In the course of a conversation some time since, speaking of the money subscribed for the erection of thy statue, it was observed that a more effectual way of perpetuating the estimation in which thou wast holden by the contributors, would be by converting the money into a captial sum, the interest of which should be applied to the reduction of the national debt. This, though cursorily mentioned, has, after mature observation, appeared to me so feasible, and so likely to comport with thy own patriotic regard for the nation, over whose concerns thou so long presided, that having heretofore, at the recommendation of the Marquis of Stafford and thy instance by George Rose, attended on a committee of the Privy Council, when the Irish propositions were under consideration, and since that time taken the liberty to address thee on some other occasions, I flatter myself thou will excuse the present, which I believe will be the last, and allow me to submit to thee that, as having benefited the nation during thy administration is the assigned reason for the proposed erection, thou would by this means benefit it in perpetuity, and toward which some might contribute who could not concur in the other mode of exhibiting their approbation. It would be as impertinent as presumptuous in me to prescribe to one so much more competent to determine the manner in which effect should be given to the proposal I have ventured to make. I doubt not, if the thought is approved, a little consideration will enable thee to adopt such a plan as shall give it permanency by a Parliamentary sanction. Whether it be that the interest accumulated in a given number of years should then be applied to the discharge of so much of the national debt by direction of the House of Commons, and noticed as such among the ways and means at that time, which would as often remind the nation, and by the

pen of future historians, succeeding generations and the world
at large, of the man who made his fame substantially conducive
to the benefit of his country, as his endeavours intentionally had;
or whether some other mode shall be adopted by thy better judgment, I hope thou will accept this suggestion as the effect of the
regard and respect with which I am

Thy faithful friend,

RICHARD REYNOLDS.

To LORD SHEFFIELD.

Ketley, 21st of First Month, 1786.

I returned from Bristol last night; and when I acknowledge
that I received thy favour of the 28th past, the 2nd of the present month, it appears necessary that I should account for my
delay by informing thee, it was occasioned partly by my being
obliged to go to Bath before I could make, or rather attempt to
make, the inquiries recommended in thy letter, and partly from
being prevented by a close attention to a very troublesome, but
to me, an important business, from sooner seeing the very few I
know in that place, and from whom I at last received but little
information, not being able to tell them what was proposed by our
government on one side, or by the French on the other, as the
terms of the commercial intercourse between them.

I took an early opportunity to communicate thy letter to our
mutual friend William Gibbons, who expressed himself much
obliged by thy attention. I recommended to him, as much
better acquainted with the inhabitants of Bristol than myself,
who have left it nearly thirty years, to make the proposed inquiries and to write to thee, which I hope he hath done or will
do, though he was at that time very busy taking an account of
his stock and settling his accounts to the year's end. With respect to the iron trade, I apprehend the intercourse between the
two nations cannot be too free. From its most imperfect state as
pig iron, to its highest finish in the regulating spring of a watch,

we have nothing to fear if the importation into each country should be permitted without duty. And if, as has been apprehended, this must be purchased with a reduction of the duties on their wines and brandies, that it would be a good purchase for this country. As to thy observation, that with French manufactures the same kinds from all the world will find their way to our market; admitting, as I do, the truth of it, I think it is obviated by a conclusion as fairly drawn, that our manufacturers will likewise find their way to all the rest of the world, with those of France of the same kinds.

Supposing the linen manufacture as likely to be affected by the proposed intercourse with France as most others, I conferred with an intelligent and respectable person in that trade, but he did not apprehend much danger. He, as well as others, asked me on what terms the importation of French cambrics was to be admitted; I could not tell him. He said the consumption in England would not, in his opinion, be much more than it now is; for those who would then wear them generally did so at present, and if they were admitted at a moderate duty they would be bought in the shops instead of being purchased of the smugglers —that we had nothing to fear from France, or from Holland or Germany, through France, with respect to other linens.

I was disappointed in not seeing a gentleman who is by much the best informed of any one I know respecting the general commerce of both countries, as well as particularly that to the West Indies, in which the French have of late years made an amazing progress, and the wines and brandy of France, being himself largely concerned as a sugar-baker and wine merchant. He was a few years since high sheriff of the county of Somerset, and is at present at Montpellier. I saw his partner at Bristol, who encouraged me to hope that, if he was requested, he would be likely to attend William Eden, Esq., at Paris; for he is a gentleman of a liberal mind, loves his country, and is as capable as well-disposed to serve it. He has been in Spain and spent much time in France, and if he is prevailed upon to give his assistance or information, I doubt not I shall not be entitled to the thanks of this country, as I flatter myself, if he cannot come to Paris, I shall obtain his excuse for informing thee that if William Eden, Esq., is pleased to apply to him he may direct to " James Ireland, Esq., Montpellier." Passing through Worcester, I conversed with a friend who employs many hands in making gloves, and which is a manufacture as likely to be hurt by that of France, as most, if not of any other. He was of opinion that, if we could have the skins at a moderate duty, it might be advantageous; but I know so little what articles are intended to be admitted in lieu of those they will consent to take from us at reduced duties, that I could say nothing to it.

It gave me great pleasure to find that my reasoning in support of what I advanced, respecting the worth of every workman in the iron works to the revenue, met thy approbation. I have been so much otherways engaged of late, that I do not know, even from the papers, whether or not William Eden is gone to Paris. There was a report that Lord Carlisle was to be joined with him on the occasion: will thou oblige me by letting me know, and also if there is any reason to expect that so desirable and judicious an indulgence is about to take place, as an allowance of the landing and re-exportation of foreign commodities without paying any duty, which is only to be exacted when they are taken out of the ware-houses for sale, or for home consumption. Fearing to be too late for the post, I have only to add, that I am with much respect and esteem,

Thy faithful and obliged friend,

23

RICHARD REYNOLDS.

To John Wilkinson

Ketley, 14th of Twelfth Month, 1787.

On the effect of a law for making book debts carry interest.

RESPECTED FRIEND,

I received the inclosed letter the 10th inst. I went from home the next morning and returned last night. As the time limited for an answer is so short, and the uncertainty of its being convenient to the few to be consulted to meet for that purpose is so great, I have concluded to send thee my opinion as briefly as possible, and to request thee to let me know in what thine is different, and I shall be glad to improve mine by it. I do not know that my brother Rathbone is returned from Liverpool, but I shall be obliged to thee to communicate it to Banks and Onions, or any others thou shalt think proper, and to let me have it again, with your opinions, by to-morrow night or the next morning.

I am against the proposed measure for the following reasons: —At present there is a little, though indeed but too little, regard paid to reputation in the punctual discharge of debts owing: the entitling creditors to legal interest, from the time their debts become due, will I apprehend lessen that inducement to the debtor to pay, and increase the odium unjustly incurred by those, who, however necessary it may be for them, shall insist upon being paid; because they will be told the law provides them a consideration, and prevents their suffering by their forbearance, though every tradesman knows, as well as the purchasers of land or of government securities, that the interest for money is not at all times, or rather is but very seldom, an adequate compensation for a delay of payment. To renters, whether of mines or works, whose landlords *will be paid*, and to manufacturers whose workmen *must be paid*, the extension of credit to the purchasers of their produce would be highly injurious; because it would require an increase of capital incompatible with the circumstances of many of them, as well as increase the risk of bad debts to all, and thereby check the spirit as well as lessen the means of enterprise and exertion, of late years so conspicuously displayed in the extension, and so essential to the continued prosecution, of the various mines and manufactures of this kingdom.

If it was allowed in cases of bankruptcy, those who had given the longest credit would prove the largest debts in proportion; but as it would not increase the effects to be divided, I think its only operation would be to increase the number of bankruptcies, by holding out an inducement to the extension of credit, which already contributes so much to a circumstance rendered less scandalous than it ought to be by its frequency. I have only time to add that I am very respectfully,

Thy assured friend,

RICHARD REYNOLDS.

To GEORGE FORESTER, ESQ.

Ketley, 2nd of Fourth Month, 1788

RESPECTED FRIEND,

I desired Egerton Leeke to inform thee how much I thought myself obliged by thy message to me on this day week. I have consistently therewith essayed a sketch for a petition against the Slave-trade, which I shall be very glad to find meets thy approbation, or that thou will be pleased to make such improvements in it as thy better judgment shall suggest.

I presume it will be expected that some reason should be assigned for petitioning, and I have confined myself to such as I apprehend must strike all men equally forcibly. An immediate abolition of the trade would be very injurious to many individ-

uals and perhaps to the nation at large, and therefore is not to
be asked; but I believe it is very possible to subject it to such
regulations as shall gradually diminish, and, by the encouragement of population, at length totally do away, the necessity of
supplies from the coast of Africa, and thereby extinguish the
trade without loss to individuals or to the nation.

I am, very respectfully,

Thy obliged friend,

RICHARD REYNOLDS.

To the Honorable the COMMONS of GREAT BRITAIN in
Parliament assembled.

The humble Petition of the Bailiff, Recorder, and Burgesses
of the town and liberties of Wenlock, in the county of
Salop, in Common Hall assembled,

Sheweth,—

That your petitioners understanding that the Slave Trade on
the coast of Africa, in America, and the West Indies, is about
to come under your consideration, are desirous to join the very
great numbers of their fellow-subjects, who, from a just abhorrence of the inhuman traffic, have petitioned against it.

That it is inconsistent with that most equitable rule of doing
to others as we would they should do unto us, every man will
acknowledge, who for a moment, and that but in idea, substi-
tutes his parent, his wife, his child, or his friend, in the place
of one of the miserable victims, which avarice and acquired necessity subjects to separation, to disease, to slavery and to
death.

That your petitioners presume not to prescribe to your honorable
house what measures they shall adopt, but to express their hope
they will be such as in due time shall extinguish a trade which they
apprehend to be disgraceful to the nation, as Christians and as
men.

And your petitioners, &c.

To Sarah Trimmer.

Ketley, 80th of Eighth Month, 1788

RESPECTED FRIEND,

The box of books which I expected to receive from James Phillips was detained some time at the carrier's warehouse through a mistake of the book-keeper; notwithstanding which I might, I confess, have acknowledged the receipt of thy favours of the 16th and 19th of last month which came in it, as well as have thanked thee sooner for thy *Sunday School Catechist*, and the spelling book and *Easy Lessons*, had not company and many other engagements prevented me. I wish I could give thee a better account of our school. I believe it doth not much decline; but, from its being situated where the few who can be procured to act as teachers are almost wholly without the aid of visitors, it doth not flourish, as I am glad to hear the schools do in many other places, and as I hoped this would have done. Another attempt is about to be made in the town of Wellington, in the extremity of which parish ours also is: that being in a market town, I expect will succeed better, were it only from its being undertaken and patronised by several.

I had sent for all the books thou hast published, excepting those I possessed before, and as a circumstance that may increase the satisfaction thou must have received from the success of thy attempts to promote the cause of virtue and the good of thy fellow-creatures, I may inform thee, that having for some time past intended to do something of the kind, I was animated and excited to an immediate determination by the considerations urged in page 107 of thy *Economy of Charity*, and have made the bricks, &c., to build six comfortable little habitations, and glad shall I be if, when they are erected, I can find six such poor men or women as are there described to inhabit them. I shall be under some difficulty to establish such rules as will be best

23 *

adapted to insure peace, religious sobriety, and cleanliness among them; but as I am apprehensive the houses will not be habitable before next spring, perhaps, with thy leave, I may take the liberty of consulting thee on my plan when I have thought more of it, and reduced it to writing : but of *this*, permit me to request—may I say *to insist?*—that thou takes no further notice ; not having yet told the workmen employed for wha tpurpose they are intended.

I have taken in thy magazine for the benefit of our servants. I observe the paper I left with thee is inserted in one of them, and in a manner that may lead some who have seen it in the detached form in which that was printed, to apply a certain character to me, to which, being so inferior in every other particular as well as circumstance, the mistake would give me much uneasiness, even if the whole of that paper had been of my writing, whereas I only had it reprinted, with the addition of the second paragraph, and that in the forepart of the third, respecting prayer. It was originally written, I believe, for a school at Barr, near Birmingham, by one thou would call a lady of our Society, and a relation of Robert Barclay, whose wife is of thy acquaintance. I took the liberty of making a few remarks, of little importance I confess, on that publication, when I had the pleasure of seeing thee at Brentford. I doubt not thy intention was as disinterested in the magazine as in thy other books for the use of the lower classes of the people, and I as little fear offending thee by suggesting, whether it might not improve that work, if occasion was taken to apprize the readers of the absolute necessity there is for them to experience a change of heart, a restoration from their fallen nature, which is so emphatically and explicitly declared by our Saviour to Nicodemus. This appears to me to be the root from which alone is to be expected the fruits of the Spirit, as described by the Apostle, and opposed to the works of the flesh in the 5th chapter of his Epistle to the Galatians. An attention to outward conduct or exterior deportment is certainly very good in its place, and by no means to be omitted ; but a prior, a superior attention to " the ingrafted word," will ensure success to the labour bestowed in training and pruning. Sensible of the inferiority of my own attainments and attempts, I only venture to drop the hint, as confidently hoping thou will improve it as believing thou will excuse it; and permit me to recommend to thy inspection, as likely to furnish some observations which perhaps may not be improperly introduced into thy magazine, a little book printed by James Phillips, entitled *The Grounds of a Holy Life*, by Hugh Turford.

I am obliged to thee for sending the anniversary sermon to the Humane Society; but where no good end is answered by the publication—and I know of none there would be in my being a life-director—I think our Saviour's injunction respecting alms-deeds should be observed, were it only for the very important condition annexed thereunto; but in the present instance I could not comply with it literally. Thou will approve of my doing it as nearly as I can.

If thou considers the military origin of the addition thou hast been pleased to make to my name in the direction of thy last letter, thy good sense will discover its incongruity with the peaceable principles I profess, even were I legally qualified to assume it; but as I am not, it is still more improperly applied, nor will my disclaiming it, I trust, be attributed to an affected humility, or prevent thy still permitting me to subscribe myself, though simply, very sincerely,

Thy respectful and obliged friend,

RICHARD REYNOLDS.

To THOMAS ADDENBROOKE.

RESPECTED FRIEND,

As thou informed me thou expected to see Lady S—— soon, I take the liberty to address this to thee on the following occasion. Some time ago, J. C—— rented of the Commissioners of the turnpike roads, one of the gates adjoining to the town, and with his wife resided in the house, which, though small, is neat, and had with it a good garden much improved by his cultivation. When his term expired, he, depending on the promises of some who were to take it for him, was disappointed; it was let to another person. He then opened a little school for his wife to teach young children to read; but being Roman Catholics, the clergyman of the parish interfered and would not suffer them to teach, threatening the parents of the children, as well as the poor man and his wife. They then set up a little shop; but, living among very poor people, *their* necessities in the late time of scarcity pleaded more strongly with this benevolent pair than the risk they ran by trusting those who had nothing to pay, and a few bad debts were more than equal to the profit of many such customers. I was at —— a little after Midsummer, and making some inquiry after them, was informed as above related. I called to see them, hoping they might have been under the notice of some more opulent Roman Catholics; but was told there was only one family left in the neighbourhood, about four miles from thence, and they, though kind and well-disposed according to their ability, were not in circumstances to do much for others. Having the pleasure of being a little acquainted with J D——, Esq., I took the liberty on my return of mentioning the case to him. He was pleased to say, he should have been glad had it been in his power to have been of service to them, but it was not; and upon my mentioning that the poor woman was the daughter of a clergyman, and had resided some time in France with Lady C——, he said I should do well to apply to Lady S—— (the daughter of Lady C——). Now though Lady S——'s charitable disposition is experienced and acknowledged so evtensively, and I believe her condescension and affability would prevent her from being offended if I had applied immediately to herself, yet as the claims on the benevolent generally increase in proportion to their abilities, and as I have not the honour of being known to Lady S——, I shall only take the liberty of submitting to thy better judgment, the propriety of the application I wish to make, for those I believe to be very worthy, and against whom I never heard anything alleged but their religion.

John C——, formerly lived in the capacity of a gentleman's servant, and I suppose has had a tolerable education, and knows something of music. His wife appears to be a respectable character, and I understand was treated by Lady C—— with much confidence and tenderness while she lived in France with her. Both of them are middle aged, or perhaps near fifty years old, without children. I should think them very capable of a house-steward's and house-keeper's place in a good family, but I question whether they would choose to live in any family, who were not Catholics, or near a chapel without liberty of attending it. Not being willing to raise expectations I could not fulfil, I did not tell them I should attempt to serve them in this manner; and, as it would have appeared impertinent to ask many questions without assigning a reason for my inquiries, I am not qualified to say much more than that I believe them to be perfectly honest, inoffensive people, who evince the sincerity of their religious persuasion, by risking their scanty subsistence, and relying upon Providence to support them in their upright profession of it.

APPENDIX.

FROM THE REPORT OF "REYNOLDS'S COMMEMORATION SOCIETY."

Bristol, October 2nd, 1816

At a General Meeting of the inhabitants of this city, convened by public advertisement, for the purpose of forming a charitable institution to perpetuate the memory of the late Richard Reynolds, the following resolutions were unanimously agreed to—

1.—That in consequence of the severe loss society has sustained by the death of the venerable Richard Reynolds, and in order to perpetuate, as far as may be, the great and important benefits he has conferred on the city of Bristol and its vicinity, and to excite others to imitate the example of the departed philanthropist, an association be formed under the designation of "Reynolds's Commemoration Society."

2.—That the members of this society do consist of life-subscribers of ten guineas or upwards, and annual subscribers of one guinea or upwards.

3.—That the object of this society be to grant relief to persons in necessitous circumstances, and also occasional assistance to other benevolent institutions, in or near this city, to enable them to continue or increase their usefulness, and that especial regard be had to the Samaritan Society, of which Richard Reynolds was the founder.

II.

EXTRACT FROM THE "DEED OF TRUST FOR CHARITABLE PURPOSES."

The clear residue or surplus of the rents and profits, &c. &c. shall be paid, applied, distributed, or divided, to, between, or amongst, all, or any one, or more, of such only of the seven following charitable institutions at present subsisting in, or in the vicinity of, the city of Bristol aforesaid, as for the time being shall be supported by voluntary contributions, that is to say : the *Bristol Infirmary*, situated in Marlborough Street; the *Bristol Samaritan Society;* the *Stranger's Friend Society;* the *Asylum for poor Orphan Girls;* the *Society for the Discharge of Persons Confined for Small Debts;* the *Bristol Dispensary;* and the *Bristol Female Misericordia;* and if to more than one of the said institutions, then in such shares and proportions as shall be resolved upon by the trustees for the time being. And the sum of money which shall by such resolution be directed to be paid to any of the said charitable institutions, shall either be paid to the treasurer, governor, &c., or shall be by the said trustees themselves applied for the benefit of the objects of the same institution, or any of them, &c. &c. * * * * Provided always, and in case any of the said seven charitable institutions herein before named, shall at any time or times hereafter, invest or lay out any part of the annual revenues, subscriptions, &c. (except legacies) in the purchase of lands, &c. or of stock bearing interest, or in any other manner whatsoever, with an intention of increasing the future revenue or income of such institution : then, and in that case, the trustees of those presents are hereby directed and required to withhold from such institutions any part, &c. ————

EXTRACTS FROM A MS. BOOK CONTAINING REFLECTIONS, &c., BY REBECCA, WIFE OF RICHARD REYNOLDS.

I reconcile myself to the disagreeable qualities of servants, and bear with their unfaithfulness from a consideration that were they more perfect, they probably would not be my servants, but filling a more useful situation than that of gratifying all my desires, which may often be more than is necessary to comfortable accommodation, and hurtful in their consequences. Were we as wise as our great Pattern and Law-giver directs, instead of studying to gratify our desires, we should consider what superfluities in our possession might be spared, and how to deny ourselves of them in future, and also render servants less necessary by addicting ourselves to employment, by which, if in the bounds of moderation, our health would improve, and our peace be secured from the interruptions we are incident to by the common mode of living.

———

Children are very early susceptible of religious ideas, and there is no sort more comfortable and pleasant to such as are not diverted from them by the objects of sense—their culture illuminates the understanding, increases the capacity for knowledge of natural things, and facilitates the exertion of the reasoning faculty beyond the most elaborate endeavours independent thereof. Solomon had this conception of its efficacy when he prayed for wisdom from God—he knew it to be His gift, and he desired it above all things. It is in the acknowledgment and obedience to its dictates that piety consists, and such ideas cannot be inculcated too early in the minds of children—not by creeds and catechisms and the like, but by a watchful care to keep them from corrupting company, and to discourage everything in them that is contrary to the purity of the Christian religion.

WRITTEN APPARENTLY ON THE MARRIAGE OF HER SON.

MY DEAR CHILDREN,

My heart follows you to your habitation, where I am desirous to greet you with a testimony of my love, which longs for your permanent happiness. Methinks I behold you in the mutual enjoyment of each other's affection; the idea is pleasant to me beyond expression. May you live near to the Fountain of Love and Source of all Comfort! so shall you from day to day participate thereof in sweet fellowship, experiencing it to be your chiefest joy; then will it be your chief pursuit. There is no safe walking but in the fear of the Lord. It is the beginning of wisdom —by it the mind is instructed to follow the things that make for peace, while those who lean to their own understanding stumble as in the dark, for we are no longer enlightened, than while we are sensible that illumination proceeds from the great Author of our being, and that it is His will we should walk in the light which discovers the necessity of submitting to its manifestations; first, in little things, to which if you are faithful, you will be made rulers over much—over all inordinate affections for the things of this life, which is a great victory and a dominion superior to that of the whole world. May it become your portion!

Those whose minds are subjected entirely to the divine will have no difficulty to discern what is required of them by the Lord, because he works in them to will and to do of his good pleasure; such walk in the light of the Lord, are united to him and his will becomes their will; they speak and act with confidence, because he upholds such in all they say and do—they have no need of repentance, or to mourn on their own account, but go on their way rejoicing, or patiently suffering the contradiction and opposition they sometimes meet with, from such as are not in subjection to his divine will; which will, is the true harmonizer of Society, giving a quick discernment by the light accompanying its manifestations, what to say and what to do for the promotion of this harmony and when to be silent.

24

VERSES TO THE MEMORY OF THE LATE RICHARD REYNOLDS

BY JAMES MONTGOMERY.

Strike a louder, loftier lyre;
　Bolder, sweeter, strains employ;
Wake remembrance!—and inspire
　Sorrow with the song of joy.

Who was he, for whom our tears
　Flow'd, and will not cease to flow?
Full of honours and of years,
　In the dust his head lies low.

＊　　＊　　＊　　＊　　＊　　＊

He was one, whose open face
　Did his inmost heart reveal;
One who wore with meekest grace,
　On his forehead Heaven's broad seal.

Kindness all his looks express'd,
　Charity was every word;
Him the eye beheld, and-bless'd,
　And the ear rejoiced, that heard.

Like a patriarchal sage,
　Holy, humble, courteous, mild,
He could blend the awe of age
　With the sweetness of a child.

As a cedar of the Lord,
　On the height of Lebanon,
Shade and shelter doth afford
　From the tempest and the sun;—

While in green luxuriant prime,
  Fragrant airs its boughs diffuse,
From its locks it shakes sublime,
  O'er the hills, the morning dews.

Thus he flourished, tall and strong,
  Glorious in perennial health;
Thus he scattered, late and long
  All his plenitude of wealth.

This, with free unsparing hand,
  To the poorest child of need,
This he threw around the land,
  Like the sower's precious seed.

In the world's great harvest day,
  Every grain on every ground,
Stony, thorny, by the way,
  Shall an hundred fold be found.

Yet, like noon's refulgent blaze,
  Though he shone from east to west,
Far withdrawn from public gaze,
  Secret goodness pleased him best.
  *   *   *   *   *   *
Oft his silent spirit went,
  Like an angel from the throne,
On benign commission bent
  In the *fear* of God alone.

Then the widow's heart would sing
  As she turned her wheel, for joy;
Then the bliss of hope would spring
  On the outcast orphan boy.

To the blind, the deaf, the lame,
  To the ignorant and vile;
Stranger, captive, slave, he came,
  With a welcome and a smile.

Help to all he did dispense,
  Gold, instruction, raiment, food,
Like the gifts of Providence,
  To the evil and the good.

Deeds of mercy, deeds unknown,
  Shall eternity record,
Which he durst not call his own,
  For he did them to the Lord.

As the earth puts forth her flowers,
  Heaven-ward breathing from below;
As the clouds descend in showers,
  When the southern breezes glow

Then his renovated mind,
  Warm with pure celestial love,
Sheds its influence on mankind,
  While its hopes aspired above.

Full of faith at length he died,
  And victorious in the race,
Wore the crown for which he died,
  Not of merit, but of grace.

NOTES

BY A

ᴀ.. ... OF RICHARD REYNOLDS.

. have been invited to contribute something, of my own personal knowledge, to the preceding Memoir of my grandfather; but, after much retrospective consideration, I am astonished, and feel almost ashamed, that I have so very little, that can possess any general interest, to communicate. In fact, my grandfather, though cheerful, was not communicative with children; he would often talk with us freely, but he very rarely conversed with us. His greatest happiness, next to that of promoting the happiness of others, was in intimate communion with the cherished few who, like my mother and like himself, were possessed of large minds, warm hearts, generous sympathies, and uncompromising integrity—with such he was open and confiding as a child—and with such he delighted to converse.

My earliest recollections of my grand-father are of his visits to Green Bank—of the pleasure with which these visits were anticipated by my mother—of her care and thought that everything should be arranged for his comfort in the best manner possible—of her anxiety, as the time for his arrival (never, barring accident, either forestalled or delayed) drew near, that nothing should have happened on the road—that he should be in good health—and that he should not have been over-fatigued. All these things are as present with me now as when, after the first greetings, I sat in silence, "like a good little boy," at my mother's knee. We were thus brought up from infancy, by the influence of first associations, to regard my grand-father with

24 *

the most profound reverence; and, although he always met us with almost parental kindness, I am persuaded that this impression never left any one of us at any after period of our lives. The general gravity of his demeanour, his dignified carriage, and, above all, his playful satire, which we understood much better than he supposed, and felt much more keenly than he desired or intended, all combined to associate with our feelings of affection and gratitude, a never banished consciousness of awe in his presence. Yet, he was indeed *very kind* to us, and when we accompanied our father and mother, as we frequently did, to his house at Coalbrook Dale, he would take us into his workshop, and show us his turning-lathe, and turn spinning-tops for us, and make lashes for our whips, and teach us how to set up our tops, with a liveliness and cordiality which charmed and surprised us about equally.

He was a dear lover of humour, and it would be difficult to do justice to the comic expression of his usually serious face, while listening to a good story or, as was not seldom the case, when he was himself the narrator. I cannot resist the temptation to repeat one of his stories, because whenever I think of it, he is brought before my mind's eye, as palpably as in his bodily presence. It was of a man who walked the streets of Bristol, crying lustily "Hot mutton pies! hot mutton pies!"—then, suddenly stopping for a few seconds, he would hold up his forefinger, and cry with an eager kind of hurried impetuosity, "Only think of the relish!" Often as my grandfather had told us this story, the sparkle of his eye, and the fun of his whole manner, were always irresistible.

During a season of extreme scarcity two extensive Millers, who lived in his neighbourhood, excited no small dissatisfaction, by holding back for extravagant prices, their stocks of grain and flour, and my grandfather used greatly to amuse us, by quoting the following distich, composed, I believe, by an acquaintance for the occasion:—

Two millers thin, called Bone and Skin,
Would starve us all, or near it;
But be it known to Skin and Bone,
That Flesh and Blood won't bear it.

We also enjoyed very much our grandfather's account of a visit paid to the Ketley Iron Works, by Lord Thurlow, the then Lord Chancellor. My grandfather, having gone through the works with his lordship, and given him all requisite information and needful refreshment, proposed to accompany him part of the way on his return, which offer his lordship gratefully accepted, and the horses were ordered to the door accordingly. They were, both of them, good riders, and were, both of them, well mounted. The Lord Chancellor's horse, no doubt a little instigated thereto by his owner, took the lead, and my grandfather's horse, nothing loth to follow the example, kept as nearly neck and neck with his rival as *his* owner considered respectful. The speed was alternately increased, until they found themselves getting on at a very dashing pace indeed! and they became aware that the steeds were as nearly matched as possible. At last, the Chancellor pulled up, and complimenting my grandfather upon his "very fine horse," confessed that he had never expected to meet with one who could trot so fast as his own. My grandfather acknowledged to a similar impression on his part; and his lordship, heartily shaking hands with him, and thanking him for his great attention, laughed, and said, "I think, Mr. Reynolds, this is probably the first time that ever a Lord Chancellor and a Quaker rode a race together!"

It will readily be supposed that earnest was the desire, and numerous were the applications of relatives and friends to obtain some likeness of one so highly esteemed,—some resemblance of that countenance on which they had so often affectionately gazed, —something to recall that smile, so full of sweetness, which ever appeared to me to be one of the most expressive that I had ever seen;—but all our entreaties were in vain, and he resolutely refused to accede to our wishes. Under these circumstances, an attempt was made to obtain a likeness, without his knowledge:

one dark evening, a miniature-painter was introduced into the garden behind the house, where my grandfather was reading by candle-light, in a little back parlour, with the window blinds up, and all unconscious of what was going on without. The miniature so taken, and another sketch which was made while he was at the Friends' Meeting, were not considered very flattering,—in which opinion our grandfather *entirely coincided*: and, as he saw that "it could not be helped," he was at last persuaded to gratify us, by sitting to Mr. Hobday for a regular oil portrait, with no other condition on his part, than that my mother should be with him during the whole of the sittings. I happened to be also at this time in Bristol, and she, in like manner, desired that I would accompany her, and endeavour, as Mr. Hobday said, to "keep up a lively conversation;" our success on the first day was very indifferent indeed. We were constrained and uncomfortable, and my grandfather was writhing under an infliction, to which he, of all men, perhaps, would be the most sensitive. We were, in fact, all discomfited; and he "cadidly admitted that it was very fatiguing and disagreeable." The next day (I could only remain in Bristol long enough to attend this second sitting) when my grandfather had re-taken his seat, I mentioned to my mother the contents of letters which I had that morning received from Liverpool, giving a fearful account of the heavy failures which were taking place there, and spreading far and wide devastation and distress. I spoke under strong excitment, while contrasting the unprincipled conduct of many houses with the unswerving honesty of others, and the generous readiness of some to assist at great risk to themselves their less fortunate but not less honest neighbours. My grandfather listened attentively, and soon became so deeply interested, that his countenance, losing its constrained expression, glowed with feeling and animation; and when we were leaving the room, Mr. Hobday expressed his regret that I could not be present at the remaining sittings. "Oh! Mr. R——, if we could but engage the attention of Mr. Reynolds away from himself, as you have done this morning, it would be quite invaluable to me."

In conclusion of these, very unsatisfactory, notices, I shall only further record, that it was my privilege (having been hastily summoned, with my sister, to Cheltenham) to be present during my grandfather's last moments. The scene on our arrival, is deeply impressed on my memory—the tranquillity which breathed around the little group of mourners, who were quietly assembling, to behold the death of the righteous—the inexpressible peacefulness of those last moments, when my grand-father, by the slight inclination of his head, expressed to my mother his wish that she should come to the other side of the bed. Speechless, but quite conscious, he took her hand, looked earnestly in her face—and died. There were, then, in the room, his only daughter, his only surviving son, his nephew, Dr. Ball, my sister, and myself, his faithful cousin and companion, Sarah Allen, and his intimate friend Priscilla H. Gurney.

Woodcote, Liverpool, 18th May, 1852.

THE END.

CPSIA information can be obtained at www.ICGtesting.com
Printed in the USA
243756LV00011B/97/P